PEPPERS
The Domesticated Capsicums

PLATE I

Capsicum annuum var. *annuum* 'Anaheim'
(LONG GREEN / RED CHILE)

Illustration from specimen grown by John Anderson from W. Atlee Burpee seed

PLATE 2

Capsicum annuum var. *annuum* 'Ancho'
(POBLANO)

Illustration from specimen grown by Roy Nakayama

PLATE 3

Capsicum annuum var. *annuum* 'Banana'
(HUNGARIAN WAX)

Illustration from specimen grown by Lorraine Wilson

PLATE 4

Capsicum annuum var. *annuum* 'Bell'

Illustration from specimen grown by John Anderson from W. Atlee Burpee 'Fordhook' seed

PLATE 5

Capsicum annuum var. *annuum* 'Carricillo'

Illustration from specimen grown by Jean Andrews from seed supplied by José Laborde Cancino

PLATE 6

Capsicum annuum var. *annuum* 'Cascabel'

Illustration from specimen grown by Jean Andrews from U.S. Southern Regional Plant Introduction Station PSRD 281-388 seed

PLATE 7

Capsicum annuum var. *annuum* 'Catarina'

Illustration from specimen grown by Jean Andrews from U.S. Southern Regional Plant Introduction Station PSRD 281-388 seed

PLATE 8

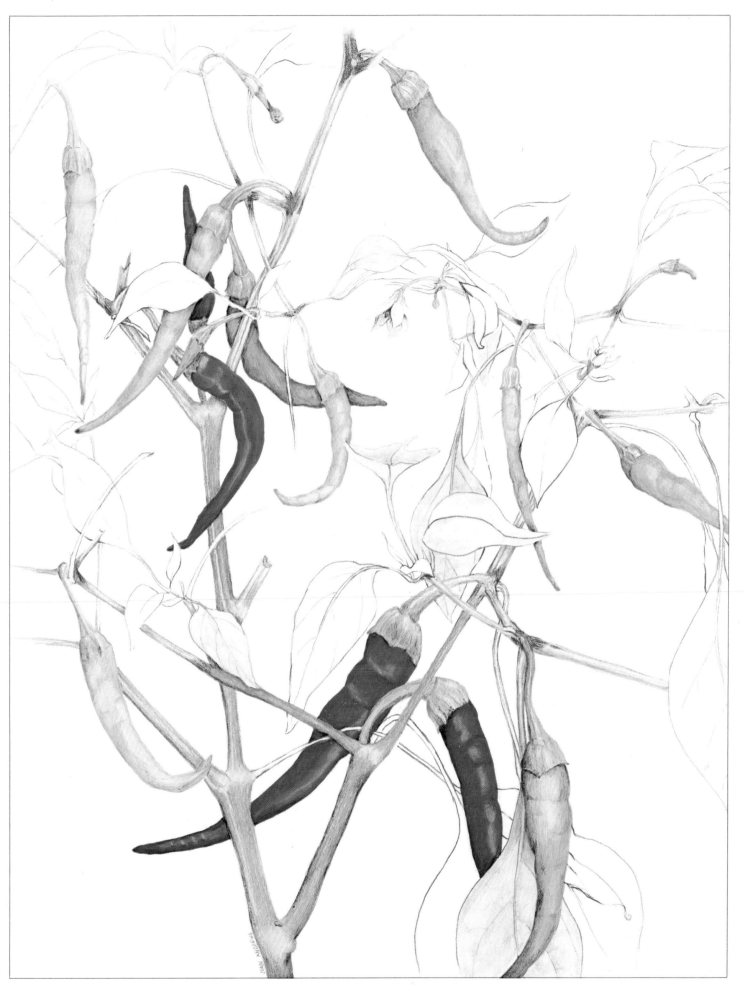

Capsicum annuum var. *annuum* 'Cayenne'

Illustration from specimen grown by Jean Andrews from Stokes Seeds, Inc., seed

PLATE 9

Capsicum annuum var. *annuum* 'Cherry'

Illustration from specimen grown by Roy Nakayama

PLATE 10

Capsicum annuum var. *annuum* 'Cubanelle'

Illustration from specimen grown by Jean Andrews and Carol Kilgore from Stokes Seeds, Inc., seed

PLATE II

Capsicum annuum var. *annuum* 'Fips'

Illustration from specimen grown by Jean Andrews from Geo. W. Park Seed Co. seed

PLATE 12

Capsicum annuum var. *annuum* 'Floral Gem'

Illustration from specimen grown by Jean Andrews and Nelwyn Anderson from seed supplied by Dale Marshall

PLATE 13

Capsicum annuum var. *annuum* 'Fresno'

Illustration from specimen grown by Jean Andrews from Horticultural Enterprises seed

PLATE 14

Capsicum annuum var. *annuum* 'Jalapeño'

Illustration from specimen grown by Lillian Murray

PLATE 15

Capsicum annuum var. *annuum* 'Mirasol/Guajillo'

Illustration from specimen grown by Jean Andrews and Carol Kilgore from U.S. Southern Regional Plant Introduction Station PSRD 281-389 seed

PLATE 16

Capsicum annuum var. *annuum* 'Pasilla'

Illustration from specimen grown by Jean Andrews from Horticultural Enterprises seed

PLATE 17

Capsicum annuum var. *annuum* 'Pepperoncini'

Illustration from specimen grown by Jean Andrews and Carol Kilgore from seed supplied by Benigo Villalon

PLATE 18

Capsicum annuum var. *annuum* 'Peter'
(PENIS PEPPER)

Illustration from specimen grown by James Fontenot

PLATE 19

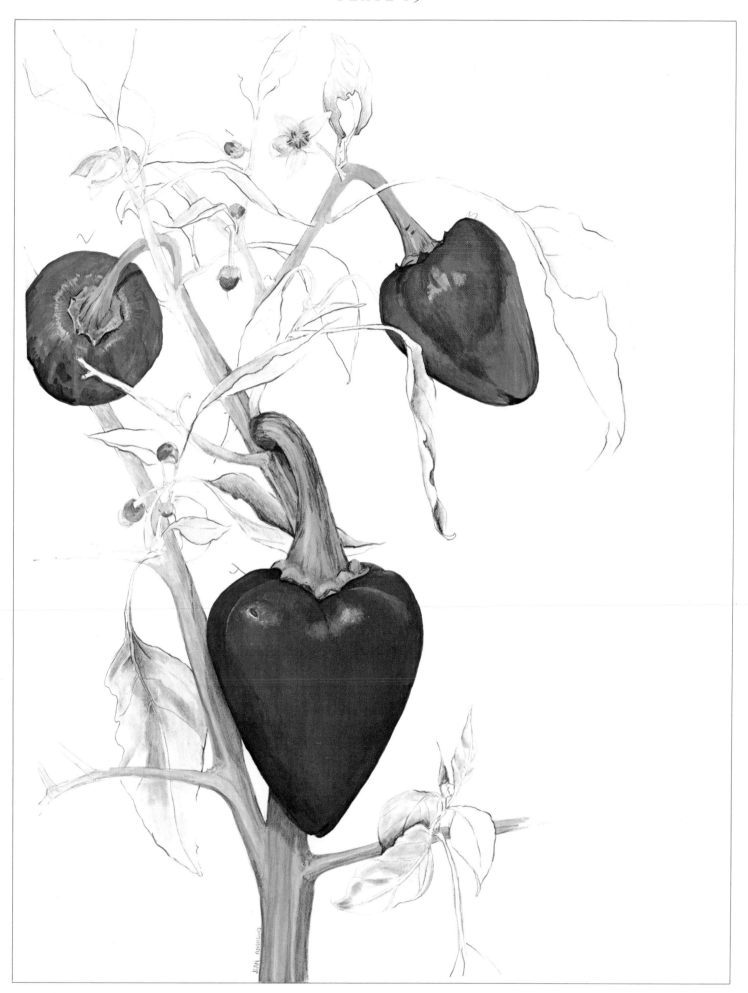

Capsicum annuum var. *annuum* 'Truhart Perfection'
(PIMENTO)

Illustration from specimen grown by Jean Andrews and Carol Kilgore from seed supplied by A. Hugh Dempsey

PLATE 20

Capsicum annuum var. *annuum* 'Santa Fe Grande'

Illustration from specimen grown by Jean Andrews and Carol Kilgore from seed supplied by Roy Nakayama

PLATE 21

Capsicum annuum var. *annuum* 'Serrano'

Illustration from specimen grown by Jean Andrews from seed supplied by Benigo Villalon

PLATE 22

Capsicum annuum var. *annuum* 'Texan'

Illustration from specimen grown by Jean Andrews from seed supplied by the Nixon Courts, Port Aransas, Texas

PLATE 23

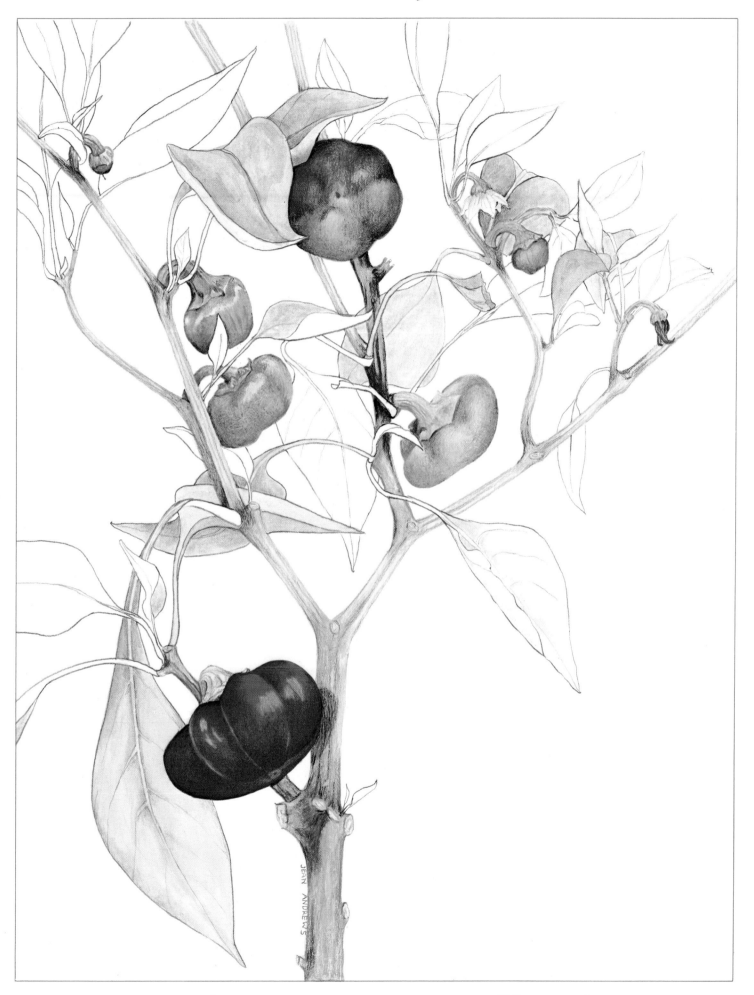

Capsicum annuum var. *annuum* 'Tomato'
(SQUASH)

Illustration from specimen grown by Jean Andrews from seed supplied by Roy Nakayama

PLATE 24

Capsicum annuum var. *aviculare*

(CHILTECPIN)

Illustration from specimen growing wild at Port Aransas, Texas

PLATE 25

Capsicum frutescens var. *tabasco*

Illustration from specimen grown by Jean Andrews and Carol Kilgore from R. H. Shumway Seedsman, Inc., seed

PLATE 26

Capsicum frutescens var. *uvilla grande*

Illustration from specimen grown by Jean Andrews and Carol Kilgore from U.S. Southern Regional Plant Introduction Station PSRD 188-477 seed

PLATE 27

Capsicum baccatum var. *pendulum* 'Kellu-uchu'
(AJÍ AMARILLO/CUSQUEÑO)

Illustration from specimen grown by Jean Andrews and Carol Kilgore from seed purchased in the Cuzco, Peru, market

PLATE 28

Capsicum baccatum var. *pendulum* 'Puca-uchu'

Illustration from specimen grown by Jean Andrews and Carol Kilgore from Walter Greenleaf PI 152-234 seed

PLATE 29

Capsicum chinense var. *chinchi-uchu*

Illustration from specimen grown by Jean Andrews and Carol Kilgore from Walter Greenleaf ACC 1554 seed

PLATE 30

Capsicum chinense var. *habañero*

Illustration from specimen grown by Jean Andrews from seed supplied by José Laborde Cancino

PLATE 31

Capsicum chinense var. *rocotillo*

Illustration from specimen grown by Jean Andrews and Carol Kilgore from Walter Greenleaf ACC 1774 seed

PLATE 32

Capsicum pubuscens var. *rocoto*

Illustration from specimen grown by Jean Andrews and Nelwyn Anderson from seed supplied by Otto Gastelumendi, Lima, Peru

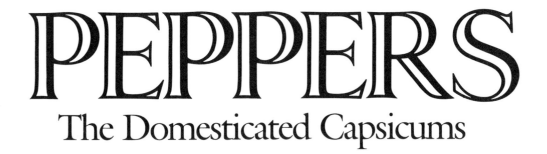

PEPPERS

The Domesticated Capsicums

Written and Illustrated by
Jean Andrews

FOREWORD BY W. HARDY ESHBAUGH

UNIVERSITY OF TEXAS PRESS, AUSTIN

First Edition, 1984

Requests for permission to reproduce material
from this work should be sent to
Permissions, University of Texas Press,
Box 7819, Austin, Texas 78713.

LIBRARY OF CONGRESS
CATALOGING IN PUBLICATION DATA

Andrews, Jean.
  Peppers: the domesticated Capsicums.

  Bibliography: p.
  Includes index.
  1. Peppers.   I. Title.
  SB307.P4A53   1984   633.8′4   84-7380
  ISBN 0-292-76486-3

To the discoverer of peppers, Christopher Columbus,
who may not have been the first citizen of the Old World
to reach the New World but was the first to document his discoveries
and to deliberately and accurately return to lay claim,
thereby opening a vast new frontier that altered the world

CONTENTS

ILLUSTRATIONS

FOREWORD

THE AMERICAN affair with chili peppers has been a growing romance ever since their discovery by Columbus on his maiden voyage to the New World. The Indian knew the value of this spice and independently domesticated four to five species that were used to complement a bland and often saltless diet.

The Amerindian knows many varied uses for these plants. Natives of southern Colombia often mix powdered pepper fruits with coca before snuffing with the knowledge that the increased mucous membrane irritation accelerates the uptake of the stimulant in the hallucinogenic snuff. In several Peruvian tribes nursing mothers apply pepper juice to their nipples when it is time to wean their infants. Modern parents have been no less inventive using chili pepper in "NOTHUM," a preparation applied to keep children from sucking their thumbs. Modern chemical mace uses chili pepper as its active ingredient.

The discovery of the red pepper in the late 1400s led to its eventual distribution and establishment in the Old World where it has assumed a role as important as that in the New World if not more so. In twentieth-century America the chili pepper occupies a significant place in our diet. Production has increased at the rate of 15 percent a year for the past decade. Demand for chili has led to several successful distributors and fast-food chains. The industry believes that both the American military and a wider traveling and more sophisticated public have led to a knowledgeable populace that demands to know more about chili peppers and consumes ever increasing quantities of the fruit in its diet.

As a native and resident of the Southwest, Jean Andrews has had a long acquaintance with chili peppers. What planted the germ of an idea to write and produce a book about peppers is Jean's secret. But, it is fortunate for us and she has given us a book that blends art, history, science, and a compendium of recipes into a single intriguing volume.

I first came to know Jean through her correspondence. Many letters crossed my desk asking a myriad of searching questions about the history, taxonomy, and genetics of the group. My later responses contained packets of seeds, which she grew for study and illustration. Some of my scientific papers reached her desk and they generated many thought-provoking questions. As her interest in the subject grew she sought information from the many experts on the genus.

Those of us who were privileged to see her early renditions of the different pepper species were impressed by the quality of her artwork. Not since Fingerhuth's 1832 *Monographia Generis Capsici* has such an outstanding collection of paintings of chili peppers been assembled by an individual artist. The end product of Jean Andrews' effort is a volume filled with discovery about the world of chili peppers. The delight of trying the many recipes included in the book will pique the palate of the most ardent gourmet. We are all in Dr. Andrews' debt for enriching our lives with this unique work.

—W. HARDY ESHBAUGH

PREFACE

DURING the eight and one-half years that I have worked on this "pepper project" I have been asked repeatedly, "What got you into peppers." Well, why are you reading this book? Peppers just get to you. I am primarily an artist and artists deal with shape, form, line, texture, value, and color. More years ago than I like to remember I became entranced with the sea shell because it so satisfied my artistic sensibilities with its variform shapes, subtle colorings, perfect proportions, and tantalizing textures. After the shell enticed me into the molluscan world I began asking questions—How was it made? Where did it live? What was its name? and on and on—enough questions to fill a three-and-a-half-pound book. And now, it has happened again.

Some time ago I began growing peppers for pleasure, attracted not only by their visual appeal but also by their usefulness. I soon began to look upon the colorful pepper pod as the sea shell of the plant kingdom with its myriad forms, multicolors, exciting textures, and on top of that a pugnacious personality . . . when you bite one, it bites back. When I began asking questions about the puzzling pod, I learned that it was, among many things, the most used condiment and spice in the entire world, having dethroned black pepper, and that all peppers on this earth belong to but one genus—the *Capsicum*. In searching the literature for material on the captivating *Capsicum*, I became quickly aware of a strange state of affairs for such a popular and common member of the vegetable world: the genus *Capsicum* had never been adequately illustrated. To rectify the situation I proposed to illustrate peppers myself. But, which ones, how many, and which medium? The provoking pod had thrown down its gauntlet and I accepted its challenge.

And challenge it was! I began reviewing the literature in order to determine just which of the many varieties I should illustrate. This was no easy task when I lived in a small city two hundred miles from a major library. I turned to a little-known service offered the reading public—interlibrary loan. It can bring the world to your doorstep and without it this work never would have been possible. Three years later I moved to Austin, which made the University of Texas library available, but I still had to depend on interlibrary loan because so much of the *Capsicum* literature has been published in rather obscure journals.

For example, in the abbreviated section of this book dealing with a review of the modern literature on peppers, twenty-eight articles appearing in eighteen journals and two dissertations were reviewed. Neither dissertation and only eight of those journals are to be found in the University of Texas at Austin science library, which services the top graduate botany department in the United States. One can well imagine the difficulty in acquiring these sources in far-flung agricultural experimental stations and smaller universities and cities. It is my hope that busy people in such places will benefit from this review and the accompanying bibliography. My praises go to the librarians whose careful and patient searching made this book possible, especially Anna Carillo, Ann Graham, and Bonnie Grobar of the Texas State Library; Betty White in the Science Library at the University of Texas at Austin; and the interlibrary loan staff at La Retama Library in Corpus Christi, Texas.

It was not easy to determine the names of the pepper cultivars that I would include because it was apparent that none of the authorities on the subject was certain of how they were to be named. Nevertheless, I came up with a tentative list and the realization that I was going to have to grow each variety myself in order to paint it. The first roadblock was in obtaining the seed. I will not belabor the sordid details that caused me and several of my friends to become *Capsicum* growers. Much of the pleasure I have derived from the preparation of this book has been in sharing the project with friends and fellow enthusiasts who have tried to help me in so many ways.

By mid-July of the first of my five growing seasons I had eighty-one different cultivars of four species vying for my attention all at one time under the broiling South Texas sun. I only managed to get ten painted that first year. Over the next five years I selected thirty-two picturesque pods of those that survived flood, drought, hurricane, and the Texas heat to represent the five species of domesticated capsicums.

Studying capsicums as a hobby can bring pleasure to many—to the cook, the gardener, the flower arranger or florist, the nursery operator, the gourmet, as well as those who value the plant heritage of the New World. It may seem difficult to the lay person to learn to distinguish one from the other. However, it is possible to do so without being a botanist through familiarity and developing powers of observation. We amateurs are dependent on the knowledge assembled by the scientific botanist who studies taxonomy, distribution, genetics, and chemistry, among other things. However, we amateurs are not inhibited by the exact demands of science or the protocol that accompanies it, so we can go on and assemble what is known up to the time of writing. We can be faulted for being presumptuous or overly ambitious in our eagerness to share assembled facts when the expert would have waited until the details were wrapped up. I deeply regret that what must be an enormous amount of pepper lore from the northern and eastern parts of South America was unavailable, making it necessary for me to have to slight those vast pepper-growing areas. I have endeavored to present the *Capsicum* to a public that might be rewarded by seeing the illustrations, as well as learning more about the history, dispersal, cultivation, and uses of this fascinating plant. A search of the facts to assure the scientific validity of the material presented was essential as a basis for understanding the genus.

The decision to write a text to accompany the paintings was basically a way to answer my own questions. Like Topsy, it just grew. Although much of the information presented in this book has been published, it is not readily available to the average researcher, much less the average reader. This, then, is a compilation of the literature interspersed with a few personal observations. I also regret that I had to distract the reader's eye with the insertion of so many source citations, but I believe that the usefulness to those who would investigate further outweighs esthetics.

I have met and had the cooperation of many of the contemporary horticulturists, taxonomists, virologists, geneticists, and botanists who have done the research presented here. Knowledge cannot be copyrighted, but when someone has spent his or her life studying and reporting data, credit for that work is both desired and deserved. It is my sincerest hope that I have properly credited those tireless researchers and writers, both living and dead, who have toiled through the ages. Any oversight has been unintentional. I try to paraphrase, but it is often difficult with a succinctly written scientific statement. I have attempted to read a body of literature, digest it, and present it in such a way that it would be readable by the lay person while being acceptable to the scientific community. I have borrowed heavily and am greatly indebted. I hope the scientist will enjoy my illustrations and the lay person will enjoy both the pictures and the details about the individual cultivars.

During the years that I have worked on this I have received help and encouragement from so many people that I can name but a few. Those who have shared freely with me the results of many years' study and experience represent a wide segment of university horticulturists, government agencies, industry horticulturists, seed suppliers, growers, processors, and many others in this country and Latin America. It has been a privileged association that I will never forget.

I would be remiss if I did not acknowledge special help from Dr. Lowell L. Black, Louisiana State University; Dr. W. Hardy Eshbaugh, Miami University; Dr. Verne Grant, University of Texas; Dr. Walter H. Greenleaf, Auburn University; Dr. Charles B. Heiser, Jr., Indiana University; Dr. Ernest Kaulbach, University of Texas; Dr. José Antonio Laborde C., CIAB, Celaya, Mexico; Thomas D. Longbrake and the Extension Service of Texas A&M University; Dr. Tom J. Mabry and the Department of Botany of the University of Texas at Austin; Dale E. Marshall, Michigan State University; Dr. Ramiro Matos, Universidad San Marcos, Lima, Peru; the McIlhenneys of Avery Island, Louisiana; Dr. Roy M. Nakayama, New Mexico State University; the Honorable J. J. Jake Pickle, Washington, D.C., and Austin, Texas; Dr. Paul G. Smith, University of California, Davis; the Trappeys of New Iberia, Louisiana; Dr. Philip L. Villa, Heublein Food Group, Oxnard, California; and Dr. Benigo Villalon, Texas A&M University.

Those who grew and nursed plants year after year for me were Nelwyn and John Anderson and Lillian Anderson Murray of Corpus Christi, Texas, and James L. Carson of Alamo, Texas. Janet Harte not only translated but also acted as liaison, along with a Peruvian friend, Otto Gastelumendi, with the Museo Nacional in Lima, Peru. My right arm, Carol Isensee Kilgore, not only grew my plants on her farm at Clarkwood, Texas, but also allowed me to usurp her dining room for a photography lab during a peak season. Of most importance, she read and reread the manuscript with her unerring eye. Helen Simons played a similar role with the bibliography. I could not have covered Central America without my son, Robin Wasson. A

special thanks goes to my husband, C. B. Smith, Sr., for not carrying out his threat to shoot my word processor until after I had completed this task. His patience and support are appreciated.

Repeating the words of historian-philosopher Walter Prescott Webb, ". . . in the last analysis no book is a primary source either of knowledge or culture." Nevertheless, I tried to find and use as many as I could. By way of saying thank you to all who made this book possible, I tender my illustrations. This book is offered in humility to those who love peppers.

"Will my song still be sung tomorrow."

—Miguel León-Portilla,
Pre-Columbian Literature of Mexico

I hope so!

SOME GUIDELINES FOR THOSE WHO WOULD BE SCIENTISTS:

". . . when you understand all about the sun and all about the atmosphere and all about the rotation of the earth, you may still miss the radiance of the sunset."

—Alfred North Whitehead

". . . to see what everyone has seen and think what no one has thought."

—Albert Szent-Györgyi

PEPPERS
The Domesticated Capsicums

1. The landing of Columbus. (S. A. Mitchell, *New Universal Atlas*;
photograph from the Cartographic History Library,
the Library, University of Texas at Arlington)

I

HISTORICAL BACKGROUND

"IN 1492 Columbus sailed the ocean blue," so goes the ditty. It was Christopher Columbus who first introduced peppers to a world hungry for spices. These pungent berries that had been a staple in the diet of New World Indians since prehistoric time were rapidly accepted and dispersed to the far reaches of the globe. Today they are the most used condiment in the world. The spice, black pepper, once ranked in first place, was one of the primary reasons that Columbus received sponsorship for his venture over uncharted seas.

Certainly all of us are familiar with the story of the Genoese mapmaker and navigator who was employed by the Spanish rulers, Ferdinand and Isabella, to find for them a direct route to the Orient so that Spain might gain the upper hand in the spice trade and a little gold on the side in order to finance their crusades against the infidel. There is no reason to question the traditional concept that Columbus' objective was to reach the Orient by sailing to the west, but there is ample evidence that the idea was not original with him. In addition, physical proof of land to the west was not unknown to his fellow seafarers in the area of the Azores. In 1492 the authority of learning favored rather than opposed venturing into unknown seas (Sauer 1966, 7).

Some have thought that Columbus was merely following directions received from another mariner. The story of the "Unknown Pilot" was first related by Oviedo (1526) and then perpetuated by Garcilaso (1609), Gómara (1552), and Acosta (1590). They alleged that in 1484, while Columbus was living on the Portuguese island of Terceira in the Azores, five sick and starving seamen stumbled to his home with a tale that was to fire his imagination and ambition. The Azores,

discovered by Europeans in the early fourteenth century, lost toward the end, and rediscovered in 1418, are a good third of the way westward from Europe across the Atlantic without intermediate land.

Before those mariners died, shortly after talking with Columbus, one of them, Alonzo Sánchez de Huelva, a Spanish pilot, related a harrowing story. Huelva was part of a Spanish coastal community of sea-hardened sailors and masters who knew the caprices of the open ocean and understood them at different latitudes. Supposedly, their small interisland trading ship was caught in a vicious storm that drove them from the Canaries to a distant uncharted island, probably Santo Domingo. After taking on water and food, they attempted to return, sailing blindly eastward. Of seventeen men aboard, all but these five had perished and they survived just long enough to inspire Columbus in his quest for things never heard of or seen before. With the information received from these men he was able to promise much to his prospective sponsors. The narrative of Alonzo Sánchez de Huelva is said to have given Columbus the direction to take in a vast ocean; without that information, only a miracle would have taken him to the West Indies in sixty-eight days. S. E. Morison (1942, 62), Columbus' biographer, minces no words when he objects to this story with ample testimony that the eastward voyage is a meteorological impossibility. The tale, he says, gained currency "because of an unfortunate human tendency to pluck at the laurels of the great."

Even if Columbus had been fortified with "secret knowledge," he had been unsuccessful for eighteen years in his petitions to the crowned heads of England and Portugal, as well as to many minor rulers, before he, with the support of the Franciscans of La Rabida at the mouth of the Río Tinto near Huelva, convinced the Spanish Catholic majesties of the worthiness of his dream, with its prospect of new wealth to continue their fight for the Christian cause. He offered them only a vision and a theory, not a record of accomplishment, status, or means, although he was a seasoned veteran of sea journeys to Guinea, Ireland, and Iceland (S. E. Morison 1942). Even then he had to wait until the expulsion of the Moors from Spain was complete. The conclusion of that struggle, ending an eight-hundred-year occupation, led to the conquest of America and the subsequent opening of the road to gold, silver, and spices.

The palates of the Greeks and Romans had been excited by aromatic spices that came to them from Arab traders by way of Egypt. Later, European taste buds grown tired of the dull, bland medieval diets craved the costly, aromatic bits of leaves, bark, and seeds from Arabian warehouses.

The fabled Venetian, Marco Polo, began a twenty-four-year odyssey to the Orient in 1271 that was to open the doors of the lands of spices to Europeans, breaking the Arabs' monopoly on that rich trade. Only the very wealthy could afford the spices that were laboriously brought to them by plodding caravans struggling along the trade routes of antiquity or by frail ships hugging the treacherous coast. They paid dearly for those cargos, which were used in every conceivable way: for curative, culinary, and, as incense, religious purposes. Black pepper, the most sought after, was so costly that it was counted out peppercorn by peppercorn.

The Arabs had kept secret the source of their spices, but the journeys of Marco Polo lifted that veil and led to the breaking of the powerful Moslem domination, the opening of trade with the Orient, and the discovery of the New World. Christopher Columbus and those who followed him were in search of spices and a direct route to their source.

No botanists were with Columbus on the journey, but his crew included two men whose special skills were expected to be of value upon his arrival in the Indies. One was Luis de Torres, whose knowledge of Hebrew, Aramaic, and Arabic would help the admiral converse with Orientals. The other was seaman Rodrigo de Xeres, who had met a native king in Guinea and who, therefore, was an expert in dealing with pagan royalty. Columbus was so confident in his goal that he called the land they reached the "Indies," unaware that he had not met his objective. The people who inhabited these lands were consequently called "Indians." The pungency of the berry from the spice plant being used for seasoning their food reminded the explorers of black pepper; thus it was called pepper, to the confusion of generations to come. In his day, Columbus was considered to be more or less a failure, but he opened the way for the success of others. His death in 1506 was scarcely noted.*

Ferdinand Magellan followed Columbus in time and his ships did reach the East by sailing west. Then came Cortez and the other audacious conquistadors. Fired by the glittering ornaments worn by Columbus' Indians, the search by these adventurers led to discovery of gold in Hispaniola in 1502. Spain then changed the thrust of her interests from spices to gold, selling her rights to the Far Eastern spice islands to Portugal in order to devote all her energies to that more spectacular treasure nearer at hand.

Actually the quest of Columbus was not a failure. Although he did not find the particular spices he was seeking, he did find quantities of two new aromatic plants that enriched the world's repertory of seasonings. Those two were peppers and allspice, both of which the Europeans labeled *pimiento*. However, only the first was recognized at the time as a useful spice. Later, others were to add a third, the vanilla-producing orchid, *Vanilla planifolia*. It is at this point that we shall leave the larger world of spices and concentrate on the hottest item introduced to the "civilized world" by the Admiral of the Ocean Sea, peppers, which have long been used by native peoples of the New World and which were cultivated from northern Mexico south through South America.

In his first letter to Ferdinand and Isabella and the treasurer of Aragon, Columbus described the many things he had seen. Although he did not call peppers by name, there can be little doubt that he was referring to them when he penned: "In these islands there are mountains where the cold this winter was very severe, but the people endure it from habit, and with the aid

---

*In July 1983 I made a pilgrimage to the monastery of La Rábida at the mouth of the Río Tinto near Huelva, Spain, and to the nearby towns of Palos de la Frontera and Moguer in order to pay homage to Columbus and his crew, for these were the places where he got his support, his men, and his ships. From there I went to Bayona in Galacia, the spot where the *Pinta* made the first continental landfall on the return of the voyagers from the New World. It surely must have been here, also, that peppers made their first stop in the Old World on a fantastic journey that would carry them to the far corners of the earth. The citizenry of Bayona celebrate March 1, 1493, as the date of the *Pinta*'s return.

Jalapeño seeds were scattered in the yard of the church, Ex-Colegiata Santa María, where the crew of the *Pinta* gave thanks for its safe return, thus recording my visit to that shrine.

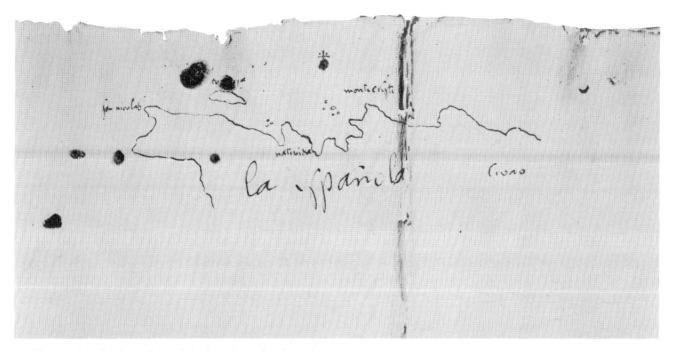

2. Hispaniola. This lyrical sketch is thought to be the only surviving map drawn by Columbus. (*Mapas españoles de América, cent. XV–XVII*; photograph from the Cartographic History Library, the Library, University of Texas at Arlington)

of the meat they eat with very hot spices" (Columbus 1493, 27).

On his second voyage, Columbus was accompanied by a learned man, Dr. Diego Alvarez Chanca, physician to the fleet, who gave us our first written account of the peppers of the West Indies. At the end of January 1494, Chanca sent a letter back to his hometown from the port of Isabella on the island of Hispaniola, now the Dominican Republic and Haiti. The letter was written to the municipal council of Seville, Spain. The document left Isabella on February 2, 1494, in care of Don Antonio de Torres, commander of the twelve vessels sent back to Spain by Columbus with the news of the discoveries. It arrived there April 8, 1494. The observations that Dr. Chanca reported had all been made in a three-month period. Concerning the voyage itself, he wrote: "By the grace of God and the good knowledge of the Admiral we came as straight as though we were following a known and established route." About peppers, he had this to say: "Their principal food consists of a sort of bread made of the root of a herb, half way between a tree and

grass, and the *agé*,* which I have already described as being like the turnip, and a very good food it certainly is. They use, to season it, a vegetable called *agí*, which they also employ to give a sharp taste to the fish and such birds as they can catch, of the infinite variety there are in this island, dishes of which they prepare in different ways" (Chanca, 1494, 68).

Chanca gets the credit for the first written record of peppers; however, an Italian cleric and historian in the service of the Spanish court in Barcelona as tutor of the royal princes, Pietro Martire de Anghiera [Martyr], 1455–1526, who was present when Columbus arrived there in April of 1493, wrote about them in September of that year. Martyr never visited the New World but obtained the information for his chronicle from those who had been on that first voyage, principally Melchoir Maldonado. Unfortunately for his place in history, this first book on America was not published until 1511, long after Chanca's letter had been received. In

---

* *Agé* is a tuber-bearing vine, *Ipomea batatas* (L.) Lam., the sweet potato (Merrill 1954).

the "Fifth Decade" of Martyr's *Decades of the New World, or West India*, we learn more of the pepper of the Indies. Originally written in Latin, the *Orbe Novo* was translated in 1555 by Rycharde Eden. Of peppers it said: "Something may be said about the pepper gathered in the islands and on the continent—but it is not pepper, though it has the same strength and the flavor, and is just as much esteemed. The natives call it *axi*, it grows taller than a poppy—When it is used there is no need of Caucasian pepper. The sweet pepper is called *Boniatum*, and the hot pepper is called *Caribe*, meaning sharp and strong; for the same reasons the cannibals are called *Caribs* because they are strong" (Anghiera 1904, 5: 225–226).

On the West Indian island of Hispaniola, which is Española* Latinized, Columbus and his men found that the native Arawak Indians called the much-used plant *axi*. The Spanish *ají* (*ajé, agí*) came from that now-extinct Arawakan language. Today in the Caribbean and much of South America the pungent varieties are still called *ají*.

The Spanish labeled the new plant *pimiento* after *pimienta*, the black pepper. It might be less confusing if we had another name for what we call peppers, in order to distinguish them from the pepper of the spice merchants, which is obtained from the dried fruit of *Piper nigrum* Linné, 1753, a climbing shrub of the family Piperaceae, native to India, whereas our peppers are of the genus *Capsicum* Tournefort, 1719, a member of the family Solanaceae. In English-speaking countries of the Eastern Hemisphere they are commonly referred to by their generic name, *Capsicum*. However, the use of the common name "pepper" for the capsicums is further proof of the linguistic dictum which finds that usage simply identifies a recent discovery with an already known thing somewhat resembling it.

The fruit of the sacred fig tree, the *peepul*, was known in ancient India as *pippali*. When the long black pepper, *Piper longum*, was discovered, for some reason the ancients called the fruit *pippali* also. Perhaps its shape suggested the fig; more likely there was a religious connotation, such as an association with the Buddhist rites in honor of the fig tree. After many centuries the English word *pepper* was derived from *pippali*, the name of the long pepper of India (Quinn 1942, 96).

In their quest for black pepper, the Spanish confused matters further by trying to make the second indigenous American spice into "pepper." They discovered the island of Jamaica to be covered with thirty-

foot trees bearing aromatic berries that, when dried unripe, somewhat resembled oversized black peppercorns. It is hard to believe that the explorers actually thought the berries were peppercorns; nonetheless, they called the new spice *pimiento*. Thus, allspice is now frequently referred to as pimenta, pimento, or Jamaican pepper. The aroma of allspice reminds one of a blend of cinnamon, nutmeg, and cloves, hence the name. Dictionaries list both *Capsicum* and allspice under pimento. Botanists did not help matters when they gave this member of the family Myrtaceae its scientific name, *Pimenta dioica* (Linné, 1753) Merrill, 1947. Allspice is not related to the true black pepper or even to peppers. In many recipes calling for pimiento, it is not always easy to determine whether the sweet red *Capsicum* pepper or allspice is intended.

In the New World, Spanish padres accompanying the explorers and conquistadors opened their knapsacks and removed the packets of seed they had brought from Spain: oranges, lemons, melons, and grapes. Before long their interest in gardening turned to the native plants, especially those being used for food and medicine by the Indians. As seeds of these plants matured, the padres gathered them, packaged and labeled them neatly, and sent them to Spain. Every returning ship, laden with gold, silver, and pearls, carried many kinds of seeds for monastery gardens (Quinn 1942, 187). From the Iberian peninsula and Brazil, peppers spread over the rest of the world as they were carried to West Africa, India, and Indonesia by early Portuguese traders.

Although amateur botanists and growers of medicinal plants obtained the first pepper seeds and seedlings from the Iberian peninsula as a spice and foodstuff,* the red capsicums first arrived in Europe from the Balkan peninsula, where they had been brought by the Ottoman Turks during their occupation of that territory. In all likelihood, the Ottoman Turks made their contact with peppers during their seige of the Portuguese colonies of Ormuz, Persia (1513), and Diu, India (1538). Thereafter, the Ottomans, and later others, carried the spice to the Balkan peninsula over established medieval trade routes from the Malabar coast of India through the Persian Gulf (Barraclough 1982). From there peppers made their way to Germany to be recorded as Indian or Calicut peppers by Fuchs in 1543. We have seen that the pepper was called *pimiento* or *pi-*

---

*A word coined by Martyr.

---

*The original use in Spain was primarily as ornamentals. Even today, I found the small, hot varieties being grown almost exclusively as ornamentals in pots in Spain.

mienton, depending on size, by the Spanish. Even today in Spain the sweet pepper is called *pimiento*,* while the ground or powdered form is *pimienton*, but those names did not stay with the peppers in Europe.

After acquiring peppers, seafaring Greeks, who used the old name for black pepper, called them *peperi* or *piperi*. The Slavic people in the Balkans called them *peperke*, *piperke*, or *paparka*, and by 1569 the Hungarians had changed the name to *paprika*. During the next one hundred years peppers revolutionized Slavic cooking as they had altered the cuisines of India and Indonesia. An embargo imposed by the tyrannical Bonaparte during the Napoleonic Wars was a windfall for the Hungarian paprika growers when pepper-hungry Europeans sought a substitute for the excluded black pepper.

Botanically, peppers are classified among the Solanaceae and are closely related to the tomato, nightshade, potato, and tobacco. They belong to the genus *Capsicum*, which was first described by a French taxonomist-botanist, Joseph Pitton de Tournefort (1656–1708) in 1700. The origin of *Capsicum* is obscure. Leonhard Fuchs (1543) and others who followed him mistakenly believed that Actuarius, who wrote in the thirteenth century, named the genus in Latin *Capsicon* after *capsa* or *capsula*, meaning chest or box, because of its shape. The pods do enclose the seeds very neatly as in a box. Others have proposed that the name is Greek, from *kaptein* or *kapto*, meaning "to bite," on account of its pungent quality. The first derivation would seem more suitable but it is quickly apparent that Actuarius could not have been referring to peppers because Columbus had not made his voyage of discovery at that time. We have been unable to determine where Fuchs got the name *Capsicum* but we have definitely determined that it is a modern Latin word and not from Theophrastos, Dioscorides, Avicenna, Actuarius, or Pliny.

The early fifteenth-century writers, led by Fuchs, a professor of medicine, confused the *Siliquastrum* and *Piperitus* of Pliny (A.D. 70) with *Capsicum*, referring to peppers, black pepper, and cardamon indiscriminately under such names as *Piper hispanum*, *Piper indicum*, and *Piper calecuthiamum*. Fuchs labored under the misapprehension that they were natives of India. Charles de

l'Escluse, or Clusius (1526–1609), a professor of botany at Leiden, was the first to give botanical descriptions of the New World peppers (l'Escluse 1611).

So far, we have established that the American capsicums were known in Spain in 1493, in Italy by 1526 (Oviedo 1950), in Germany by 1543 (Fuchs 1543), in the Balkans before 1569 (Halasz 1963), and in Moravia by 1585 (l'Escluse 1611). The Portuguese explorer-traders, who had first discovered the African Cape of Good Hope in 1486, probably introduced them to Africa and, after their first voyage to India in 1498, to the Far East. By 1542, three races of peppers were recognized in India (Purseglove 1968). They were known to be in Goa, India, in the middle of the sixteenth century under the name of Pernambuco* Pepper (Deb 1979; Watt 1908); that Brazilian placename documents a Portuguese presence.†

Extrapolating the dispersal of capsicums to the Far East, we will substitute *aji* for *agé* in Brand's (1971) theory for the dispersal of the American sweet potato. Assuming that peppers were cultivated in Portugal and Spain by 1500, we may surmise that they were taken from Portugal (or picked up in Brazil)** to the Malabar coast of India by the Portuguese over the direct trade route they operated from 1500 to 1665 from Lisbon to Brazil, around the Cape of Good Hope, then to Goa; from there they were joined by Persian, Arab, Hindu, and other traders, who carried the peppers to Indonesia, thence to the Moluccas. Moluccan and Papuan traders carried them along the north coast of New Guinea in the first two decades of the sixteenth century. From northern New Guinea they moved gradually eastward into eastern Melanesia; and there they were when the Europeans arrived . . . logical, but unproven. However, we do know that in India the American peppers are called *achar*, derived from *achi*, which was the Portuguese way of writing the West Indian name *axi* (*aji*), and that the prefix *capo* or *capro*

---

*In Spain today both the hot and sweet types are referred to as *pimiento*. *Pimenta* is black pepper. However, any large sweet, round, or blocky variety is called *morrón*, while the long, narrow, Anaheim-type cultivars are known as *guindilla* when small and *guinda* when large. *Guindas* are strung in *ristras* to dry.

Although I had heard that peppers were still called *aji* in Spain today, I did not get any response when I asked for *ajíes* in the markets of western Spain in 1983.

---

*Modern Recife, Brazil, is the place that the Portuguese knew as Pernambuco. It was a regular stop on their voyages to the East Indies and in their slave trade with Africa.

†Freyer (1966, 318) reports that Pernambuco (modern Recife and now the name of a state) and Bahia (modern Salvador), both founded by 1507, rapidly became ports of call for refitting and supplying all ships going to and returning from the Far East with heavy cargoes of valuable merchandise. Pernambuco was also the headquarters for Portuguese and Dutch slave trade, which was primarily with Angola, Mozambique, and the Ivory, Gold, and Slave coasts. Slaves were brought in to work sugarcane, which was introduced to Pernambuco in 1532.

**Brazil, which had native peppers, was a regular stop for reprovisioning on that route. Several early writers, such as Rheede (*Hort. Mal.*, 1679, p. 109); Bontius (*Hist. Nat. et Med. Ind. Or.*); Pizo (*Ind. Utri re Nat. et Med.*, 1658, pp. 130–131); and Clusius (*Hist. Exot. Pl.*, 1605, p. 340), refer to peppers in India as Brazilian Pepper.

3. Post-Columbian trade routes, 1492–1600: the probable avenues for the worldwide distribution of the genus *Capsicum*. Until 1600 other European nations did not break the Spanish-Portuguese monopoly of world trade; however, peppers were already established in Africa, India, the Far East, and Europe. It was not until much later that European colonists introduced peppers into their North American possessions, completing the capsicums' circumnavigation of the world.

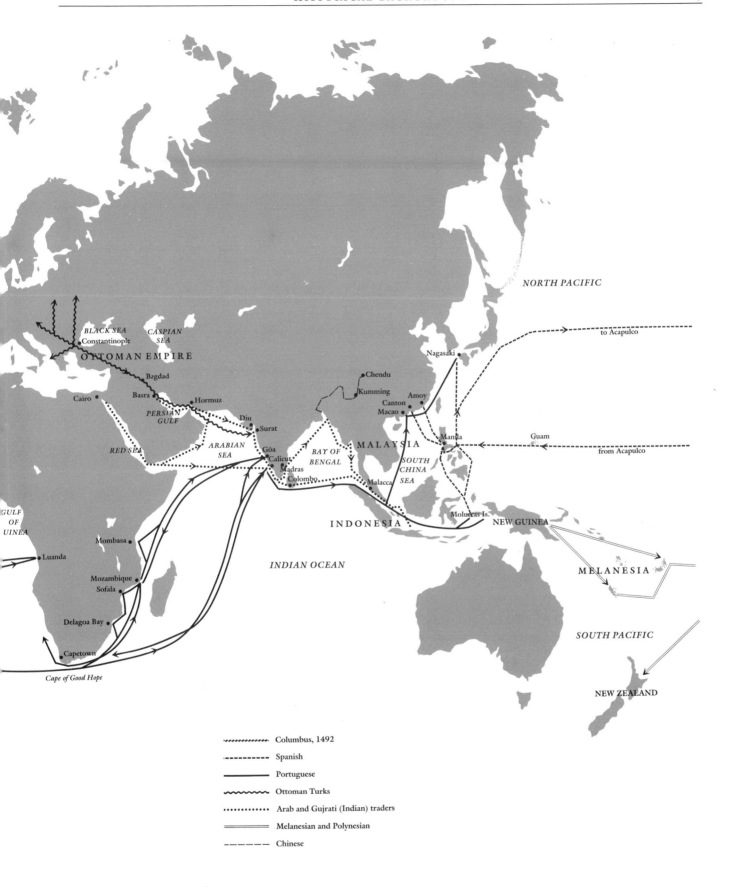

NORTH PACIFIC

BLACK SEA
CASPIAN
SEA
Constantinople
OTTOMAN EMPIRE
Bagdad
Cairo
Basra
Hormuz
PERSIAN
GULF
Diu
Surat
RED SEA
ARABIAN
SEA
Gôa
Calicut
Madras
Colombo
BAY OF
BENGAL
MALAYSIA
Chendu
Kumming
Canton
Macao
Amoy
Nagasaki
to Acapulco
Guam
from Acapulco
Manila
SOUTH
CHINA
SEA
Malacca
INDONESIA
Moluccas Is.
NEW GUINEA
GULF
OF
GUINEA
Luanda
Mombasa
Mozambique
Sofala
Delagoa Bay
Capetown
Cape of Good Hope
INDIAN OCEAN
MELANESIA
SOUTH PACIFIC
NEW ZEALAND

Columbus, 1492

Spanish

Portuguese

Ottoman Turks

Arab and Gujrati (Indian) traders

Melanesian and Polynesian

Chinese

used in pepper names denotes its introduction by Arab traders (Watt 1908).*

During the early period of European exploration peppers were carried into Africa by Europeans. The Portuguese were responsible for the introduction of peppers into western Africa and the Congo Basin. Later they found their way from European botanical gardens to the colonies of the Netherlands, Great Britain, and France. The introductions into Africa before the early nineteenth century are poorly documented (Miracle 1967). McClure (1982) has suggested that captains of slave ships returning to the west coast of Africa from the New World introduced many West Indian plants, including perhaps *Capsicum*; then Arab slave traders transported the peppers to East Africa.†

So enthusiastically was this blistering spice received in those hot lands that its New World origin was completely forgotten and it was long regarded as native to tropical Africa and India. Early English colonists brought peppers with them to their new American possessions, thereby reintroducing it to the North American continent.

As previously noted, the Spaniards found the natives of the Caribbean Islands calling the peppers *ají* (pronounced ah-hée). Today that is the common name in the West Indies and South America, but it is not clear whether the Spanish introduced the term to South America or if it was already in use. Heiser (1969a) suggests it is likely that peppers went from South America to the West Indies in prehistoric times with the name *ají* already attached. Linguists, however, consider this unlikely (F. Karttunen (1982, personal communication). Although *ají* is now in general use in the territory formerly governed by the Inca, the original word in Quechua, the language of the Incas, was *uchu* (*ucho, ucha*). It is still employed by some Indian groups. In Aymara, the other language spoken in parts of the Incan empire, the pepper was known as *huayca*.

When the Spaniards arrived in Mexico they heard the *ají* being called *chilli*, a Nahuatl word; Nahuatl was the language of the Aztecs, the dominant group at the time of the Conquest. The stem *CHIL* refers to the *chilli* plant. It also means "red." *TLI* is a suffix without significance denoting closure, as is the custom in Nahuatl. To the generic word, *chilli*, the term that described the particular *chilli* cultivar was added (e.g., *quauhchilli* = tree chilli, *chiltecpin* = flea chilli). Dr. Francisco Hernández (1615) was the first to use the term *chilli* in print.

In Mexico today, the term *chile*, which was derived from the Nahuatl, refers to both hot and sweet types and is used in combination with a descriptive adjective, such as *chile verde*, or a word that indicates the place of origin, such as *chile poblano*. The same variety can have different names in different geographic regions, in its various stages of maturity, or in the dehydrated state. Consequently, the names of peppers in Mexico can be very confusing.

Today in the Far East, *chillie* or *chilly* is generally used as the English name for the pungent types, while the larger mild ones are called capsicums. In the United States the spelling of this ancient word varies and two forms of the term are used. Both the anglicized spelling *chili* and the Spanish *chile* are used by some for the pungent or hot berries of the *Capsicum* plant, while *chili* (minus one *l*) also applies to a variously concocted mixture of meat and peppers. However, most English-speaking countries use *pepper* as the popular term. *Pimento*, the anglicized version of the Spanish word for pepper, is the accepted spelling for the thick-fleshed, sweet, red capsicums.

---

* As a result of Papal Bulls of Demarcation in 1493 and 1494, which set a line 370 leagues west of the Cape Verde Islands as the boundary between Spanish and Portuguese fields of exploration and conquest and which barred Spain from the route around Africa via the Cape of Good Hope, each country exercised a monopoly on a vast territory for almost one hundred years. Consequently, it is highly probable that during those years the peppers introduced by the Portuguese to the lands in their sphere of influence (Africa, India, Indonesia, Moluccas [Spice Islands], Mallaca [near modern Singapore], Macao, and Japan) were *C. frutescens* and *C. chinense*, which were of Brazilian origin, and *C. annuum annuum*, which was brought to the Iberian peninsula by the Spanish. The Spanish would have brought Mesoamerican types (*C. annuum annuum* and *C. frutescens*) with them to their colonies in the Pacific (Philippines and Guam) and to their major trading points in China (Canton and Amoy); Nagasaki, Japan; and Mallaca. Later, when other European nations entered the East Indian trade and commerce became general, the more favored varieties of these species would move throughout the vast area.

† Captains of slave ships were indeed instrumental in transporting peppers. We read in Mannix (1978, 115) that on British slavers in 1783 the second meal of the day served to the slaves consisted of "horse beans" ground to a pulp and then covered with "slabber sauce," which was a mixture of palm oil, flour, water, and red peppers. Although there is no documentation, I feel certain that the Portuguese introduced peppers to west Africa early in the sixteenth century when they held a monopoly on African trade just as it has been recorded that they did in India. It also stands to reason that the British did not originate the addition of peppers to the slaves' diet at a time so near the end of legal slavery.

Freyer (1966, 318) documents an active exchange between the New World and Africa via slave ships from the inception of that shameful practice soon after 1532 until the abolition of slavery in Brazil in 1888. This commerce between the slaves' homelands and Brazil provided those uprooted thousands with religious objects and other favored articles for their personal use. The year after slavery was abolished the Brazilian minister of finance ordered the burning of the archives of slavery (Freyer 1966, 301).

Table 1. Various Names for Peppers

Place/Language	Name	Place/Language	Name
		Tamilnadu & North Sri Lanka/Tamil	Mulagay, mollagu
AFRICA			
French Guiana	Furtu	**EUROPE**	
Gold Coast	Mako	France/French	Piment de Guinée, poivre d'Inde, poivre du Brézil
Kenya/Swahili	Piri-piri or peri-peri		
Liberia	Mano	Germany/German	Spanischcher oderkercher pheffer
Nigeria (North)	Barkono		
Nigeria (South)	Ata-jije	Greece/Greek	Piperiĕs
Senegal	Foronto	Hungary/Hungarian	Paprika
Sierra Leone	Pujei	Italy/Italian	Peperone
		Netherlands/Dutch	Bzefilie peper
ASIA (BRITISH-INFLUENCED)		Portugal/Portuguese	Pimento, pimentão
Australia & India/Latin	Capsicum	Russia/Russian	Struchkovy pyerets
Australia & India/from Nahuatl, Anglo-Indian	Chillies	Sweden/Swedish	Spansk peppar
ASIA (ORIENTAL)		**LATIN AMERICA**	
Bali	Tabia	Brazil/Indian	Auija or quiya
Burma/Burmese	Nayu·si, na yop	Chile/Indian	Thapi
China/Chinese	La-chio	Costa Rica/Bribri	Dipá-boró-boró, tiesh
China/Cochin-Chinese	Lat-tsiao	Haiti/Arawak	Ají (axí, agí, achí)
Japan/Japanese	Togarashi	Mexico/Huasteco	Itz
Java/Javanese	Lombok	Mexico/Mayan	Chac-ic, Max-ic
Malaysia/Malay	Lada mira	Mexico/Nahuatl	Chilli
Philippines/Tagalog	Pa sitis	Mexico/Otomi	Ng-i
		Peru/Aymara	Huayca
ASIA (SOUTH)		Peru/Quechuan	Uchu
Andhra/Telegu	Mirapakaya, merapu-kai		
Bengal/Bengali	Lankamarich, lalmarich	**MIDDLE EAST**	
Gujarat/Gujarati	Lilun marchu	Arabia/Arabic	Filfile, ahmur; filfilianhar
Karnataka/Kannada	Menasina-kayi (kai)	Egypt/Arabic	Filfil-achdar
Kerala/Malayalam	Kapu-mologu or Kappal-melaka	Iran/Persian	Filfile súrkh
Maharashtra/Marathi	Mirsinga	Yemen/Arabic	Dar feller
North India & Pakistan/Hindu & Urdu	Lal mirch, gachmirch, hari mirch		

There is probably a word for both sweet peppers and chili-peppers in every language in the world. Many have separate names for the different varieties. These are only a few that have been found in such sources as Watt 1889–1896, Pickering 1879, Roys 1931, Standley 1938, and others.

This chart was prepared with the assistance of Dr. Bharat Bhatt, University of Texas at Austin.

In this book, *pepper** will be used when speaking of the fruit of the *Capsicum* in general, both sweet and hot; *chili-pepper* for the pungent types; *chili* for the hot, spicy meat dish; *pimento* for the sweet, thick-fleshed, heart-shaped red pepper; and *Chile* for the South American country. If *chile* (always in italics) is used, it will refer to a native Mexican cultivar or the long green/red chile type. Wherever possible the specific cultivar name or type will be used. It is hoped that the reader will follow suit, thereby helping to stabilize a rather troublesome situation among the followers of the pungent pod. However, if one is set on being perverse, another name might be selected from Table 1.

All the names for peppers listed in Table 1 occur in modern languages; there is no name for the genus in early Latin, Greek, Hebrew, ancient Sanscrit, or Chinese. In the reports of his travels in the Far East, the observant Marco Polo (1286–1296) made no reference at all to *Capsicum*, although he discussed black pepper and cardamon (Watt, 1908). No word for the Ameri-can pepper has been found in a language outside the Western Hemisphere predating the voyage of Columbus.* Dr. Chanca's letter is the first recorded mention of this plant, which today ranks as the most used condiment in the entire world.

To date, the oldest known records of peppers come from the desert valley of Tehuacán, Mexico, 150 miles south of Mexico City. From studies of seeds found in ancient cave dwellings and from human coprolites in those caves, we know that the indigenes were eating peppers as early as 7000 B.C. (MacNeish 1964; C. E. Smith 1967). The first peppers consumed presumably came from wild plants, but, apparently, between 5200 and 3400 B.C. the Indians were actually cultivating them, although the actual date of domestication remains obscure. We do know that peppers were among the first plants to be domesticated in the Americas. In South America peppers recovered at the archaeological site of Huaca Prieta in the Chicama valley of northern Peru have been dated at 2500 B.C. (Bird 1948). Some whole fruits are preserved and, although they are rather small, they are clearly larger than wild peppers, making it reasonable to assume that they represent varieties selected and cultivated by people. Botanists cannot identify species of peppers with certainty from seeds alone; nevertheless, it is quite likely that species cultivated in Mexico were different from those cultivated in South America at that period (Pickersgill 1972).

---

* I had wanted to use chili-pepper as the common name for capsicums; however, after much soul searching, literature searching, letter writing, etc., etc., I bow to convention and the International Board of Plant Genetic Resources. Eleven international leaders in the study of the genus *Capsicum* met in Turrialba, Costa Rica, August 13–15, 1980, to formulate a global plan of action for *Capsicum* genetic resources. One of their recommendations was to provide uniform usage of specific names and terminology. In their initial report, the capsicums in general are referred to as peppers or chili peppers. The fact that the term "pepper" was used more frequently than the latter in that report is my criterion for using the conventional term "pepper." We are reminded that it is a mistake to legislate common names. Otherwise, they cease to be genuinely "common," that is, the names that ordinary people give to the plants they know and cultivate (J. McNeill 1983, personal communication).

This is a very sensitive subject to the members of the National Pepper Conference (U.S.A.) and will be one of the primary topics for discussion at the next meeting in Washington, D.C., in 1984. Unfortunately, the results of that conference will come too late to meet my deadline. I hope my choice will not offend. In any case, we can blame it on Columbus!

---

* Some writers provide botanical support for the hypothesis of prehistoric trans-Pacific human contacts, while others give evidence that plants could have been self-transported by oceanic drift of their fruits. If trans-Pacific contact proves true, there should be a pre-Columbian name in the language used in the area of contact for peppers and other plants claimed to have been transported (Heyerdahl 1963, 1964; Pickersgill & Bunting, 1969).

PRE-COLUMBIAN DOMESTICATION

ALTHOUGH there are still areas on this earth that have not been explored, we can now safely claim that peppers originated in South America (Pickersgill 1969*a*, 443). To date twenty-two wild species and three varieties as well as five domesticated species and four varieties related to these have been collected and studied (Eshbaugh 1980*a*). Twenty are strictly wild, and the wild ancestral forms of all but one of the domesticated species have been identified.

Despite the diversity of names and the differences in size and shape, all pepper cultivars found in markets derive from only five domesticated species and none are substantially different from those raised by the pre-Columbian Indians of the Americas. Most of the commercial capsicums are *Capsicum annuum*, which is the species best known in North American and European markets. Long before Columbus, some of the South American peppers had reached Central America, Mexico, and the Caribbean where they were grown for seasoning and as vegetables. Wherever they are raised, countless local forms exist because they hybridize readily. The tendency to hybridize has helped the pepper develop new forms as it was dispersed around the world, plus the fact that the plants are naturally weedy colonizers. No other spice ever spread so quickly. The seeds were readily transportable, they remained viable for several years, and they found hospitable climatic conditions in almost every country in the world.

Peppers share with *Phaseolus* beans (e.g., pinto, lima), maize (corn), and the cucurbits (e.g., squash, gourd) the distinction of being among the first plants cultivated in the New World (Heiser 1973). Archaeologists have found their remains in sites in both Middle and South America. Excavations in Tamaulipas and Tehuacán, Mexico, revealed pepper remains at the earliest levels, dating back to about 7000 B.C. (MacNeish 1964, 1977). The events at those levels occurred at least 1,000 years after the disappearance of the Bering land bridge caused migrations from Asia to cease. The closing of that land bridge antedates the development of New World agriculture, implying that wild plants were already being harvested. In South America, peppers have been found in sites on the coast of Peru. The prehistoric people at the site known as Huaca Prieta did not possess the knowledge of pottery but they practiced, with only the most primitive stone tools, some of the earliest agriculture in America (Bird 1948, 302). Huaca Prieta levels dated from about 2500 B.C. contain pepper remnants (Bird 1948, 335). The only plant remains found at other preagricultural sites are of the widely distributed bottle gourd. There are no records in those sites of such favorites as squash and peppers, suggesting they were not wild locally but were introduced after domestication elsewhere (Pickersgill 1969*b*).

Based on the fact that there are wild pepper plants related to most domesticated varieties, all of which are separated genetically, Pickersgill (1969*a*) opined that it is probable these species existed before the development of agriculture and that each was domesticated independently in different areas by different groups, with peppers occupying a privileged status as tolerated weeds in the initial stages of their domestication.

The development of agriculture is considered to be one of the most significant events in human social evolution. Vavilov (1949–1950, 20) suggested eight independent ancient main centers of origin. Later a theory was advocated that agriculture originated independently in three distinct areas and that, in each case, there was a system comprising a center of origin and a noncenter, in which processes of domestication were dispersed over a span of 5,000 to 10,000 kilometers (Harlan 1971, 473). Heiser (1976b) agreed that agriculture was invented at least three times in that many different parts of the globe: in Southeast Asia, in the Middle East, and in the New World.

Another theory argues that agriculture was not an invention in the sense of a "creative flash" but was a long process in which hunting-and-gathering people reduced their ranges and the numbers of plants and animals they depended on. These resources were shielded from natural selection by humans, who in turn selected for characters favorable to their needs (Flannery 1965). It is not known just how and why people "invented" agriculture but we do know it was highly successful, spreading over the ancient world and forming the material basis of all civilizations.

About 60 million years ago the Cenozoic Era began. It was marked by the emergence of flowering plants, grasses, and deciduous trees and shrubs. The passing of the dinosaurs and the emergence of the mammals also characterized the period. During the Cenozoic, evolution was profoundly affected by the emerging and submerging of various great land bridges that united or separated continents throughout the world. The Bering Strait of Alaska and the Torres Strait between New Guinea and Australia are two examples.

Humans had been around since the end of the Cenozoic, about a million years, and anatomically modern people have existed for at least forty thousand years (C. A. Reed 1977). Some of the plants and animals that were later to become their principal foods were available for domestication by the Late Miocene, about 10 million years ago. However, "the proper hand and the proper brain" did not come together to develop agriculture until the end of the Pleistocene (11,000 years ago) when the extinction of many large animals made hunting unprofitable (MacNeish 1977, 794). The last humans had crossed over the Bering Straits before the development of agriculture occurred (Manglesdorf et al. 1964, 428).

The sites where agriculture is thought to have originated are in semiarid, somewhat hilly or mountainous country, not the verdant river valleys where there had been an abundance of natural food. To such marginal areas, people migrated from more favorable regions where climatic and environmental changes had upset their established options for subsistence causing stress and/or stimulation in populations (C. A. Reed 1977;

MacNeish 1977). Why and how people "invented" agriculture may be unknown but it is felt that "Necessity" was not the mother of that invention but Mother probably was. Sauer (1952) credits women with the domestication of both plants and animals.

The origin of a domesticated plant, such as the Jalapeño, is a process, not an event (Anderson 1960, 71). Multiple origins are already known with certainty for some crop plants, including peppers. "Reticulate relationships" with a cultivated plant's progenitors and with the weeds derived from them are provisionally documented. Like "which came first, the chicken or the egg?" the weed-to-cultivated-plant relationship is no longer something that can be taken for granted. Anderson points out that selecting a closely related weed as the probable precursor of a cultivated plant poses two additional problems: (a) the origin of the weed and (b) the nature of the relationships between the weed and the cultivated plant. Different wild plants were domesticated by different peoples inhabiting different areas. It has been unusual for humans to domesticate the same or closely related plants in areas not in contact with each other (Carter 1950). Consequently, the presence of a plant, such as peppers, in archaeological digs in both Peru and Mexico is not proof of contact between the two areas, because different species of peppers are known to have been domesticated in Mexico and Peru (Pickersgill 1972). However, Jett (1973) retorts that genetic difference in species is not proof that there was no contact because ideas and techniques of plant cultivation could be introduced by substituting a local plant for the plant grown in the "idea-donating" area. Local environmental differences would favor the use of a local pepper rather than one from a distant homeland. Today the study of plant origins requires the support of each and any field that can provide working information.

As archaeological findings continue to produce botanical evidence, it will become possible for ethnobotanists to make more accurate analyses of the interplay between diverse areas of the Western Hemisphere on the basis of changes in the cultivated plants. The real and considerable differences between the domesticated plants of Mesoamerica and South America point to agriculture in the Americas having developed along independent lines in Peru and Mexico (Pickersgill & Heiser 1977; MacNeish 1977). Within Peru one would think that the arid coastal area would have been effectively separated from the humid Amazon region by the imposing Andes Mountains, but cultivation of the same species of *Capsicum* occurred on either side of

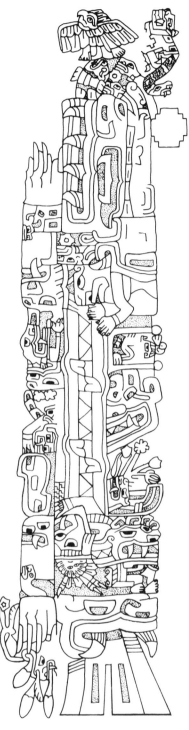
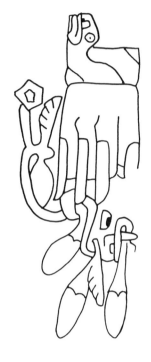

4. Tello Obelisk. Chavín de Huantar is the modern name for a small town located in a fertile valley on the northwestern slope of the main range of the Peruvian Andes at an altitude of 3,135 m (10,200 ft.) at the headwaters of the Amazon River. Outside the town are the ruins of a great temple where a carved, rectangular granite shaft was found early in this century by a farmer, who took it home. It was later moved to a church, where Julio C. Tello rediscovered it in 1919. The Tello Obelisk is an idol on which are depicted two representations of a mythical being in the form of a black caiman (*Melanosuclius niger*). In the claws of one caiman are the blooms, leaves, and four pods of the genus *Capsicum*. This stela (8 ft. 3 in. tall, 12½ in. narrowing to 10½ in. wide), which is now in the Museo Nacional de Antropología y Arqueología in Pueblo Libre, Lima, is from the early Chavín culture, 800–1000 A.D., probably making the carving thereon one of the earliest known representations of capsicums. (Lathrap 1973; Tello 1960; Pickersgill 1969; photograph from Museo Nacional de Antropología y Arqueología, Lima, Peru)

5. Ceramic vessels. *Top*, following a common practice of the Nazca culture in pre-Columbian Peru of making vessels in the form of fruits and vegetables, this vase (850–1425 A.D.) is made up of a group of pepper pods. (Photograph from the Museo Nacional de Antropología y Arqueología, Lima, Peru) *Bottom*, this shallow polychrome vessel decorated with a painted border of stylized chili-peppers is Classic Nazca, dating between the fourth century and the end of the sixth century A.D. (From the author's collection)

them, which suggests that contact between the two regions has been effective and prolonged.

During the last twenty years archaeological, cytogenetic, and morphological studies have been employed to determine the evolutionary history of the capsicums. Such studies tell us that when the Spanish invaded the New World there were at least four species being cultivated, all of which appear to have undergone parallel but independent domestication and selection in different areas (Pickersgill 1969*a*). Peppers are among the most ancient cultivated plants in the Americas and may prove as valuable as some inorganic artifacts in tracing cultural contacts. Other significant New World plants are maize, amaranth, *Chenopodium* herbs, *Phaseolus* beans, peanut, squash, bottle gourd, tobacco, cacao, coca, rubber, manioc, sweet potato, *achira canna*, potato, and cotton (Safford 1927).

New World agriculture was found to be quite different from that of Europe.* The first pre-Columbian cultivars (peppers, squash, beans, zapote, avocados, early maize, and possibly amaranths) were domesticated by nonsedentary people who still roved about hunting and gathering, for they were dependent for more than half of their subsistence on the harvesting of wild plants (C. A. Reed 1977, 926). Most of the New World's domesticated native plants, the potato being the principal exception, prefer a warm start, summer rains, and a dry fall with lowered temperature. They start and mature late and most are planted at the beginning of summer and harvested at the end of fall (Sauer 1936, 1285). New World domesticates do not have the deeply developed root systems common to dry-land vegetation and some Old World crops.

When pre-Columbian people finally developed agriculture, it was basically gardening by planting individual seeds as opposed to Old World broadcasting of seed in tilled fields (Heiser 1969*c*). The house garden that can still be seen in Peru is the ancestral type of cultivation in the New World (Lathrap 1977). In the Old World, field crops were not harvested until the fruit matured and green vegetables were grown in separate plots. However, in the New World, various parts of the plants were consumed at different stages of development (Sauer 1950, 519).

The first objective of primitive agriculture is to produce a more adequate supply of starches. The competitive domestication of several species of the same plant in the same area may be considered improbable. Such

*Crosby (1972) presents a fascinating discussion of the effect of New World foods on Old World demography.

evidence as we have on the origin of the basic, or starch-food, domestications in the New World indicates that each has a center of origin distinct from the others; in other words, there may be as many American centers of plant domestication as there are domesticated starch plants. The basic starches may be interpreted as alternative domestications, coming from various climatically differentiated centers (Sauer 1936).

In time other desired plants were domesticated as auxiliaries to the cultivated starch crop. In the geographical area of an unrelated specific starch, similar auxiliaries are found that could have been other members of that genus which served the same dietary uses, for example, for spice: *C. annuum* in Mexico and *C. chinense* in South America. It is almost inevitable that people would have found similar uses for similar plants in response to similar needs (Mangelsdorf 1953).

Not only peppers but also other groups of plants, among them tobacco, beans, cotton, squash, and amaranth, consist of two or more domesticated species, grown for the same product and used in the same way in different locations. This presents a question, according to Pickersgill (1977*a*, 591), "of whether speciation preceded domestication (which implies that the individual cultivated species were domesticated independently, from wild ancestors which were already specifically distinct), or whether speciation followed domestication (in which case each crop may have been domesticated once only).* This question must be answered separately for each crop."

"Chili peppers," she continues, "present a more complex situation." Of the five domesticated species, *C. baccatum* and *C. pubescens* are morphologically and cytogenetically so different that it is probable they were domesticated independently from at least two distinct wild species. Numerical taxonomic studies confirm the probable independent domestication of *C. baccatum* but suggest that domesticated *C. annuum*, *C. chinense*, and *C. frutescens* all arose from different parts of the same complex of wild forms, which was not completely differentiated. Speciation in certain peppers preceded domestication and in other instances was accentuated by it.

According to Eschbaugh (in press), the domesticated capsicums now have a worldwide distribution but at the time of Columbus' discovery of the New World there was a much narrower distribution. *C. pubescens* was a midelevational (2,000–2,500 m) An-

6. Nazca embroideries. The figure of a man holding chili-peppers shown here is from a garment called the Nazca shirt, representing the textile art of the early Nazca period (400–600 A.D.). Two rows of figures on the front and back contain 23 figures of agriculturalists with some of the principal crop plants of the time done in 14 hues of wool yarn on cotton cloth. Not only is this farmer (fig. 12) holding peppers, but he also has two pods hanging from his neck. These embroidered capsicums predate the Tello Obelisk. (O'Neale & Whitaker 1947; photograph from the Lowie Museum of Anthropology, University of California, Berkeley)

---

* According to Candolle (1964), no basic food plants have been domesticated in historical times.

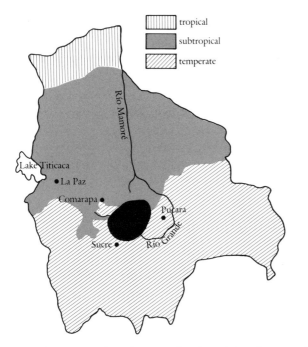

7a. The proposed nuclear area for the origin of peppers in central Bolivia just north of Sucre in an area crossed by the Río Grande.

dean species (Eshbaugh 1979). *C. baccatum* var. *pendulum* was restricted to areas east and west of the Andes (Eshbaugh 1970; Pickersgill 1971). *C. frutescens* and *C. chinense* were Amazonian (Pickersgill 1971), while *C. annuum* var. *annuum* was Mesoamerican (Pickersgill 1971).

No matter where or by whom plants were first domesticated, certain changes took place during the process. Peppers are a good subject for the study of evolution under domestication because most of the species contain both wild and cultivated varieties. The two types can be crossed and the genetic bases for differences within them analyzed.

The wild peppers have certain common characters: small, red, pungent fruits, which may be conical, globose, or elongate; the attachment position is erect; they are easily separated from the calyx (deciduous or soft fleshed); the seeds are dispersed by birds. As humans began to grow the plants for their fruits, they selected, unconsciously or perhaps even consciously, those that were nondeciduous, since they held the fruit until harvest and the fruit was more difficult for birds to steal. Most cultivated peppers have pendent instead of erect fruits. Being pendent has come about not only from selection for increased weight of the fruit but also because it protects the fruit from bird damage by hiding it amid the foliage (Pickersgill & Heiser 1976).

As is the case in all domesticated plants, the color, shape, flavor, and size were altered considerably under selection by growers. The greatest morphological alterations occur in that part of the plant that is most valued (Harlan 1975). Wild capsicums have styles exserted beyond the anthers to make pollination by insects easier. The domesticated cultivars have been selected for short styles, which promote self-pollination. A self-pollinating variety can be grown in a small area with several other distinct types without danger of cross breeding, whereby its identity would be lost.

We have already discussed the fact that the domesticated peppers had several centers of origin in the New World and that in each center distinct species were domesticated. This is a unique evolutionary history because seldom have five species been domesticated independently in different geographical regions from one small genus (Eshbaugh, in press). The four or five species that were known to be cultivated at the time of the Conquest were each developed along similar lines with selection for nondeciduous fruit, pendent attachment position, self-pollination, and desired shape, color, and size. After domestication the different species spread from their original ranges.

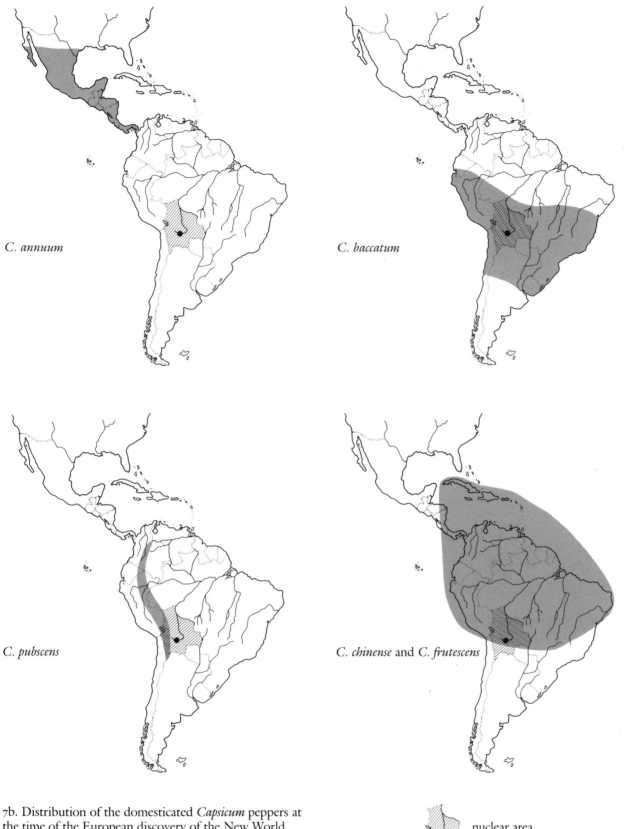

C. annuum

C. baccatum

C. pubscens

C. chinense and *C. frutescens*

7b. Distribution of the domesticated *Capsicum* peppers at the time of the European discovery of the New World. (After Heiser 1976*a*; McLeod et al. 1982)

 nuclear area

A perceptive hypothesis regarding the early evolution and dispersal of peppers from a nuclear area in central Bolivia has such logical appeal that it merits presenting. It is certainly food for thought. Admitting the highly speculative nature of their data-supported "scenario" McLeod et al. suggest "that *C. chacoense* or its ancestor gave rise to both the purple- and white-flowered groups in this nuclear area. The purple-flowered group (*C. eximium*), which also includes some white corolla forms, then migrated into the Andean highlands where subsequent directional selection and genetic drift yielded *C. cardenasii* as a local founder event and *C. pubscens* as a domesticate" (1982, 366). They go on to say: "We suggest that the white-flowered ancestor migrated out of the nuclear area and gave rise to the *C. baccatum* group in the relatively dry area of southern Bolivia. The wild form then continued to migrate along the river system and, in the wetter Amazon Basin, developed into the wild progenitor of the *C. annuum* group."

To confirm or deny this hypothesis will require additional detailed collecting from the nuclear area and its surrounding regions as well as from Brazil and the Amazon. We hope this can be accomplished before land development and the destruction of forests in those areas destroy the natural habitat of the *Capsicum*.

Let's return for a brief look at the world picture of agriculture's beginnings. As previously stated, humans, in small bands of hunter-gatherers, have been on this earth at least a million years, but grasses and flowering plants are even more ancient. During those eons many of the plants that were available for domestication were equipped with natural means of dispersal. With so much time and adequate means it is highly likely that prehistoric plants could have been naturally transported great distances. A plant with seed-bearing fruit known to float in sea water for long periods, such as the coconut and gourd, would only have had to establish itself once to explain its presence in the New World (Whitaker & Carter 1954; Camp 1954; Heiser 1973). Indeed, this is a rare event but given a couple of million years in which to accomplish this, it is a probability.*

About ten thousand years ago the means of acquiring food employed by those hunter-gatherers began to change as they began domesticating plants and animals. In reference to the New World, Heiser (1973, 10) queries: "Could the idea of agriculture have come from the Old World?" Answering his own question, he asserts that the New World was peopled by migrations of Asian hunters crossing the "Bering Strait long before agriculture was known. . . . it seems highly unlikely that agriculture had but a single origin. It is in fact likely that it had several origins in both the Old and the New World." In the New World, agriculture developed a few thousand years later than in the Old World, with dual origins in Mexico and Peru at about the same time.

Scholars are examining every proposed theory in their efforts to trace prehistoric plant distribution. In the case of plants that bear seeds not adapted to distribution over vast expanses of water, some authors appeal to the theory of continental drift to explain how those plants might have reached their niches by dispersal across land masses with a dry climate; however, evidence to date suggests that the continents began drifting apart before or during a period when flowering plants were still very primitive (Heiser 1979, 101). Yet another possibility is an ancient transantarctic distribution of seed plants in a preglacial period when arid conditions prevailed in much of Antarctica (Merrill 1954).

Ethnobotanists study the dispersal of cultivated plants and their relationship to humans, or ethnic groups. The science of ethnobotany became established in the early decades of this century to study plants in relation to the needs and customs of a given ethnic group. There is a movement toward the isolationist's view as a result of two things: (*a*) the increased demand for scientific evidence and fact rather than speculation and (*b*) the discovery that parallel phenomena within two separated areas may be a result of independent evolution along parallel lines.

The critical proof of prehistoric voyages across the Pacific will come from domesticated plants, such as peppers, because these do not have characteristics necessary for "natural long distance dispersal and cannot establish themselves in wild habitats" (Pickersgill & Bunting 1969, 227). They continue by saying: "Evidence from only four species (Cotton, Sweet potato, Bottle gourd, Coconut) does not constitute a proof of significant cultural contact between the Americas and Asia or Africa after the invention of agriculture and before the time of Columbus's discovery." Merrill (1954) and others omit cotton. A diffusionist explorer, Heyerdahl (1964, 131) of Kon Tiki fame, adds: "As a marked contrast to the multiple evidence of South American voyages to Polynesia, the botanical support for aboriginal American contact with Asia or Africa is

---

*Chapters 8, 9, and 10 in *The Gourd Book* by Heiser (1979) are recommended for those desiring further discussion of plant dispersal.

very vague and as yet quite vulnerable."

If we suppose that Heyerdahl's (1964) alleged documented evidence listing the pepper as being among several American plants growing on Easter Island at the time the first Europeans arrived in about 1768 is a fact, then the presence of these American plants would present several alternatives: (*a*) pre-Columbian Amerindians sailed to Polynesia, (*b*) Polynesians sailed to pre-Columbian America and returned with peppers, (*c*) the plant was introduced into Polynesia directly from America during the 250-year interval between Magellan and Captain Cook (Harlan 1975), or (*d*) capsicums made a complete post-Columbian circumnavigation of the world via the Cape of Good Hope and the Far East before Cook's voyage. Whether one is an isolationist or a diffusionist, one has to admit that *if* domesticated peppers were there it was due to contact, either pre-Columbian or post-Columbian. However, most botanists do not take Heyerdahl seriously. Ten years earlier, Merrill (1954) had marveled at the complete absence of *Capsicum* from the list of seed-bearing plants reported by the botanists who accompanied Captain Cook on his voyages to Polynesia from 1768 to 1780.

Another plant said to be found in both places was the sweet potato (*Ipomea batatas*). Before 1864 in Polynesia it was called *kumara*, which was thought to be derived from an alleged Quechuan word, *cumar*. Many have considered that to be evidence proving the plant came from Peru (Carter 1950, 163). The origin of *cumar* has become suspect in recent years and Brand (1971, 363) affirms that the word is not a Quechuan name for sweet potato. The word may be of Polynesian origin instead of Quechuan, being introduced to Peru in early post-Columbian times (Heiser 1973, 144). Regardless of how the plant got there, by natural means or artificial, people would have had to carry the plant name and quite feasibly its usages across the same sea. That is why diffusionists strive to find these types of bonds and are disappointed when one of them is disproved.

The likelihood of transoceanic contact with aboriginal America is very limited, but some (Heyerdahl 1963; Sauer 1952; Carter 1950) argue that it is possible. There are no natural departure routes to the Old World on the Atlantic side of America but there are two on the Pacific. One of these sets of prevailing winds and currents, known as the North Equatorial Current, leads across the Pacific from Mesoamerica to the Philippines. The second, called the South Equatorial Current, carries from Peru to Polynesia and New Guinea

(Jett 1971, 15). Either premeditated or forced crossings outside these naturally occurring routes would demand exceptional navigational skill and, without a doubt, the certain knowledge that land was ahead (Heyerdahl 1963).

Going from Asia to America, the most direct route is the Japan–North Pacific–California current originating in the Philippines, following the coast of Asia north, crossing the Pacific, and then flowing along the coast of North America and Mexico to Costa Rica. This is the route of the annual Manila galleon that traveled from Manila to Acapulco between 1565 and 1815 (Schurz 1939). A second, but less dependable, direct route is with the Equatorial Counter Current.

A Spanish navigator, Andrés de Urdaneta, discovered the Japan Current in 1565, thereby making the round trip possible. Prior to that ships had been able to sail from America to the East Indies but were unable to return. The outbound voyage from Acapulco took the vessels well south of the Hawaiian Islands, while the return carried the trading ships far to the north of that group of islands (E. K. Reed 1971, 108); as a consequence, the Pacific Ocean south of the Equator was virtually unknown to Europeans prior to Cook's voyage in 1768.*

Granted that there were rare prehistoric transpacific contacts with America at long intervals, what effect did they have? We know that drift voyages between Asia and America not only are clearly possible but actually have occurred repeatedly in historic time (Schurz 1939, 227). We also know that Orientals have had the capacity to construct and maneuver ocean-going craft for over two thousand years. By analogy, we might conclude that prehistoric people also made such voyages. Doran (1971, 136) comments that "the ocean gap that has been such a barrier to acceptance of the derivation of American traits from the Old World is a lesser obstacle when the sea worthiness of rafts, their sailing ability, and the fortitude of man are demonstrated as adequate for transpacific crossings."

Why wasn't the influence of those prehistoric voyagers more pronounced and widespread in the New World? Many writers have inferred that the influence is plainly visible in the art and architecture, even the

---

*In the 250 years of its operation, the Manila galleon was under strict orders never to deviate from its established route. As a consequence, the Hawaiian Islands and many others in the South Pacific remained unknown and unexplored by Europeans until the three scientific voyages of Cook between 1768 and 1780 (Schurz 1939). The Spanish policy of exclusion, which barred all commerce with foreign countries, resulted in the Pacific being virtually a Spanish lake for almost two centuries.

languages, but it is a fact that there is *no* reliable evidence that these oriental contacts had significant influence on indigenous populations. In fact, excluding Viking contacts, no verified archaeological finds of artifacts from one hemisphere in pre-Columbian context have been found to date in the other hemisphere (Riley et al. 1971, 448).

The concensus of botanical evidence given in the American Archaeology Society symposium on pre-Columbian contacts concluded that "*there is no hard and fast evidence for any pre-Columbian human introduction of any single plant or animal* across the ocean from the Old World to the New World, or vice-versa. This is emphatically *not* to say that it could not have occurred" (Riley et al. 1971, 452).

When we were children we would "play-like"; as a consequence, a childish elision was formed to identify that type of play—"pl'ike." Let's "pl'ike" by surmizing that even one small vesselload of people had reached a New World shore in prehistoric times armed only with the superior cultural traits that would have made a premeditated or even a chance voyage of such proportions possible. The influence of the survivors of such a voyage could have been widespread if we use the well-documented activities of the sixteenth-century Spaniards as an example of possible accomplishment.

Those hardy or perhaps foolhardy conquistadors in relatively small bands or singly (as was the case of Cabeza de Vaca), living off the land, covered a vast area, ranging from the Grand Canyon of the American west to Argentina in only twenty years (1519–1540) after their first invasion of the New World mainland (Carter 1950, 178). Thus, one person's lifetime, without establishing a colony or producing heirs, would be time enough to traverse two continents.

Given that the invention of agriculture predates the invention of ocean-going craft, prehistoric mariners would have had the knowledge of plant cultivation. If these ancient voyagers had landed with the knowledge of agriculture and had moved overland like the conquistadors, it would seem likely that the various species of cultivated plants, both native and introduced, would have been more widespread throughout the New World than they were at the time of the first documented Old World contact in 1492. Carter (1950) maintains that plant contact is not a fleeting contact. Any exchange of crop plants involves reciprocal learning. He contends that plants must be used to be appreciated. Each plant has its own method of cultivation and use. Learning such things about a plant involves prolonged association and exchange of knowledge,

at least through a growing season. However, the incipient farming in the New World, as indicated by cultivated plant remains, is not indicative of the growth pattern one would anticipate if the knowledge of agriculture came to the New World fully developed (Phillips 1966).

In proclaiming the origins of pre-Columbian art, Grieder (1982) theorized that the Americas were populated from Asia in three waves and that the "Third Wave" of migrations carried a still more developed cultural stage (than those of the first two) to Polynesia and the Americas between 5000 and 1500 B.C. If the people making these migrations had been of such a high cultural development as he purports, they would have had fully developed knowledge of plant cultivation and domestication, but so far archaeological-botanical evidence does not support such "migrations." Excavations in the Tehuacán Valley of Mexico demonstrate a transition over a period from 7200 B.C. to A.D. 1540 from a hunting-and-food-gathering subsistence to full-fledged agriculture (MacNeish 1964). Migrants after 5000 B.C. would have been met by neophyte agriculturalists. Before that date, humans lacked the technology for such overseas migrations from Asia (Doran 1971). Even such a diffusionist as Gordon Ekholm (1964) states that the absence of concrete evidence indicates there was no large-scale migration from Asia and, even if there had been, there was no long and continuing contact. There was no "Pacific Regatta" (Mangelsdorf & Oliver 1951).

It is difficult to extend dates to other areas but if, as an example, we look at those established for Middle America, we find that the "Third Wave" would encounter not only sedentary agricultural villages linked to established agriculture but also some with nascent temple and ceremonial centers. The year 1500 B.C. is accepted as the beginning of the Pre-Classic Period of Middle American civilization, the era that witnessed the temple-center rise to importance. These centers provided leadership, which gave impetus for the development of arts, crafts, and formal learning (Willey et al. 1964).

Styles or artistic traditions can be equated with domesticated plants: both are diffused by the movement of objects by people capable of making the object, or by people capable of teaching others to make the object (Phillips 1966). A style is a complex phenomenon, like culture. One style can be influenced by another, resulting in something unlike either. To propose that a particular style can be adopted by an alien people without serious modification is rather dubious. In addition, to consider that it could be preserved in "purity" for a thousand or more years—until the Conquest—is unpractical.

No object of Old World origin has been found in the New World to carry on a style and even if it had been brought it is inconceivable that an idea of an object, carried across the sea, given to a person of a different culture, who in turn gave it to another and so on for a thousand years, would still be traceable.

Try this exercise with a group of eight or more people. Give each person a piece of tracing paper and a pen. Let the first participant carefully trace a simple line drawing and then pass on the tracing, without the original, to the next, who traces that tracing, and so on until the circle is complete. The result is unrecognizable from the original, even more so if the first drawing is complex and the group is large. If each "artist" represented a period of time, it is obvious that the longer the time the greater the difference between the original idea and the finished product. According to Kubler (1962, 71), "every man-made replica varies from its model by minute, unplanned divergences, of which the accumulated effects are like a slow drift away from the archetype." Selection, planting, and harvesting are representative of this type of replication.

We contend that a style is unlikely to have lain dormant for a thousand years and suddenly reappeared in a new context unless, after a long burial, the resurrected artifact sat before an accomplished artist. Nor could it have been maintained in wood carving for hundreds of years as Ekholm (1964) suggests. Replication by humans, not machines, does not permit this. Each person makes his or her selection based on personal sets of perceptions.

It might seem to those of us who have been "pl'iking" that, since botanical scholars propose that agriculture

developed independently in at least three centers throughout the world, the various cultural features that evolved from agriculture would have developed independently, also. Astronomy-astrology, and the associated development of calendrics, is said to be a key to Grieder's "Third Wave" symbolism. Astronomy and calendrics were probably an outgrowth of agriculture as the agriculturist became more aware of the seasons and time in relation to plant growth, one development following the other as the need occurred in a universal sequence (Enc. Americana 1976, 2: 570). The famous Aztec calendar came after, not before, agriculture.

I don't deny that there could have been contacts or influences from Asia that activated civilization in Middle America even though archaeological findings do not support them at this time. What I do question is the degree to which they influenced development in the New World. We will all await the future results of continued study to present the evidence needed to resolve the question, if indeed it can be resolved. Phillips (1966, 297) clarifies the case by maintaining: "Before any assertions can be made about unity of New and Old World civilizations, it will be necessary not only to produce evidence of historical contacts with some degree of precision as to time, place, and means of transport, but also to show that the role of such contacts was decisive in the development of Nuclear American civilization *in their formative stages*, that without such contacts the level of civilization would not have been attained."

Regardless of future findings, we can be certain that the genus *Capsicum* originated and was domesticated in the Western Hemisphere before there was an opportunity for outside influence. We will end on a word of caution—those who theorize on transoceanic contacts, ignoring the plant evidence, do so at great risk.

3
EARLY EUROPEAN OBSERVERS

IMMEDIATELY following the Conquest, Spaniards began to document the happenings in their new-found realm. The vast archives relating to the Spanish dominion of the New World may still be studied by diligent scholars in the Casa Lonja of Seville, Spain, where the general archives of the Indies have been accumulated and stored for almost five hundred years. Among the 35,793 items pertaining to the conquest and colonization of Hispano-America can be found material relating to the flora and fauna of the Americas.

The first group of documents referring to the New World were written as personal testaments of the Conquest by men of arms, who felt nothing but contempt for everything aboriginal. They spoke only of the most common plants, calling them by European or Antillian names, which replaced local names in many cases (Yacovleff & Herrera 1934). However, in 1526 that trend changed with the publication of the first part of the great work by Oviedo, *Historia general y natural de las Indias.*

The early post-Columbian writers' references to *Capsicum* are presented here, along with comments on peppers by other observant visitors to the various parts of the colonial empire of Spain. These are followed by what was set forth by early European herbalists and writers who came into contact with *pimientos de las Indias* after their introduction in the Old World. Since Oviedo was the first important historian after Chanca and Martyr, we shall begin with him.

GONZALO FERNÁNDEZ DE OVIEDO Y VALDÉS

Historia general y natural de las Indias (1526) was the work of a Spanish *caballero*, El Capitán Gonzalo Fernández de Oviedo y Valdés (1478–1537), who reached tropical America at Darién, Panama, in 1513. He is considered to be the first official chronicler of the New World and the first to document peppers in Tierra Firme.* During the thirty-four years he spent in different parts of the Spanish Main,† he found that the pepper, or *ají*, was very well known and was used both in the West Indies and on the mainland. "The Indians everywhere grow it in gardens and farms with much diligence and attention because they eat it continuously with almost all of their food" (Oviedo 1950, 235).

He was quick to report that the "Christians" did not use it any less than the Indians. Oviedo, who had uncommon powers of observation and a strong interest in natural history, goes on to describe the plant, flower, and fruit, adding that the size was dependent on the fertility of the soil and whether or not it was irrigated. After describing several varieties, he comments on its having been taken to Spain, Italy, and many other places because it was considered to be a very good spice; it is healthful, especially in the wintertime; and it is better with meat and fish than "good black pepper."

BARTOLOMÉ DE LAS CASAS

Two major manuscripts written by Bartolomé de las Casas (1474–1566) were not published during his lifetime. His *Historia de las Indias, 1520–1561,* was used by

---

*Tierra Firme is the southern coast, or littoral, of the Caribbean Sea: the continent or mainland, not the islands, extending from the peninsula of Paria, opposite the island of Trinidad, westward into Central America.

†Spanish Main is the English translation of the Spanish mainland, or Tierra Firme. Later the whole of the Caribbean area, including the sea, came to be known in English as the Spanish Main. This later meaning included the Tierra Firme, the West Indies, and the sea between them.

other historians before it was printed in 1875–1876 in Madrid. His *Apologetica historia de las Indias* remained in manuscript until 1909, at which time it was published in Madrid by Marcelino Menéndez y Pelayo in *Historiadores de Indias*.

Few, if any, have known the Spanish Main and its natives so well for so long. His father and uncle had been to the New World before he came with Ovando in 1502. He campaigned in Hispaniola for ten years before going to Cuba with Narváez. He became a Dominican friar and the bishop of Chiapas, being the first priest to be ordained in the New World. His work among the Indians was such that he was known as the "Father of the Indians" and the "Apostle of the Indies." Many years later he began his writings while in a convent in Hispaniola, but he did most of the work on his two histories during an unusually long lifetime in Valladolid after his return to Spain.

Las Casas was an acute and careful observer; his identifications are important because he took great care to give location data for what he described. He gathered documents of the period, such as the journal of Columbus, wherever he could find them—originals when possible or copies he made himself or had made. He and Oviedo met but clashed over Indian policy.

Peppers were among the many plants he documented. He tells us that orchards and kitchen gardens did not occur in Hispaniola as they did in Tierra Firme. Capsicums were common seasoning; two kinds were described as domestic, and a third as wild. One cultivated *ají* was long, red, and finger shaped; a second was globular like a cherry and more pungent; the wild form bore very small fruits, which were most certainly *C. annuum* var. *aviculare*.

LEONHARD FUCHS

In his *De historia stirpium*, 1543, Leonhard Fuchs (Fuchsius, Fuchsen) (1501–1566), a Lutheran professor of medicine at the University of Tubingen, introduces some of the first scientifically accurate illustrations of plants. The woodblocks were prepared from drawings done from nature by artists Albert Meyer, Heinrich Fullmaurer, and Veit Rudolf Speckle. The prints by Hans Weiditz in Otto Brunfel's herbal of 1530–1536 were the source of Fuchs' inspiration. In the text, which was based on Dioscorides, he presented his mistaken belief that the new peppers were native to India because they had been introduced to Germany a few years prior to 1542 from that distant country and were called Calicut pepper. He was also confused in thinking peppers were *Grana paradisi*. Grains of paradise is

Guinea pepper, *Amomum melequeta*,* a native of western tropical Africa, allied to ginger. After it was discovered in 1460, it was once used as a substitute for black pepper and is the reason Guinea has a "Pepper Coast" (Macmillan 1962).

Other herbalists were to depend on Fuchs' book and to republish its influential illustrations for years to come. The woodblocks, done in a simple line designed to be hand colored, show bloom, fruit, and roots. The three prints depicting Calechutifcher Pfeffer, Greyter Indianifcher Pfeffer, and Langer Indianifcher Pfeffer are the first published illustrations of peppers. Fuchs himself is shown in an elegant fur-collared brocade cape holding a small plant.

HANS STADE

During a period from 1547 to 1555, Hans Stade, a Hessian, was a captive of Indians in eastern Brazil. His observation that the peppers of the continent of America (Brazil) were of two kinds—"the one yellow, the other red; both, however, grow in like manner"—was perhaps the earliest report from that area.† He also noted: "When green it is as large as the haws that grow on hawthorns. It is a small shrub, about half a fathom high and has small leaves; it is full of peppers which burn the mouth. They pluck it when it becomes ripe, and they dry it in the sun" (Stade 1874, 166).

REMBERT DODOENS

Rembert Dodoens' (1517–1585) *History of Plants*, or *Cruydtboeck*, was originally written in Flemish and was published in Antwerp in 1554. Dodoens was physician to the court of Maximilian II in Vienna. The early botanists were nearly all physicians because plants were valued and studied for their curative and medicinal potential. Three years later the *Cruydtboeck* was translated into French by Clusius. Next, Henrie Lyte translated the French manuscript into English. That amended and edited version was dedicated to Queen Elizabeth I in 1595.

The book, like other herbals from the second half of the sixteenth century, was illustrated with woodcuts that had originally been prepared for the octavo edition of Fuchs' *De historia stirpium* in 1541. Dodoens,

---

*In Cassell's *Spanish Dictionary* there are two words defined as grains of paradise—*malagueta* and *amomo*, obviously corruptions of *Amomum melequeta*; they are sometimes applied to the *chiltecpín*, the wild "bird pepper" or flea chilli, in northern Mexico.
†The cultivation of peppers is listed as one of the cultural traits of the indigenous tribes of central Brazil at the time the first Europeans arrived sometime after it was first sighted by Cabral in 1500 and the time the first colony was established before 1507 (Freyre 1966, 90).

who was a Belgian physician, describes three "sorts" of peppers and proclaims their medicinal virtues, but in so doing he cautions the reader of "The Danger," warning that it is dangerous to eat them if one is bled very often or in great quantity and "it killeth dogs, if it be given them to eat" (Dodoens 1595, 730–731).

CHARLES DE L'ESCLUSE (CLUSIUS)

Charles de l'Escluse (1526–1609) was a Dutch botanist of world reknown who, among a host of accomplishments, introduced the mideastern tulip to Holland. Besides being the first translator of Dodoens' *History of Plants*, or *Cruydtboeck*, he wrote other important books concerning plants, was the director of the imperial gardens at Vienna, a professor of botany at the University of Leiden, a lawyer, a philosopher and a historian. He traveled extensively in foreign lands, no small feat in that day. Although his travels were facilitated by his ability to speak eight languages, they were fraught with accidents, which finally crippled him.

Flanders, especially the University of Leiden and the city of Antwerp, was the center of botanical learning in the late sixteenth and early seventeenth centuries and Clusius (his Latin name) was its foremost botanist (Rix 1981, 39–49).

His description of peppers reads as follows: "This capsicum, or Indian pepper, is painstakingly grown in Castilia both by gardeners and by housewives. Instead of pepper it is used all the year round as a seasoning, either dried or in the form of the freshly picked green pods. It has several varieties. . . . I remember having seen, in 1585, vast plantations of it in the suburbs of Brunn, this famous town of Moravia; pepper means a considerable income for the gardeners, because it is commonly used by most people" (l'Escluse 1611, 104).

Plants from far afield were represented in his collected works, *Rariorum plantarum historia*, published in Antwerp in 1601, including plants from Mexico, among them the *Capsicum*. In 1611, two years following his death, another book of interest to a follower of the pod, *Curae posteriores* (*Curaposter*), was published. Previously he had thought the *Capsicum* came from India, but here he says, ". . . some call the American pepper and other the Piperitis or yet others think is the Siliquastrum of Plinius." In this work he credits the Reverend Father Gregorius of Regium, a Cappucine monk from Italy, as being the most learned authority on the subject of *Capsicum*. Regium (Reggio) sent Clusius thirteen plates showing branches of individual species with their fruit. Clusius condensed these plates

8. Fuchs, *De historia stirpium*. (From the Rare Books and Manuscripts Library, Harry Ransom Humanities Research Center, University of Texas at Austin)

to three by dispensing with the representation of the foliage as being repetitious. He grouped the illustrations into plates based on the three classes set up by Regium—straight, erect fruit; pendent, round fruit; pendent oblong pods. To these he added a plate showing the entire plant of the "common Siliquast." These engravings were used repeatedly by writers for years to come. It was the custom of the publisher, Plantin of Antwerp, to pool the woodblocks used for illustrations in the books the company published; as a consequence, the same prints are found in books by different authors. Dodoens, Fuchs, and Clusius were among those.

JOSÉ DE ACOSTA

At the end of the sixteenth century, Jesuit priest, poet, historian, and cosmographer Father José de Acosta (or de a Costa) (1539–1600) informs us that:

They had not found at the West Indies any kinde of Spices proper or peculiar to them, as pepper, cloves, cinnamon, nutmegges or ginger . . . but the naturall spice that God hath given to the West Indies, is that we call in Castille, Indian pepper, and in India *Axi*, as a generall worde taken from the first land of the Ilands, which they conquered. In the language of Cusco, it is called *Vchu*, and in that of Mexico *Chilli*. This plant is well knowne, and therefore I will speake a little, onely wee must understand, that in olde time it was much esteemed amongst the Indians, which they carried into places where it grew not, as a marchandise of consequence. . . . When *Axi* is taken moderately, it helps and comforts the stomacke for digestion: but if they take too much, it hath bad effects, for of its self it is very hote, fuming, and pierceth greatly, so as the use thereof is prejudiciall to the health of young folkes, chiefly to the soule, for that it provokes to lust. . . . it is mockery to say it is not hote, seeing it is so in the highest degree etc. etc. (Acosta 1970, 239)

BERNARDINO DE SAHAGÚN

In 1529 another Spanish friar, Franciscan Bernardino de Sahagún (?–1590), arrived in Mexico. About 1569 he put down for posterity his *Historia general de las cosas de la Nueva España*, which has come to be known as the Florentine Codex. In this fascinating work, written in both the language of the Aztecs and Spanish with profuse illustrations, he documented the daily life of the Indian as it was before the Conquest. In the work he refers to the pepper more than any other condiment. One might say that he was the first to classify *Capsicum*. The pepper was such an important item in the daily life of the Mexican Indians that when they fasted to appease their gods a man did not lay with a woman or a woman with a man . . . and they ate no peppers. In speaking of the foods eaten by the lords,

Sahagún tells us that red or yellow peppers are in almost every dish. Some of the foods the lords ate were "frog with green chillis; newt with yellow chilli; tadpoles with small chillis; maguey grubs with a sauce of small chillis; lobster with red chilli, tomatoes and ground squash seeds; winged ants with savory herbs" (Sahagún 1963, 14 [9]: 37).

The Aztec ruler directed the market place, where everything to be sold was placed separately in its own station. Thus, in the food section one could find the pre-Columbian *chilli* vender selling "mild red chillis, broad chillis, hot green chillis, yellow chillis, *cuitlachilli, tenpilchilli, chichioachilli*. He sells water chillis,* conchilli; he sells smoked chillis, small chillis, tree chillis, thin chillis, those like beetles. He sells green chillis, sharp-pointed red chillis, a late variety, those from Arzitziuacan, Tochmilco, Hauxtepec, Michoacan, Anauac, the Huaxteca, the Chichimeca. Separately he sells strings of chillis, chillis cooked in an olla, fish chillis, white fish chillis" (Sahagún 1963, 14 [8]: 68).

JOHN GERARD[E]

About the same time, the end of the sixteenth century, the most famous but not the most reliable English herbal was published. *The Herball or General Historie of Plantes* by John Gerard (1545–1607), an apothecary, is a compilation including translations of Dodoens' work; however, the book is filled with additions of his own "eye-witness" incredibilities. These flights of fancy can be better understood by recalling that the art of healing had always been involved in magic; as a consequence, herbals, up through the Renaissance, were filled with fable. The invention of printing changed the entire aspect of science. Among the first printed books were the herbals, which presented plants for their usefulness in medicine or as food. As a result of European exploration in the sixteenth century, many new plants were introduced.

Previously, plants had been cultivated for food and for their medicinal properties; now they came to be grown for their ornamental value as well. Books showing these flowers are known as florilegia. As mentioned earlier, the publishing house of Plantin in Antwerp pooled the woodblocks used in the works of Clusius, Dodoens, l'Obel, Fuchs, and others and then loaned them freely to followers. Gerard used such il-

---

*"Water chillis" may be comparable to the thick-fleshed sweet peppers similar to the Bell peppers, which are currently called "de Aguas," or "of water," in southern Mexico.

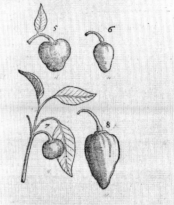
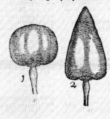

9. L'Éscluse, *Curae posteriores*. (Photographs from the Missouri Botanical Garden Library, St. Louis)

Table 2.   Nahuatl Names for Seven Pre-Columbian Peppers with Descriptions by Hernández*

1. QUAUHCHILLI: *Quahu* = tree. *Chilli árbol*, or tree *chilli*; Haitians call it *chillimontes*. The smallest and hottest of all; leaves smaller than any other *chilli* species; similar in shape to olives. Bears fruit all year. Used as a condiment, not as a vegetable.
   cf. CHILTECPIN: has woody, treelike stalks and very small leaves; leaf size, fruit size, and pungency are not those of the long, cylindrical, pointed *chile de árbol* we know today.
2. CHILTECPINTLI: *Tecpin* = flea. Size and bite of a flea. There are three forms, which differ only in location, harvest season, or pungency. All bear three times during the harvest season from December to April. Sometimes seems more burning than *quauhchilli* but loses its heat more readily.
   1. TOTOCUITLATL: *Toto* = bird; *cuitla-tl* = excrement; Haitians call it *huarahuao*; largest of the three.
   2. TLILCHILLI: *chilli negro* = black. Turns dark; three sizes, smallest in last harvest.
   3. TZANALCHILLI: grown irrigated in August; smallest of the three.
   cf. CHILTECPIN = ovoid; CHILIPIQUIN = elongate.
3. TONALCHILLI: *Tonal* = heat of the sun. *Chilli del sol* because it fruits during the summer months only and is the color of the sun, pale yellow. Haitians call it *chili blanco*. Green at first, turning pale yellow, finally red.
   cf. CARRICILLO or TORNACHILI.
4. TZINQUAUHYO: *Tzin* = stump; *quauh* = wilderness, mountain forest; also *tzin* = one's rump. Some authors say it means "wild," "from the mountain." In Hispaniola it is called *ají coral* = like coral. Thin, five fingers long, red when ripe.
   cf. *Capsicum violaceum* DC. Hort. Monsp. 87, 1813, according to Herrera (1904, 102); however, it does not match that description. A comparable modern species has not been determined.
5. TZONCHILLI, TEXOCHILLI, TEPOCHILLI: *Tzon* = head; *texo* = ground, like flour; *tepotz* = rump. Also *pochilli*. *De masa* (dough) *chile* because it is sweet and bland and can be eaten with tortillas. Long, narrow, some sweetness, red color, of a smooth bitterness. Soft flesh (pericarp) must be preserved by smoking, thus *pochilli* (*pochilli* = smoked; invert root word for *chi pocli*).
   cf. JALAPEÑO: cannot be dried; it may have seemed sweet to early Mexican Indian tastes by comparison; also there has been time for growers to have increased the pungency through selection.
6. CHILCOZTLI: *Co* = yellow. Foods cooked with it take a saffron color. Six fingers long; bears all year. Called *ají azafrán* (saffron pepper) by Spaniards in Haiti. Reddish, sometimes turning raisin color.
   cf. GUAJILLO: a strong coloring agent.
7. MILCHILLI: *Mil* = field (not specifically corn field). Long, narrow, ending in a sharp point. Red when ripe. Smaller than *texochilli*. Sown and reaped in corn season, thus "field of corn."
   cf. CHILE DE ARBOL or perhaps another Cayenne type.

*Cf. = my comments and comparisons with modern cultivars.

lustrations, some being those found in an earlier work by Clusius that depicted thirteen individual peppers. According to Gerard the capsicums were "verie well knowne in shoppes at Billingsgate by the name of Ginnie Pepper" (1974, 292–293).

FRANCISCO HERNÁNDEZ

Dr. Francisco Hernández (1514–1578), who was physician and historian to King Felipe II of Spain and the Indies, was the first European to collect plants in America. He lived in Mexico from 1570 to 1577, and in about 1615 he produced *Quatro libros de la naturaleza y virtutes de las plantas y animales que estan recevidos en el uso de medicina en la Nueva España*, the medical parts of which were translated into Latin by Antonio Reccho and published in 1651. The majority of the original manuscript and all of the colored drawings for the Hernández book were destroyed by a fire in the Escorial near Madrid in 1671. Several mutilated and abbreviated versions appeared after this. Later, a lay brother, Fray Francisco Ximénez, found the Reccho translation. Recognizing its value, he "acquired" and translated it in an effort to correct errors in numerous corrupt Hernández manuscripts. That translation, published in Mexico in 1888, was unknown in Europe for many years. A translation of the 1651 edition was issued in Mexico City in 1942.

In speaking of peppers, Hernández affirmed that they were used not only to season food but also to stimulate appetite. He continued by naming and describing seven peppers that were used by the Indians, giving them their Nahuatl names: *quauhchilli, chiltecpin, tonalchilli, tzinquauhyo, tzonchilli* (or *texochilli* or *tepochilli*), *chilcoztli,* and *milchilli* (Hernández 1943).

Because he was a physician, his interests lay in the medicinal qualities of the plants; consequently, he enumerated what were considered to be the virtues of peppers. He recorded that they arouse intestinal gases or cause flatulence, they incite the appetite, and they tend to provoke bowel movements although not without some strain. In addition, when cooked, they ease and soften the bowels as well as provoking urination. They were thought not only to provoke the menstrual period but also to comfort a stomach and help digestion that is feeble due to a cold.

GARCILASO DE LA VEGA

Garcilaso de la Vega, El Inca, was born Gómez Suárez de Figueroa, son of a Spanish nobleman and a royal Incan princess. His *Royal Commentaries of the*

Incas, 1609, is significant because it is the first written account by someone with Incan blood and sympathies. His is the first book about America by an American author.

He was able to communicate with the Indians and learn their way of life. Garcilaso described the Incan hierarchy, relating that Manco Cápac was the first king, or Inca. To the Indians, *uchu*, the pepper, represented the delight they received from the teachings of those first Incan kings. Annual tribute was paid to the kings, the principal tribute being the tilling and fertilizing of the lands assigned to the Inca, who personified the Sun God, as well as the harvesting and storing of crops produced. One of the principal crops was the *uchu*, which the Spaniards call *ají* or *pimiento*; therefore, it was an important element in the tribute system—so important that one of the three brothers of Manco Cápac was named Agar-Uchu.

The Incas had strict fasts: one consisted of only maize and water, the maize being uncooked and minute in quantity. After three days they were permitted some uncooked herbs, *ají*, and salt but nothing else with their single daily meal of maize.

In the Peru of the Incas, boys of sixteen with royal blood had to undergo rigorous tests in order to receive the insignias of manhood. The previously mentioned fasts were doubled for the initiates undergoing this ordeal, in order to show that they were men enough to suffer any hunger or thirst to which they might be exposed in time of war. After the fast they were fed to restore their strength before being subjected to tests of body agility.

Garcilaso, writing in Spain many years after his observations, describes several varieties of *uchu*—green, red, yellow, and purple. He had, however, only seen the red kind in Spain. The "*chinchi uchu*," found but in small quantities, was more esteemed than the others. He tells us: "I heard a Spaniard from Mexico say that it was very good for the sight, so he used to eat two roast peppers as a sort of dessert after every meal. All the Spaniards who come to Spain from the Indies are accustomed to it and prefer it to Oriental spices. The Indians esteem it so highly that they set it above all the other fruits we have mentioned" (Garcilaso 1966, 505). He then pointed out that "poisonous creatures" avoid the *pimiento* and its fruit.

When the Spanish conquerors arrived, subduing and killing the Indians on the way, Pizarro, their leader, was met with an envoy from the Inca king. The king begged for mercy for his people while offering gifts in an attempt to appease the invaders. The Indians came bearing meat, game, honey, articles of gold and silver, macaws and llamas, and much more, among which was "the Indian pepper called *uchu*."

PEDRO CIEZA DE LEÓN

Pedro Cieza de León (1519?–1560) left his home in Seville, Spain, at the age of fourteen to become a boy soldier in the New World. The journal he kept during the seventeen years that he marched through South America provided the material for writing his *Chronicle of Peru* after he had returned to Spain. The first part of this work was published in Seville in 1553.

He dwells at length on descriptions of Indian customs and proclaims that their lot was improved under the dominion of the Incas. Before the Incas, the Peruvian Indians practiced human sacrifice and cannibalism; afterward they only sacrificed human blood that was drawn without killing. However, in the case of a particularly vicious Spaniard, the Indians retaliated by killing and eating him. Of this episode, Cieza tells us, "God permitted that he should be sentenced to death in the same place and have for his tomb the bellies of Indians." The question occurs: "Could he have been spiced with chili-peppers?" because Cieza's chronicle reports "the consumption of *ají* is greater than that of salt; for two-thirds of the dishes, more of the former than of the latter is used. It is sometimes eaten green and sometimes dried and pounded" (Cieza de León 1864, 232).

JOHN PARKINSON

John Parkinson (1567–1680), an English apothecary-botanist, published his *Theatrum botanicum* in 1640. Much of the information it contains is from Dodoens via Clusius as translated by Lyte. He placed the *Capsicum*, which he calls Ginnie Pepper, following the nightshades, because of its form and "because it is dangerous, but in a different way. Nightshades are cold, but peppers be hot." This confusing comment appears in much of the early literature. We can understand this when we learn that the pre-Columbian American Indian classified the medicinal properties of peppers as either *frio*, or cold, meaning difficult to digest, and *caliente*, or hot, signifying easy to digest. In reference to the capsicums, they did not use hot to mean "burning or biting" as we do when speaking of the pungent principle of the chili-peppers (Gentry & Standley 1974). Parkinson discusses twenty varieties of peppers, then proceeds to detail many remedies in which they are a principal ingredient. The woodcuts illustrating the book were borrowed or adapted from continental works.

THOMAS GAGE

Thomas Gage (1597–1656) was an Irish priest of the Dominican order who wrote *The English American, His Travail by Sea and Land; or, a New Survey of the West Indies*, 1648, after serving in Guatemala. In this work he writes of four peppers, the "*chilochote, chilipiquin, tonalchile,* and *chilpaelagua.*" The last of these was reported to be used in a chocolate drink that acts medically "to open, attenuate, not to bind." Today one of the peppers sold in the Guatemalan markets is called *chile chocolate,* while in Mexico the *costeño* is used in chocolate beverages.

BERNABE COBO

A naturalist and historian who knew Acosta, Jesuit priest Bernabe Cobo (1580–1657) traveled in many parts of Spanish America during his fifty years there. In a manuscript published in 1653 but begun forty years earlier, Padre Cobo, referring primarily to Peruvian plants, affirms that, next to maize, the *ají* was the plant held in the greatest esteem by the Indians. He describes the plant in detail, observing that there were more than forty different shapes and colors of peppers. Among other things, they are used to make sauces, one of which was called *locro,* comparable to *mole* sauce in Mexico, bringing tears to the eyes of those not accustomed to eating it.

It was intriguing to read that Spanish sailors took pickled peppers (*en escabeche*) to sea with them. One wonders if they did so only to season their food or if they recognized that eating them would help to ward off the mariner's malady, scurvy, because capsicums are a rich source of vitamin C, which prevents that disease.

His description of a tamale is "*bollos de maiz con mucho ají,*" or rolls of corn with a lot of *chile,* "some are large enough to hold a whole chicken and must be wrapped in a *petate* [straw mat]." The usual corn shuck covering would not be large enough.

ROBERT MORISON

Another medical doctor–botanist was an Englishman, Robert Morison (1620–1686), who wrote the *Plantarum historiae universalis oxoniensis* of 1680 (R. Morison 1715). Some of the herbarium specimens he used were one hundred years old. He described thirty-three species of *Capsicum,* which he grouped as pendent or erect, according to attachment position. Thir-

teen of those listed were from Clusius' *Curaposter* and two were referred to as Hernández' *milchilli* and *texochilli.* Although the book was illustrated, there were no peppers represented in the plates drawn by the Dutch artist, Michael Burghers.

LIONEL WAFER

The earliest report of peppers in Panama comes to us from an English buccaneer, Lionel Wafer (1660?–1705?), when he relates his activities during the spring of 1681 on the isthmus of Panama. Wafer was a surgeon who had cast his lot with a shipload of pirates. After he had been injured by a gunpowder explosion, they abandoned him in Panama where he was taken in by the Indians of Darién. He learned much about their lives and wrote a book in which he reported that they "have two sorts of *Pepper,* the one called *Bell-Pepper,* the other *Bird-Pepper,* and great quantities of each are much used by the Indians. Each sort grows on a Weed, or Shrubby Bush about a Yard high. The *Bird-Pepper* has the smaller Leaf, and is by the *Indians* better esteemed than the other, for they eat a great deal of it" (Wafer 1970, 107).

GEORG EBERHARD RUMPF

Georg Eberhard Rumpf (1627–1702), the Dutch governor of Amboine Island in Indonesia, collected and described the plants of that area in a huge work titled *Herbarium amboinense.* His life is a prime example of the perseverance, tenacity, and strength of character that typified the early naturalists.

Better known as Rumphius, the man spent most of his tragedy-plagued life on the island of Amboine (Amboyna). After having gone blind in 1635, he lost his wife and one of his daughters in an earthquake in 1674. Undismayed, he completed his voluminous manuscript and sent it to Holland to be printed. En route it was lost when the French attacked the ship carrying it. Again, he and his surviving daughter started to rewrite it but a fire engulfed his drawings in 1687. At last, in 1690, the first three of his botanical works were ready for publication, with nine more to come. Not surprisingly, they were published posthumously from 1741 to 1750. The drawings are magnificent.

He treated peppers in the fifth volume, stating his belief that certain forms had been cultivated in India since ancient times. However, his detailed observation that the vernacular names by which they are consistently called, such as *chillie* or *chilly* and *achar,* are of foreign origin contradicts that theory. He went on to painstakingly establish the pre-Columbian New World origin of the names, thereby proving a post-Columbian introduction of *Capsicum* to the Far East (Rumpf 1741–1750).

JOSEPH PITTON DE TOURNEFORT

In 1719 a Frenchman, Joseph Pitton de Tournefort (1656–1708), gave us the *Institutiones rei herbariae*. This influential work contains the original description of the genus *Capsicum*. His definition, however, does not give us a clue to his choice of the word *Capsicum*; consequently, the debate as to its meaning continues. The *Institutiones* was one of the major pre-Linnean attempts at plant classification. Tournefort, who practiced medicine in London, visited the West Indies. His vast herbarium collection, plus that of Joseph Banks, forms the basis of the herbarium section of the British Museum of Natural History.

I could not help observing that the third volume of that trend-setting book contains very clearly drawn illustrations of five invertebrate animals: *Corallum*, *Madrepora*, *Lithophyton*, *Tubularia*, and *Spongia*, which he described as plants. This says more than my words can for the state of botanical science in 1700.

FRANCISCO XIMÉNEZ

A Dominican priest, Francisco Ximénez (1666–1721?), set forth a natural history of Guatemala in 1722 in which he reports a number of peppers. The hottest one is called *tempenchile* (*chiltecpin* in Mexico), which is so hot "it seems like a fire." He had heard of one in Havana that was so strong a single pod was enough to make "a bull unable to eat" (Ximénez 1967, 289–290). This was probably the *chile* we know today as the *habañero*, a temptingly beautiful orange pod.

PHILLIP MILLER

In an eighteenth-century work we read more of the *Capsicum* in the final edition of an early herbal written by Phillip Miller (1691–1771). The full title of that work is *Gardener's Dictionary Containing the Method of Cultivation and Improving the Kitchen, Fruit, and Flower Garden, also, the Physick Garden, Wilderness, Conservatory, and Vinyard. Interspers'd with the History of Plants, the Characters of Each Genus, and the Names of All the Particular Species in Latin and English, and an Explanation of All the Terms Used in Botany and Gardening.*

The *Dictionary* went through eight editions, each of which was revised and enlarged. In the eighth Miller incorporated Linné's new binomial system of classification. After describing ten "species" of *Capsicum* (one

10. Rumpf, *Herbarium amboinense*: the first illustrations of *C. frutescens*. (Photograph from the McIlhenny Collection, Troy H. Middleton Library, Louisiana State University, Baton Rouge)

of which sounds like he might have had a *C. chinense* from the West Indies in his collection), he details the making of cayan butter, which was a tedious method of drying pepper for use in cooking. Chili-pepper "gives a better relish to meat or sauce and is found excellent to use to break and diffuse the wind, both in the stomach and guts." He cautions the reader not to throw peppers into the fire for "they will raise strong and noisome vapors, which occasion violent sneezing and coughing and often vomiting to those near the place where they are burnt." Those eighteenth-century Englishmen had a rather warped sense of humor, for he tells us that "some mix the powder with snuff to give others diversion but it causes violent fits of sneezing as to break the blood vessels of the head, as I have observed of some to whom it has been given" (Miller 1768).

CAROLUS LINNAEUS

The great Swedish taxonomist Carolus Linnaeus (Carl von Linné, 1707–1778), the son of a poor clergyman, was a physician before his treatise on sexuality in plants gained him the position of deputy to the professor of botany at Uppsala. During his lifetime, Linnaeus exerted an influence that has had few parallels in the field of natural science.

He devised a classification system that encompassed all living things. Botanical classification was based on sexual parts of the flower, allowing plants to be arranged into some sort of order. His binomial system of nomenclature, in which every plant or animal has two names—a generic and then a specific name—was first used extensively in *Species plantarum* (Linnaeus 1753). In that treatise he maintained the name *Capsicum*, first used by Tournefort, for the genus that comprises the peppers and listed two species: *C. annuum* and *C. frutescens*.

In that revolutionary book he named every plant that was known to him, some 7,300 species. This eighteenth-century "workaholic" also developed the formalized scientific description, thereby launching modern botany.

NIKOLAUS VON JACQUIN

Another physician, Nikolaus von Jacquin (1727–1817), who was born in Holland of French parents, was a skilled draftsman and a prolific writer. He organized a botanical collecting expedition for Emperor Francis I, husband of Maria Theresa. From 1754 to 1759 he sent back a rich collection from the West Indies.

In his florilegium, *Hortus botanicus vindobonensis* (1770–1776), which contained three hundred engravings, he gave the first description of *Capsicum chinense*. The *Vindobonensis* was but one of several lavishly illustrated books on flowering plants produced by Jacquin.

EDWARD LONG

The next report came in 1774 from Edward Long, an English planter and historian who made a general survey of the island of Jamaica, where he lived. He speaks of finding fifteen peppers on the island, which were used fresh, for pickling, and in the dried form. Long even details the pickling process and advances the proposal that peppers preserved in that manner might be considered as an article of export to help commerce with North America.

SAN JUAN IGNATIUS MOLINA

At about the time Long was surveying Jamaica, the Abbe San Juan Ignatius Molina (?–1829) compiled data for his *Geographical, Natural, and Civil History of Chile*, in which he placed on record the fact that many species of the *pimiento*, called by the Indians *thapi*, are cultivated in Chile, among others the "annual pimiento which is there perennial, the berry pimiento and the pimiento with a subligenous stalk" (Molina 1808).

FRIEDRICH HEINRICH ALEXANDER VON HUMBOLDT

Between 1779 and 1804, German scientist, explorer, and natural philosopher Friedrich Heinrich Alexander von Humboldt (1769–1859), along with A. J. A. Bonpland, completed a remarkable expedition to Central and South America. His journey initiated an era of scientific exploration. In his chronicle of that experience, we find the following about peppers: "The different species of pimento (*C. annuum*, *C. frutescens*, *C. baccatum*), called by the Mexicans *chilli*, and the Peruvians *uchu*, of which the fruit is as indispensably necessary to the natives as salt to the whites. The Spaniards call pimento *chile* or *axi* (*ahi*). The first word is derived from *quauh-chilli*, the second is a Haitian word that we must not confound with *axe*, which, as we have already observed, designates the *Dioscorea alata*" (Humboldt 1814, 457). Humboldt was mistaken; it was *Ipomea batatas* that the natives called *axé* or *agé*.

WHITELAW AINSLIE

Sir Whitelaw Ainslie (1767–1837) reports on the peppers in India at the beginning of the nineteenth century. In that country the British call them "chilie" and many varieties are used extensively as a seasoning and for medicine. His discussion of the medicinal uses is very amusing, but of a more serious nature is this comment: "The Chilie plant is constantly found in its wild state in the Eastern Islands, though from its being so commonly called Chilie, Rumphius argues its American origin" (Ainslie 1826, 306–310). During this period we begin to see authors supporting Rumphius' evidence and disagreeing with early herbalists as to an origin in India for the *Capsicum*.

ALPHONSE PYRAMUS DE CANDOLLE

In 1827, *The Origin of Cultivated Plants* by Alphonse Pyramus de Candolle (1728–1847), a Swiss botanist and taxonomist, was published in France. A second edition was issued in 1886. Of considerable interest is his thesis: "I cannot refrain from stating my opinion that no *Capsicum* is indigenous to the Old World. I be-

lieve them to be all of American origin, though I cannot absolutely prove it." He continues by giving the reasons for this theory:

Fruits so conspicuous, so easily grown in the garden and so agreeable to the palate of the inhabitants of hot countries, would have been quickly diffused throughout the Old World, if they had existed in the south of Asia, as it has sometimes been supposed. They would have had names in several ancient languages. Yet neither Romans, Greeks, nor even Hebrews were acquainted with them. They are not mentioned in ancient Chinese books. The islanders of the Pacific did not cultivate them at the time of Cook's voyages, in spite of their proximity to the Sunda Isles where Rumphius mentions their very general use. The Arabian physician, Ebn Baithar, who collected during the thirteenth century from all Eastern nations, knew about medicinal plants, says nothing about it. . . . This species has a number of different names in European languages, which all indicate a foreign origin and the resemblance of the taste to that of pepper. . . . The wild nature and ancient existence of the *Capsicum* is always uncertain, owing to its very general cultivation; but it seems to me to be more often doubtful in Asia than in South America. (Candolle 1964, 288)

4

REVIEW OF THE LITERATURE

HAVING completed a brief survey of significant references to the pepper from its discovery to the beginning of the nineteenth century, we have arrived at that period, beginning with Linnaeus, which can be referred to as the Modern Era. The genus *Capsicum* was first described by Tournefort in 1719, but he gave us no clue as to his choice of the word *Capsicum* for its name. Before the genus was established, the early sixteenth-century writers, beginning with Fuchs, confused it with the *Piperitus* and *Siliquastrum* of Pliny (A.D. 70) and used the terms indiscriminately when referring to peppers, black pepper, and cardamon (Pliny 1945).

Carolus Linnaeus chose to maintain Tournefort's designation of *Capsicum* for the generic name of peppers. Since that time until the present, however, the subgeneric or specific and varietal nomenclature of the different forms of *Capsicum* has been in a state of confusion. Numerous names have been given to the plant, to the fruit of different varieties, and to the various preparations made from them, but many of those names are ambiguous.

The basis of these systematic problems centers on the parallel evolution of fruit form among the domesticated species. Assigning specific names to a variety of fruit types based on morphology has compounded the taxonomic difficulties of the genus. Various authors before the Modern Era, working only with herbarium specimens, recognized as many as fifty and as few as a single species within the genus. However, most recent authors have agreed that there are twenty to thirty species native to the New World and one dubious species (?*C. anomalum* Franch. & Sav., 1875) native to Japan and adjacent areas of the Orient, which is probably not a true *Capsicum* (Eshbaugh in press; Pickersgill 1971).

PRE-LINNEAN PERIOD OR PREMODERN

Prior to Linnaeus, botanical science was in its infancy. The primary interest in plants was medicinal and most of those who studied them were physicians examining them for curative properties that could be utilized in the emerging science of medicine. In 1543, one of those doctors, Leonhard Fuchs, set forth his belief that peppers were natives of India and that they had been called *Capsicum* by the medieval writer Actuarius. This belief, which we now know to be incorrect, was perpetuated by Dodoens, Clusius, and others who followed. It will require further investigation to determine the origin of Fuchs' concept, which would have placed American peppers in the Old World prior to the voyage of Columbus.

LINNEAN PERIOD OR MODERN

In *Hortus cliffortianus* (1737), Linnaeus presented two species of peppers. In 1753 his binomial system was introduced in the first edition of *Species plantarum*. Included therein were the same two species, *C. annuum*, a herbaceous annual, and *C. frutescens*, a shrubby perennial. His *Mantissa plantarum* (1767) adds two more, *C. baccatum* and *C. grossum*. When Willdenow edited the *Species plantarum* (Linné 1797), a fifth species, *C. pendulum*, was described. During the next one hundred years over fifty new species were proposed, most of which were based on cultivated plant material.

Early Modern, 1753–1897 By the nineteenth century, W. S. J. G. von Besser's *Catalogue des plantes* (1811) listed seventeen species. In 1832, K. A. Fingerhuth's *Monographia generis capsici* was published in Latin. In his beautifully illustrated study, Fingerhuth recognized twenty-five accepted species, together with seven requiring further examination and twenty-eight botanical varieties. Three of the species and most of the varieties were named by him.

Otto Sendtner in Martius' *Flora brasiliensis* (1846) recorded ten species and numerous varieties as occurring in Brazil alone, having named seven of the species himself. Writing in Candolle's *Prodromous* (1852), Felix Dunal recorded fifty accepted species, of which eleven were described for the first time, together with many varieties and eleven species requiring further examination, besides three doubtful ones. In extreme contrast, Otto Kuntze describes but one species in his *Revisio generum plantarum* (1891).

Late Modern, 1898–1948 In 1898, H. C. Irish proceeded to revise the genus *Capsicum* on the basis of a large collection of cultivated forms at the Missouri Botanic Garden. He recognized only Linnaeus' two original species, *C. annuum* and *C. frutescens*, basing his classification on the fact that in the former the plants are annual or biennial and herbaceous and in the latter they are perennial and shrubby; however, he does list several other species that he says need additional study. Irish also considered the shape of the fruit and the calyx but he did not take into consideration the number of peduncles (often miscalled pedicel) as a distinguishing character. (There is usually one peduncle in the case of *C. annuum* and two or three in *C. chinense* and, occasionally, *C. frutescens*.) He decided the leading commercial varieties were all *C. annuum*. Irish's work reflected the reaction against the large number of species distinguishable only on fruit morphology.

In his *Bengal Plants* (1903), Sir David Prain agreed with Irish on the number of species but declared that the number of peduncles should be the distinguishing character.

L. H. Bailey, in *Gentes herbarum* (1923), recognized only one cultivated species and chose the name *C. frutescens* in preference to *C. annuum*. He held that the herbaceous, or so-called annual, varieties found in the United States were actually races that develop in a short season and do not have time to become woody before being killed by frost. Therefore, the specific name of *frutescens* should be retained even though it did not take precedence on the page in Linnaeus' *Hortus cliffortianius* (1737) or *Species plantarum* (1753). Ac-

cording to Bailey, the name *annuum* was a misnomer, which he dismissed with a curt "I cannot allow the accident of precedence on pages to obscure a biological fact" (1923, 129). He suggested that a simultaneous study of the wild and cultivated forms would be needed to understand the genus.

In 1929, A. T. Erwin accepted Bailey's treatment and assigned all the varieties he worked with to *C. frutescens*. However, he adduced that the genetic relationship pointed to a single species and that there was every intergrade of leaf, flower, and fruit from one form to another. He concluded that the perennial and woody character is, therefore, not a suitable criterion for separating *C. annuum* from *C. frutescens*.

In Mexico, Helia Bravo (1934) supported the two-species concept of Irish. Julian Miller and A. M. Fineman (1937) adopted the species name *C. frutescens* for all varieties of peppers because, in growing plants, they found that one of the Bell cultivars became as woody as the perennial types when it was grown from April to November.

The late period of the Modern Era, starting with Irish, found most workers holding with the Bailey-Erwin one-species position. Even those who did not began considering characteristics other than fruit morphology alone when assigning species.

THE RECENT PERIOD, 1948–1982

Following World War II, a new generation of taxonomists led by Paul G. Smith and Charles B. Heiser, Jr., in the United States and Armando T. Hunziker in Argentina made great strides toward an understanding of the generic limits of the genus *Capsicum*. Men and women who have been under their tutelage, such as William A. Emboden, Jr., W. Hardy Eshbaugh III, and Barbara Pickersgill, are following their examples of scholarship, research, and teaching, which will eventually lead to a better understanding of the genus *Capsicum*.

Recent work on *Capsicum* has justified Bailey's (1923) opinion that a simultaneous study of the wild and cultivated forms is essential to the complete understanding of the genus. Improved travel and communications within the Western Hemisphere have made available for study an increasing number of collections of plant material from South and Central America. No longer are we completely dependent on herbarium specimens, for we now have living plants from the greenhouse or field to evaluate. Analysis of this living plant material has supplied some new characters of taxonomic import, notably those of corolla color and form.

The scientists mentioned previously, along with others, have studied these data and have published the results in a series of papers that have led to a better understanding of the biologically significant units of variation.

The genus *Capsicum* as recognized today (Table 3, p. 44) contains twenty to thirty species native to the New World tropics and subtropics and one doubtful species, ?*C. anomalum*, native to Japan (Hunziker, 1956). Within this genus there are five domesticated species—*C. annuum*, *C. frutescens*, *C. pubescens*, *C. chinense*, and *C. baccatum* var. *pendulum*—and at least three to five semicultivated species. The domesticated species have developed from quite different ancestral stock in three distinct centers of origin: Mesoamerica, Amazonia, and Bolivia (Pickersgill 1971).

In all probability the cultivated species were domesticated at different times within the last four thousand years (Pickersgill 1969*b*). The relatively short period of domestication and separation of these domesticated species from their wild ancestors provides the investigator with an opportunity to study the relationship of a cultivated species and its presumed wild progenitor.

At the considered risk of losing the reader who is more interested in eating peppers than in the more epistemological aspects of the pungent pod, an abbreviated review of the more significant recent studies concerning capsicums will follow.

Beginning in 1923 all capsicums were considered to be one species, that of the shrubby *C. frutescens* (Latin *fruticis* = shrubby, referring to the woody stems), which was the second species to be named by Linnaeus in his *Species plantarum* (1753). In several countries taxonomists followed the one-species view initiated by Bailey (1923) but instead of *C. frutescens* they opted for the name *C. annuum*. Consequently, some referred to all capsicums as *C. annuum*, while others used *C. frutescens*, a situation that makes reading the literature of that period very confusing.

In California, in 1948, a breeding program for disease resistance provided data supporting a second distinct species, *C. pubescens* Ruiz & Pavon, 1797 (Heiser & Smith 1948). Continued study caused a third species to be recognized, *C. pendulum* Willdenow, 1809 (Smith, Rick, & Heiser, 1951). The next year the confusing situation in which the same cultivated plant is called *C. annuum* Linné in some areas and *C. frutescens* Linné in others was resolved when Smith and Heiser (1951) rec-

11. Fingerhuth, *Monographia generis capsici*. Although it was revised by Irish in 1898, this still is the only monograph on the genus *Capsicum*. (Photograph from the Missouri Botanical Garden Library, St. Louis)

ognized both *C. annuum* and *C. frutescens* as valid species, although their specific lines are slightly different from those proposed by Irish (1898). Their conclusions were based on the lack of crossability between the two groups and slight but distinct morphological differences. The majority of the peppers of commerce at the present time are forms of either *C. annuum* or *C. frutescens*.

In Argentina, Hunziker (1950) found a wild purple-flowered pepper, which he describes as *C. eximium*. We are interested in it here because of its relationship to the cultivated *C. pubescens* Ruiz & Pavon.

In 1957 Smith and Heiser (1957*b*) isolated yet a fourth distinct domesticated species common to the Caribbean and Peru. They called it *C. sinense* Jacquin, 1776. In so doing the original spelling of *chinense* was altered. The first reference to this change in spelling is by Eshbaugh (1964, 100), who says: "Concerning *sinense* Smith & Heiser, Bull. Torrey Bot. Club, 84: 413–414, 1957*b*. Although this spelling has been widely used, according to the Rules of Nomenclature the original form must be restored." Jacquin said the reason for calling this American *Capsicum* "Chinese" was "I have taken the plant's name from its homeland" (Jacquin 1776, 3: 38), but there was no further explanation. Jacquin did not collect in China but he had done considerable collecting in the West Indies. (It would be helpful if anyone naming a new species of plant or animal would clarify the reason for the choice; however, many do not.)

Studies of plant material sent to them by Martín Cárdenas of Bolivia and described as a new species, *C. cardenasii*, prompted Heiser and Smith (1958) to recommend that the description of the genus *Capsicum* be amended to include "campanulate corollas and entire calyx margins." In stating the reason for dedicating the species to Martín Cárdenas, its collector, the authors set a good example.

Working in somewhat geographic isolation in Córdoba, Argentina, in southern South America, Hunziker (1958) proposed the division of *Capsicum* into three sections.*

1. Turbocapsicum (*C. anomalum*)
2. Pseudoacnistus (*C. breviflorum*)
3. Capsicum

---

*The validity of these divisions is in question today (Eshbaugh 1982, personal communication).

Eshbaugh (1964, 1968, 1970), continuing his study of *C. baccatum* Linné, used both quantitative and qualitative means, chromosome behavior, chromosome morphology, and breeding behavior to validate an earlier thesis (1968) that *C. baccatum* Linné has two varieties—wild *C. baccatum* var. *baccatum* and domesticated *C. baccatum* var. *pendulum* (Willd.) Eshbaugh. At one point the taxonomic confusion that has plagued the genus was compounded when the name *C. baccatum* was applied to *C. annuum* and both were called the bird pepper.

One way of grouping the capsicums is based on flower color. This artificial system recognizes two groups, white flowered and purple flowered; a chemosystematic study by Ballard et al. (1970) produced evidence for adding a third group, the purple-to-white, forming a transition between the two corolla groups. The study proposed the following groups:

Group I. Purple flowered
    a. *C. pubescens* group
Group II. White flowered
    a. *C. baccatum* group
    b. *C. annuum* group

Recent work (McLeod et al. 1983) supports three distinct clusters of taxa based on corolla type but does not hold with the purple-to-white group.

Pickersgill (1971), working in England, reports that her investigations have produced evidence favoring the hypothesis that "weedy" races of peppers are ancestral to their respective cultivated types. Heiser, Eshbaugh, and Pickersgill (1971) conclude that the progenitors of cultivated peppers are the wild forms still existing in each of the groups, and that speciation in peppers, along with *Phaseolus* beans and amaranths, provides some of the best evidence that there were independent centers of domestication in the Americas instead of a single center. Of the more than twenty recognized species of peppers, all originating in the New World, some are domesticated while others are wild, although their fruits may be collected and used.

D'Arcy and Eshbaugh (1974) review the situation, stressing the need for a workable key with stable names that could be used to advantage by the herbarium botanist, agricultural advisor, ornamental grower, or industrial specialist. They end on a hopeful note: "Unfortunately it is not yet possible to promise stable names, but reasons for their uncertainty are clarified."

Eshbaugh (1975) divided part of Hunziker's (1958) section *Capsicum* into two categories: the purple-flowered and the white-flowered species. A study of the purple-flowered species—*C. pubescens*, *C. cardenasii*, and *C. eximium*—suggests a common ancestor for the three that either has become extinct or occupies a limited range and has not yet been discovered (McLeod 1977).

In a EUCARPIA report, Pickersgill (1977*b*) states that her continued studies into the origin of New World agriculture suggest multiple origins to be likely for New World agriculture in general. That same year at the 3° Congres EUCARPIA, thirty-four other papers on genetics and selection were presented (Pochard 1977).

After stating that the purple-flowered species *C. pubescens* is morphologically and cytogenetically distinct, Pickersgill et al. (1978), using morphological data, go on to quantify and depict the relationship between wild and domesticated forms in the white-flowered taxa. This analysis confirms that *C. baccatum* is definitely distinct from the *C. annuum–C. chinense–C. frutescens* complex and that the domesticated form *C. baccatum* var. *pendulum* is probably derived from wild forms of the same species.

Pickersgill et al. (1978) conclude that *C. annuum*, *C. frutescens*, and *C. chinense* appear to be three distinct groups with a poorly differentiated ancestral complex of wild forms instead of the two distinct wild/domesticated pairs belonging to *C. annuum* and the *C. chinense–C. frutescens* complex as was assumed at the initiation of their study. This ancestral complex probably occurred throughout Mesoamerica, South America, the West Indies, and southern North America, giving rise to the domesticated peppers.

The final studies reviewed here indicate the problem facing the plant taxonomist today in dealing with the difference between the taxonomic species and the biological species. Early taxonomists did not recognize this disparity. Pickersgill et al. (1978), using numerical analysis, and Jensen et al. (1979) and McLeod et al. (1979*a*, 1979*b*), using isoenzyme analysis, agree that *C. pubescens* and *C. baccatum* var. *pendulum* are clearly defined domesticated species but provide somewhat different insights concerning the relationship of the domesticates, *C. annuum*, *C. frutescens*, and *C. chinense*.

The biological species is defined by Mayr (1970, 12) as "groups of interbreeding natural populations that are reproductively isolated from other such groups." Grant (1981, 46) concurs that "it is the reproductively isolated system of breeding populations," adding that "interbreeding is prevented by many kinds of isolating

mechanisms." The taxonomic species is based on morphology. By way of clarification, Mayr (1970, 12) adds: "The biological species concept is called biological not because it deals with biological taxa, but because the definition is biological. It utilizes criteria that are meaningless as far as the inanimate world is concerned. . . . It combines the discreteness of the local species at a given time with an evolutionary potential for continuing change."

In an experimental study based on enzyme profiles, Jensen et al. (1979) and McLeod et al. (1979*a*, 1979*b*) agree that *C. pubescens* and *C. baccatum* var. *pendulum* are clearly defined domesticated species. However, *C. annuum*, *C. frutescens*, and *C. chinense* are somewhat indistinguishable as more primitive taxa are included in their analysis. If one uses a biological species approach, there would be only three domesticated species: *C. pubescens* with the wild *C. eximium* and *C. cardenasii* as a self-contained breeding group; *C. baccatum* as another one; and *C. annuum*, *C. frutescens*, and *C. chinense* as a single unit genetically linked together from a wild ancestral gene pool (Eshbaugh et al., in press *Ethnobiology*).

Recent electrophoretic enzyme studies by McLeod et al. (1983) determined three clusters of taxa, each with at least one domesticated taxon. This finding gives support to the hypothesis that there are several wild progenitors for the domesticated capsicums and at least three centers of domestication. However, the pattern of evolution within each cluster has not been determined. This idea is not radically different from the one advanced by Pickersgill et al. (1978) and McLeod (1977) that the wild forms constitute a single, polytypic species with a large geographical range and with multiple, independent domestications of local forms from this wild gene pool.

Actually, it is not that simple. Eshbaugh (1980*a*) reminds us that these studies may not solve the taxonomic problem involving domesticated *Capsicum* but they "may well explain part of the dilemma faced by the early taxonomists who did not recognize the difference between the taxonomic and biological species." Continuing, he states that "when this is considered in light of the many varieties, cultivars, races, forms, etc., created by man the problem of developing a rational taxonomy for the plant breeder and horticulturist becomes enormous."

Below specific rank it would seem that the best approach for the horticulturist and geneticist would be the use of the category *cultivar* instead of *variety*, with

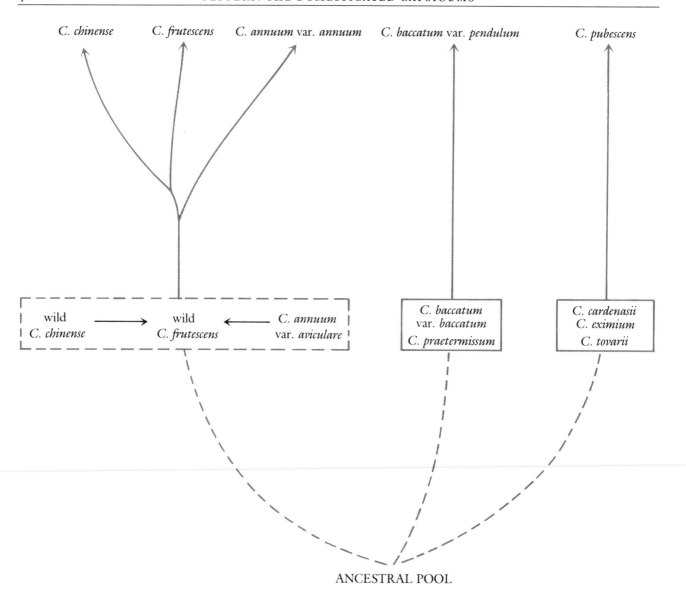

12. A synthetic model depicting the evolution of *Capsicum*
as perceived at the present time. (After Eshbaugh et al., in
press *Ethnobiology*)

the appropriate *fancy* or *common name* as outlined under the International Code of Nomenclature for Cultivated Plants (Gilmour 1969): "Cultivar = a group or assemblage of cultivated individual plants that when reproduced sexually or asexually retain their distinguishing features that have been described morphologically, physiologically, cytologically, chemically or in other ways that have significant meaning to agriculture, horticulture, or forestry." Put in a simpler way, a cultivar (short for cultivated variety) is a plant that has been selected or hybridized and probably would not persist outside of cultivation.

Is there a suitable solution to this perplexing problem so that those working with this genus can communicate effectively? At the moment it is questionable; however, it is not hopeless. A forthcoming document prepared by the International Board for Plant Genetic Resources of the Food and Agriculture Organization of the United Nations (United Nations, in press) covering the genetic resources of *Capsicum* is designed to be a global plan of action, specifically to standardize terminology in order to promote communication among those scientists who are working with *Capsicum*. It will provide descriptors designed to be computerized, keys for field identification, diagnostic descriptions of the five domesticated species, directions for collecting, and other sought-after information that will be invaluable to anyone working with *Capsicum* as well as for use in genetic resources research. A thorough monographic study on a worldwide scale is greatly needed.

5
DIAGNOSTIC DESCRIPTIONS

THE FIRST description of the genus *Capsicum* was by Tournefort in *Institutiones rei herbariae* (1700, 1: 152), but it has become so outdated that it does not bear repeating. A precise definition of the genus *Capsicum* is lacking at this time and only in the most recent studies is there agreement as to just what characters such a definition should include (C. B. Heiser, Jr., 1982, personal communication).

Studies employing modern research methods have produced data that will necessitate at least six major amendments to the original concept of the genus, thus, any definition found in the literature today is obsolete. The generic limits have been interpreted differently by various workers. This inadequate understanding of the generic limits has in part prevented the establishment of a satisfactory taxonomy of the genus *Capsicum*.

Some of the exceptions to the definition of the *Capsicum* that have been proposed follow:

Peduncle: pedicel [*sic*] not limited to three per node; some have more than three (Smith & Heiser 1951).
Calyx margin: smooth as well as toothed calyx margin (Heiser & Smith 1958).
Fruit: plants that have soft, pulp-filled berries should be excluded from the genus (Heiser & Smith 1958).
Flower: there are campanulate blooms as well as rotate (Heiser & Smith 1958).
Capsaicin: only plants with a pungent berry should be included (Morton 1938). Nonpungent berries should be excluded from the genus (Heiser & Smith 1958). Most recent authorities consider the presence of capsaicin diagnostic for the genus. However, exceptions are found in some wild species still included in the genus and a number of domesticated cultivars are nonpungent (Eshbaugh 1980, 155). Hunziker (1971) stated that *C. ciliatum* never has a pungent fruit. (Later studies based on chromosome number have shown that *C. ciliatum* should no longer be considered to be a *Capsicum* [Eshbaugh, in press *Bothalia*].)

Tables 3 and 4 are based on the studies of Hunziker (1956) and Eshbaugh (1980 & in press *Bothalia*). They are a synopsis of the genus *Capsicum* as it is known today. Eshbaugh emphasizes that significant realignments of certain of these species can be expected as Brazilian and other South American material is better studied. We can anticipate that new undescribed species will be placed within the genus *Capsicum* as well as that some species currently considered to be in that genus will be removed from it.

Table 3 presents the classification of the domesticated species of the genus *Capsicum* along with their related wild species. The authorities for the binomials are given along with a complete citation of the reference to their original description and its revision, if one has been made, in the hope of saving a harried researcher some valuable time. Table 4 is a key to the domesticated *Capsicum* species. It is hoped that these two tables will help the reader to visualize the relationships within the genus *Capsicum* and be a ready source of reference for further study.

Early botanists gave but brief accounts of new species, which sometimes led to misinterpretation by those who followed. As the science of botany developed, the quality of the descriptions improved. Original descriptions are required to be written in Latin,

Table 3.　Classification of the Genus *Capsicum*

PART I.　Domesticated Species and Hypothetically
Related Spontaneous Forms

KINGDOM:　Plant
DIVISION:　Angiospermae
CLASS:　Dycotyledonese
SUBCLASS:　Metachlamydeae
ORDER:　Tubiflorae
FAMILY:　SOLANACEAE
TRIBE:　Solaneae
SUBTRIBE:　Solaninae
GENUS:　*Capsicum*

SECTION:　?*Tubocapsicum* (?*C. anomalum*)
　　　　　?*Pseudoacnistus* (*C. breviflorum*)
　　　　　Capsicum

　GROUP 1. Purple flowered
　　SPECIES: *C. pubescens* Ruiz Lopez & Pavon, 1797
　　　Flora peruviana et chilensis, 2:30
　　　*C. eximium var. *tomentosum* Eshbaugh & Smith, 1971
　　　Baileya, 18(1):15
　　　*C. tovarii Eshbaugh, Smith, & Nickrent, 1983
　　　Brittonia, 35:55
　　　*C. cardenasii Heiser & Smith, 1958
　　　Brittonia, 10:195

　GROUP 2. White flowered
　a. *C. baccatum* complex
　　SPECIES: *C. baccatum* Linné, 1767–1771
　　Mantissa plantarum, p. 47
　　　　VARIETY: *C. b.* var. *pendulum* (Willd., 1808)
　　　　　Eshbaugh, 1968
　　　　Willdenow, *Enumeratio . . . horti . . . beroliensis*, 1:242;
　　　　　Eshbaugh, *Taxon*, 17:51–52
　　　　*C. b. var. *baccatum* Linné, 1771
　　　　Mantissa plantarum, p. 47
　　　　*C. b. var. *praetermissum* (Heiser & Smith, 1958) A. T.
　　　　　Hunziker, 1971
　　　　Heiser & Smith, *Brittonia*, 10:198; Hunziker,
　　　　　Kurtziana, 6:242
　　　　*C. b. var. *tomentosum* (Hassler, 1918) A. T. Hunziker,
　　　　　1950
　　　　Hassler, *Fedde Rep. Sp.*, 1(17):24; Hunziker, *Dar-
　　　　　winiana*, 9(2):235
　b. *C. annuum* complex
　　SPECIES: *C. annuum* Linné, 1753
　　　　VARIETY: *C. a.* var. *annuum* Linné, 1753
　　　　Species plantarum, p. 189
　　　　*C. a. var. *aviculare* (Dierbach, 1829) D'Arcy &
　　　　　Eshbaugh, 1973
　　　　Dierbach, *Archiv des Apothekervereins*, 30(1):30; D'Arcy
　　　　　& Eshbaugh, *Phytologia*, 25(6)350
　　SPECIES: *C. frutescens* Linné, 1753
　　Species plantarum, p. 189
　　SPECIES: *C. chinense* Jacquin, 1776
　　Hortus botanicus vindobonensis, 3:38

PART II.　Strictly Wild Forms of *Capsicum*

C. buforum A. T. Hunziker, 1969
Kurtziana, 1:394, f. 1

C. campylopodium Sendtner, 1846
in Martius, *Flora brasiliensis*, 10:143

C. chacoense var. *tomentosum* A. T. Hunziker, 1950
Darwiniana 9:228

C. coccineum (Rusby, 1927), A. T. Hunziker, 1956
Rusby, *Mem. New York Bot. Gard.*, 7:343–344; Hunziker, VIII
　Cong. Int. Bot. Paris, *Proceedings*, Comptes Rend, Seances
　Rapp. & Commun., Sec. 4(2):73.

C. cornutum (Hiern, 1877–78), A. T. Hunziker, 1961
Hiern, *Videnskabelige Meddelelser Knobenhaven*, p. 59; Hunziker,
　Kurtziana, 1:213

C. dimorphum (Miers, 1849), O. Kuntze, 1891
Miers, *Annals & Mag. of Nat. History*, 2:3–6; Kuntze, *Revisio gen-
　erum plantarum*, pl. 2:449

C. dusenii Bitter, 1920
Abh. Nat. Ver. Bremen, 24:520

C. galapogensis A. T. Hunziker, 1956
VIII Cong. Int. Bot. Paris, *Proceedings*, Comptes Rend, Seances
　Rapp. & Commun., Sec. 4(2):73

C. geminifolium (Dammer, 1905), A. T. Hunziker, 1961
Dammer in Engler, *Bot. Jahrb.* 36:384; Hunziker, VIII Cong. Int.
　Bot. Paris, *Proceedings*, Comptes Rend, Seances Rapp. & Com-
　mun., Sec. 4(2):73

C. hookerianum (Miers, 1849), O. Kuntze, 1891
Miers, *Annals & Mag. of Nat. History*, 2:3–6; Kuntze, *Revisio gen-
　erum plantarum*, 2:449

C. lanceolatum (Greenman, 1904), Morton & Standley, 1940
Greenman, *Field Mus. of Nat. Hist. Ser.*, 22:272; Morton & Stand-
　ley in Donnel-Smith, *Botanical Gazette*, 37:212

C. leptopodum (Dunal, 1852), O. Kuntze, 1891
Dunal in Candolle, *Prodromus*, p. 4; Kuntze, *Revisio generum
　plantarum*, 2:449

C. minutiflorum (Rusby, 1927), A. T. Hunziker, 1961
Rusby, *Mem. N. Y. Bot. Gard.*, 7:343–344; Hunziker, VIII Cong.
　Int. Bot. Paris, *Proceedings*, Comptes Rend, Seances Rapp. &
　Commun., Sec. 4(2):74

C. mirabile Martius, 1846
Flora brasiliensis, 10:144

C. parvifolium Sendtner, 1846
in Martius, *Flora brasiliensis*, 10:145
see Candolle, *Prodromus*, 13(1):419, 1852

C. schottianum var. *flexuosum* (Sendtner, 1846)
Sendtner in Martius, *Flora brasiliensis*, 10:143

C. scolnikianum A. T. Hunziker, 1961
Kurtziana, 1:213

C. villosum Sendtner, 1846
in Martius, *Flora brasiliensis*, 10:145

*Wild forms.

which at one time was considered to be the universal language of science. Today it is difficult to find anyone who reads and writes scientific Latin, even in the linguistic departments of major universities.

Of the five domesticated species of *Capsicum*, *C. annuum* is the most widely cultivated and economically the most important species today. It includes practically all of the peppers we find fresh, processed, or dried on our grocer's shelves. The cultivated forms are *C. annuum* var. *annuum*, while the wild types are designated *C. annuum* var. *aviculare*. Wild *C. annuum* can be found from the southern United States to northern South America. Evidence points to Middle America, probably Mexico, as being the area where this pepper was first domesticated (Pickersgill 1971).

There have been several attempts to classify the multitude of cultivars of this species but little agreement has been reached. P. G. Smith (1978) proposed a horticultural classification of the commercially important cultivars to the Fourth National Pepper Conference, but it, like those preceding, did not take into account the pepper cultivars from Mexico and other Latin American countries.

Although there is confusion regarding the descriptions of the various cultivars, botanists have recently reached a general agreement regarding the domesticated species so that I feel fairly secure in these descriptions of the domesticated capsicums, as set forth by the United Nations Food and Agricultural Organization (F.A.O., in press).

1a. *Capsicum annuum* var. *annuum*
   Capsicum annuum Linné, 1753, *Hortus cliffortianus*, p. 59
      (*Species plantarum*, 1753, p. 188). Lectotype: Herb. Hort. Cliff. 59 (BM).

Flowers solitary at each node (occasionally two or more). Peduncles usually declining at anthesis. Corolla milky white (occasionally purple), without diffuse spots at base of lobes; corolla lobes usually straight. Calyx of mature fruit without annular constriction at junction with peduncle (though sometimes irregularly wrinkled); veins often prolonged into short teeth. Fruit flesh usually firm (soft in certain cultivars). Seeds straw colored. Chromosome number 2n=24, with 2 pairs of acrocentric chromosomes. E.g., Bell peppers, Anaheim (F.A.O., in press).

The original range of this species during pre-Columbian times was from Mexico south into Colombia. This pepper, which probably originated in Mesoamerica, is now cultivated in virtually every country in the world (D'Arcy & Eshbaugh 1974).

Table 4. Key to the Domesticated Species of *Capsicum*

1. Seeds dark, corolla purple .... *C. pubescens*
1. Seeds straw colored, corolla white or greenish-white (rarely purple) 2
  2. Corolla with diffuse yellow spots at bases of lobes .... *C. baccatum*
  2. Corolla without diffuse yellow spots at bases of lobes 3
    3. Corolla purple 4
      4. Flowers solitary .... *C. annuum*
      4. Flowers 2 or more at each node .... *C. chinense*
    3. Corolla white or greenish-white 5
      5. Calyx of mature fruit with annular constriction at junction with peduncle ...... *C. chinense*
      5. Calyx of mature fruit without annular constriction at junction with peduncle ... 6
        6. Flowers solitary 7
          7. Corolla milky white, lobes usually slightly revolute, peduncles often declining at anthesis .... *C. annuum*
          7. Corolla greenish-white, lobes usually slightly revolute, peduncles erect at anthesis .... *C. frutescens*
        6. Flowers 2 or more at each node 8
          8. Corolla milky white .... *C. annuum*
          8. Corolla greenish-white 9
            9. Peduncles erect at anthesis, corolla lobes usually slightly revolute .... *C. frutescens*
            9. Peduncles declining at anthesis, corolla lobes straight .... *C. chinense*

Source: F.A.O., in press.

1b. *Capsicum annuum* var. *aviculare** (Dierbach, *Archiv des Apothekervereins* 30[1]: 30, 1829), D'Arcy & Eshbaugh, 1973, *Phytologia*, 25(6): 350. Synonyms: *C. annuum* var. *glabrisculum* (Dunal 1852, in Candolle, *Prodromus* 13 [1]: 420), Heiser & Pickersgill, 1975, *Baileya*, 19: 156; *C. minimum* Miller, 1768, *Gardener's . . . Dictionary*, 8th ed., p. 8.

C. a. var. *aviculare* is a wild herb or small shrub to 2 m tall, short-lived perennial, glabrous or rarely puberulent; flowers solitary, rarely 2–3 pairs; peduncles slender, enlarging just beneath the fruit; calyx mostly truncate or with small umbo in place of teeth; corolla white, rarely greenish; anthers violet to blue, filaments short; fruit green suffused with dark purple to black when immature, red when mature, erect, deciduous, small, globose or ovoid, 5–10 mm in diameter, rarely exceeding 15 mm in length; seeds cream to yellow.

*The use of the name *C. annuum aviculare* instead of *C. annuum glabrisculum* is based on the U.S. Department of Agriculture and Soil Conservation Service's 1982 *National List of Scientific Plant Names*, pp. 73–74, 359.

Commonly called the bird pepper, this species is frequently a weed along fence rows, in pastures, and in waste places. It probably originated in southern Mexico or northern Colombia but today can be found from southeastern and southwestern United States south into northern Peru and is widespread in the Caribbean. It seldom occurs at an elevation of more than 1,000 m (D'Arcy & Eshbaugh 1974).

Most authorities consider it to be the possible progenitor of the domesticated *C. annuum*. Studies of geographic distribution, karyoptypic variation, and crossability plus studies of available archaeological specimens suggest that, in peppers, the weedy forms are ancestral to the domesticated varieties (Pickersgill 1971, 684). This wild species is included because of its widespread usage.

2. *Capsicum frutescens* Linné, 1753, *Species plantarum*, p. 189. Lectotype: *van Royen* (L-902560).

C. frutescens has solitary flowers at each node (occasionally two or more). It should be noted that earlier descriptions by Smith and Heiser (1951, 362) and D'Arcy and Eshbaugh (1974, 101) include having two or more flowers per node as well as being solitary under certain circumstances as being a character that distinguishes *C. frutescens* from *C. annuum*. Peduncles erect at anthesis but flowers nodding. Corolla greenish-white without diffuse spots at base of lobes; corolla lobes often slightly revolute. Calyx of mature fruit without annular constriction at junction with peduncle, though often irregularly wrinkled; veins usually not prolonged into teeth. Fruit flesh often soft. Seeds straw colored. Chromosome number 2n=24, with 1 pair of acrocentric chromosomes. E.g., *tabasco* (F.A.O., in press).

C. frutescens is a widespread species found from southeastern United States to Argentina. It has a wide distribution as a wild or semidomesticated plant in lowland tropical America and, secondarily, in southeastern Asia. It is also grown in India and throughout the islands of Polynesia. The western Amazon River basin of lowland Colombia and Peru is its probable area of origin (Heiser & Smith 1953). *Tabasco* is the only member of this species commonly in cultivation outside the tropics.

3. *C. baccatum* Linné, 1767–1771, *Mantissa plantarum* p. 47. var. *baccatum*. Lectotype: LINN 249-3.

C. baccatum var. *pendulum* (Willdenow, 1808, *Enumeratio plantarum horti regii botanici beroliensis*, 1: 242). Eshbaugh, 1968, *Taxon* 17: 51–52. Lectotype: *Willdenow 4431* (B-W no. 9).

C. b. var. *pendulum* has solitary flowers at each node. Peduncles erect or declining at anthesis. Corolla white or greenish-white, with diffuse yellow spots at base of corolla lobes on either side of mid-vein; corolla lobes usually slightly revolute. Calyx of mature fruit without annular constriction at junction with peduncle (though sometimes irregularly wrinkled); veins prolonged into prominent teeth. Fruit flesh firm. Seeds straw colored. Chromosome number 2n=24, with 1 pair of acrocentric chromosomes. E.g., Cusqueño (Peru) (F.A.O., in press).

Until about twenty years ago this species was confused with the common bird pepper, *C. annuum* var. *aviculare*, and most references to *C. baccatum* during that period refer to the wild "bird-pepper," not the true *C. baccatum* as it is known today.

C. b. var. *baccatum* is known to occur in Argentina, Bolivia, Brazil, Paraguay, and Peru with the primary center in Bolivia and northern Argentina. The discontinuity between Bolivia, Peru, and Brazil probably reflects incomplete collecting. Unfavorable habitats in the Gran Chaco of Paraguay may be another reason (Hunziker 1950).

The variety *pendulum* is native from the lowlands to middle elevations in South America with its primary center in Peru and Bolivia. It undoubtedly arose from the variety *baccatum*, which has a distribution confined primarily to Bolivia with slight range extensions into central Peru, northern Argentina, western Paraguay, and southwestern Brazil (Eshbaugh 1970). *C. b.* var. *pendulum* was under cultivation before the Conquest (Pickersgill 1969*a*, 444). The evolution was achieved by selection, which was initially subconscious and more recently deliberate.

This widely distributed cultivated plant is found throughout western South America. During the twentieth century, it has also been introduced into Hawaii, Costa Rica, the United States, and India and is being spread to other countries (Eshbaugh 1970).

4. *Capsicum pubescens* Ruiz & Pavon, 1797, *Flora peruviana et chilensis*, 2: 30. Type not identified.

C. pubescens has solitary flowers at each node. Peduncles erect at anthesis but flowers nodding. Corolla purple (occasionally with white margins to lobes and/or white tube), without diffuse spots at base of lobes (though drop of yellow nectar may accumulate in this position and simulate corolla spot); corolla lobes usually straight. Calyx of mature fruit without annular constrictions at junction with peduncle; veins prolonged into teeth. Fruit flesh firm. Seeds dark in color. Chromosome number 2n=24, with 1 pair of acrocentric chromosomes. E.g., *rocoto* (Andes) (F.A.O., in press).

This species is from relatively high elevations, being grown from 1,500 to 2,800 m in Andean South America (D'Arcy & Eshbaugh 1974) and to 3,000 m in Ecuador (Heiser 1964). It is also in cultivation in a few places in highland Mexico and Central America, where it was probably introduced in the twentieth century (Smith & Heiser 1957*b*). Although an ancestral type to *C. pubescens* has not been positively identified, it shows affinities with the wild South American species *C. eximium* and *C. cardenasii*. It is possible that one of these species could be its progenitor (Heiser 1976*a*; Eshbaugh 1979).

This pepper is the most distinct morphologically of the five domesticated species. Its dark, rugose seeds and thicker flesh set it apart from the others. It is grown and marketed at relatively high elevations and is a cash crop in many areas, such as Arequipa, Peru, and Patzcuaro, Mexico. It is primarily grown for home consumption but the surplus is commonly sold in highland village markets and occasionally in stores in Lima, Quito, Bogatá, and San José.

5. *Capsicum chinense* Jacquin, 1776, *Hortus botanicus vindobonensis*, 3: 38, pl. 67. Type not designated.

C. chinense has 2 or more flowers at each node (occasionally solitary). Peduncles erect or declining at anthesis. Corolla greenish-white (occasionally milky white or purple), without diffuse spots at base of lobes; corolla lobes usually straight. Calyx of mature fruit usually with annular constriction at junction with peduncle; veins not prolonged into teeth. Fruit flesh firm. Seeds straw colored. Chromosome number 2n=24, with 1 pair of acrocentric chromosomes. E.g., *habañero* (Mexico), *chinchi-uchu* (Peru) (F.A.O., in press).

At best it is difficult to make a distinction between *C. chinense* and *C. frutescens*. Heiser (1976*a*) reports that a constriction below the calyx is the only morphological character that separates the two species; however, Pickersgill (1966) indicates that no one character is sufficient to distinguish these species. She finds, however, that, if a combination of characters is considered, a given sample can usually be assigned to one species or another. Clearly, *C. chinense* and *C. frutescens* are very closely related and probably should be combined into one species, in which case the name *C. frutescens* would take precedence (Heiser 1976*a*).

C. chinense is cultivated widely in tropical America and is the most commonly grown pepper in the Amazon region. It is found primarily in the Caribbean and Mexico south to and including Bolivia and Brazil. It probably originated in the lowland jungle of the western Amazon River basin (D'Arcy & Eshbaugh 1974). The varieties grown in Africa are reportedly the most pungent of all the chili-peppers.

6

BIOLOGY

Seed

The pepper seed is disclike/discoidal, flattened, and usually smooth, but some can be slightly rough/sub-scabrous, with a deep depression where the seed coats are united to the nucellus. The color ranges from straw color to blackish-brown in the various species. Old seeds become brown. Within the pod they are attached to the placenta in close rows, principally near the base of the pod. The size varies from about 2.5 mm to about 5 mm with larger fruit having the larger seeds. The number of seeds per pod varies greatly with different cultivars.

Plant Characters

The pepper plant is erect, prostrate, or compact in form with dichotomous branching. When it is young it is herbaceous, but it becomes woody with age when it is grown as a perennial in areas not subject to freeze. The pepper plant grows with a single stem until nine to eleven leaves are formed. This main stem terminates with a flower. Two or occasionally three branches grow from the axils of the highest leaves. Each of these branches forms two leaves, terminating in a flower. Thus, according to Dorland and Went (1947), there is repeated apparently dichotomous branching and the entire plant assumes an inverted conical shape with the growth following a sigmoid curve.*

---

*In *Capsicum* the initial branching is a dichotomy with an angle of 65°–110°. Subsequent branchings maintain the dichotomy and are on a plane 90° removed from the original dichotomy. This pattern is maintained as leaves develop and is interrupted only by damage, pruning, or aging (Eshbaugh 1964, 4).

LEAF AND STEM

The leaf is simple, entire, and asymmetrical. The shape varies from broadly ovate to ovate lanceolate. In most cases the apex is acuminate but it can be acute or even obtuse. The base either gradually narrows into the petiole or is abruptly acute. The leaves arise singly and usually develop alternately. They can be flat and smooth or wrinkled and glabrous or subglabrous. Some are pubescent along the veins. The color ranges from light to dark green, and occasionally purple and white variegation occurs. The thickness and size are also variable. In some instances the foliage is compact and clustered while in others it is open and scattered. The young stems are angular, becoming circular in cross section as they mature, while their color changes from green to a streaked grey, becoming brown as they become woody; some of the young stems are streaked with purple. The stem may be either glabrous or pubescent.

There is some degree of swelling at the nodes. Certain forms will manifest purple coloration at the axils of the branches and leaves, while others may exhibit purple coloration in all parts of the plant.

ROOT SYSTEM

Various root systems have been found to occur in peppers: deep tap root, shallow tap root, very vigorous fibrous root system, moderately vigorous fibrous root system, and shallow fibrous root system.

The perennial plants develop a deep tap root system. Shallow, poorly developed root systems are associated with poor aboveground growth. A well-grown six-month-old plant will have a root spread of about forty inches from the base of the plant and penetrated downward to about twenty-six inches (Paul 1940, [3]: 133).

CHROMOSOME NUMBER

It was once thought that all true members of the genus *Capsicum* are diploids and have a chromosome number of 2n=2x=24 (Heiser 1976a, 266); however, it has been shown that some domesticated *C. annuum* in Asia are tetraploid (Eshbaugh 1982, personal communication).

Floral Biology

The flowers (solitary or two or more) are produced at the axils of each dichotomy. Each flower is pendent and borne on a single peduncle. The flowers are without odor and of inconspicuous size varying from a diameter of about 1.2 cm to 3.5 cm. During the growing season they are produced continuously.

DEVELOPMENT OF THE FLOWER BUD

At the first stage of development the bud is entirely enclosed by the calyx. Development is rapid and as the bud grows it widens, leaving the tip of the corolla visible. The first sign of a bud is a protuberance arising in the axil of a pair of tiny lanceolate leaves or, in some instances, in the axil of a branch. After two or three days the peduncle begins to develop. Until the fifth day the calyx remains closed and the peduncle forms a bend at either the base or the calyx end. In another two or three days the corolla becomes apparent but it takes another seven to eight days for it to open. During the development of the bud the peduncle elongates and then curves downward so that the flower is parallel to it in the case of pendent fruit or it grows upward with the flower at right angles to it in the case of erect fruit. The peduncle is swollen where it joins the calyx and it varies in length with the various cultivars.

THE FLORAL ORGANS

Peduncle: The number of peduncles per node varies from one to three or more. *C. chinense* and, oftentimes, *C. frutescens* produce two or three or more peduncles but that many are unusual in the other domesticated species. The length varies in the different types; however, the small pods generally have long peduncles. Short peduncles are also associated with purple color in the plants (Lippert et al. 1966).

Calyx: The flower has a campanulate, subentire per-

sistent calyx, which is barely accrescent and in domesticated species is obscurely five-toothed or entire, with some wild species prominently dentate; however, the segments may range from four to six and occasionally more. In all varieties the base of the young fruit is entirely enclosed by the calyx. At maturity the base is either enclosed by the calyx or seated on it. The shape of the calyx is one of the most important characters by which a species is classified. There are two calyx shapes: (*a*) cup shaped and (*b*) pateriform or saucer shaped. Four types of the calyx have been recognized (Paul 1940, [3]: 135): (*a*) cup shaped and embracing the base of the fruit, (*b*) pateriform but slightly embracing the base of the fruit, (*c*) pateriform but not embracing the base of the fruit, and (*d*) pateriform within a depression at the base of the fruit.

In wild forms the fruit separates readily from the calyx but during domestication growers selected for the nondeciduous type. In domesticated sorts the calyx and most of the peduncle stay attached when the fruit is picked. At the present time the high cost of labor makes the removal of these stems impractical even though their presence lowers the quality in commercial usage for certain products. Ironically, attempts are being made today to breed the deciduous or soft-flesh* character back into the varieties suitable for commercial use and for machine harvesting. It is desirable that a type should be developed that needs a slight pull rather than falling at a light touch so that high winds and similar factors would not cause the pods to drop (P. G. Smith 1951, 343).

Corolla: While in the bud stage the corolla margins of the domesticated species are valvate (do not overlap), but when they fully open they are rotate. Campanulate blooms have been found to exist in at least one of the wild species (Heiser & Smith 1958; Eshbaugh 1979). The base of the flower is a short, cylindrical tube from which arise the acuminate lobes. The usual number of lobes is five but, as in the calyx, it varies from four to seven and in abnormal blossoms there can be even more. Each lobe has three veins. The color ranges from white to cream to greenish-white, while some forms may be purple and others may have greenish-yellow spots. In *C. annuum* the purple-colored flowers are associated with purple pigmentation of the stems, leaves, and immature fruit. Short petal length is

---

*Soft flesh: a character term to be used in place of deciduous; it is normal for all wild forms of the cultivated species as well as for nearly all purely wild species (Lippert et al. 1966).

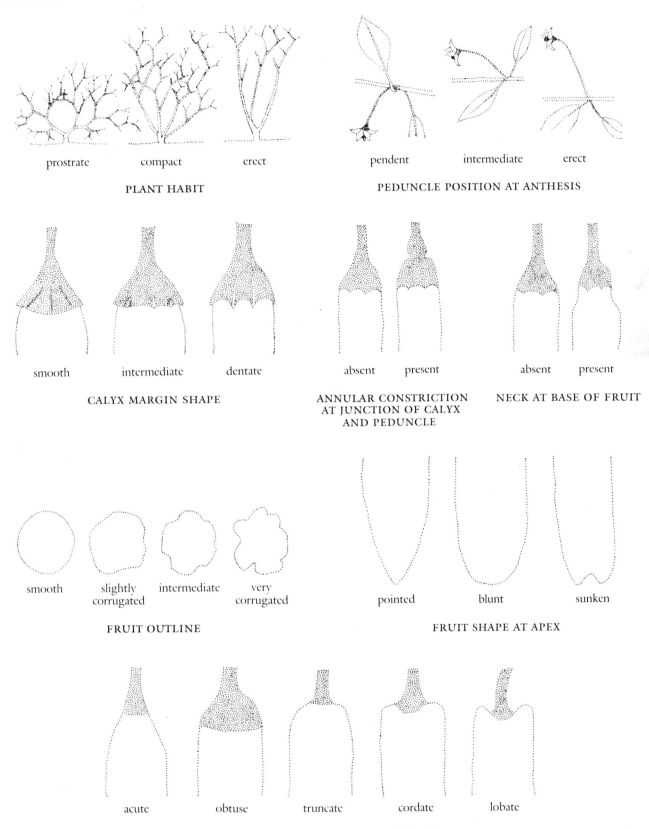

PLANT HABIT

prostrate   compact   erect

PEDUNCLE POSITION AT ANTHESIS

pendent   intermediate   erect

CALYX MARGIN SHAPE

smooth   intermediate   dentate

ANNULAR CONSTRICTION
AT JUNCTION OF CALYX
AND PEDUNCLE

absent   present

NECK AT BASE OF FRUIT

absent   present

FRUIT OUTLINE

smooth   slightly corrugated   intermediate   very corrugated

FRUIT SHAPE AT APEX

pointed   blunt   sunken

FRUIT SHAPE AT PEDUNCLE ATTACHMENT

acute   obtuse   truncate   cordate   lobate

13. *Capsicum* descriptors after the International Board for
Plant Genetic Resources. (F.A.O. in press)

also associated with purple color in the plant (Lippert et al. 1966).

Stamens: The position of the stamens is alternate with corolla lobes. They exhibit the same variation in numbers as do the lobes. The anthers, which dehisce longitudinally, are shorter than the filaments in most instances. The anther colors may be bluish-purple, violet, indigo, or brownish-yellow. The filaments may be white, greenish-white, or violet.

Pollen grains: The dry pollen grains are ellipsoidal with a longitudinal groove along the middle. After they reach the stigma, they remain inactive for some time, regardless of the environmental condition.

Ovary: In the wild forms, the ovary is two celled; however, in domesticates the number of locules may vary from two to four. In some cases as many as five locules have been reported. It is not unusual for the same plant to produce fruit with a variation in the number of locules.

Pistil: The linear style may be either straight or curved. The length may be longer than (exserted), same level as, or below the level of (included) the stamens. This variation in length may occur on the same plant. The pistils that are longer than the stamen column are not favorable to self-fertilization and are typical of the more primitive types of peppers (Erwin 1937). The color may be white with a green or yellow stigma or purple with a greenish-yellow stigma. The bifid stigma is subcapitate and becomes mucilaginous when it is receptive. Apparently it is receptive only the first day the flower is open (S. E. McGregor 1976).

Nectar: The flowers of the *Capsicum* have no odor; honey bees are the principal insect attracted to them by the nectar, which is secreted and accumulated at the base of the corolla lobes (S. E. McGregor 1976). The nectar globules are fully formed by the time the flower is completely open. The nectar, which forms in the corolla tube, passes through the filament grooves to the surface of the petals. The nectar is liquefied mucilage with sugar and other elements (Martin et al. 1932).

Curvature of the peduncle: Paul (1940, [2]: 141) tells us that, "in the early stage of the flower bud differentiation, the peduncle is erect, but as development proceeds it elongates and responds geotropically so that before the flower opens it assumes a pendent position." When the curvature in the peduncle is located close to the point of attachment at the node, it maintains that position after the fruit has matured and the fruit, therefore, becomes pendent; but when the curvature takes place near the calyx the peduncle becomes erect after fertilization and the fruit will be either erect or horizontal.

Anthesis and anther dehiscence: On the day before the bud opens it becomes swollen and turgid. Anthesis (flowering) begins very early the next day and is quickly followed by dehiscence (opening) of the anthers. The anthers may dehisce from one to ten hours after the flower opens, but frequently they fail to dehisce (S. E. McGregor 1976, 293). Observers have reported (Paul 1940, 94 [3]: 142) that the tips of the buds start to separate as early as 2:00 A.M., by 6:15 A.M. about 50 percent have opened, and by 8:30 A.M. the corollas of the majority at that stage are fully extended; however, stragglers may continue until noon but most are completely open within three hours of sunrise (Cochran 1938*b*, 408). The corollas remain open until about 4:00 P.M. and all are closed by 6:30 to 7:30 P.M. On the second day, they reopen between 5:00 and 8:00 A.M. and close between 4:00 and 6:30 P.M. As the flower opens, the anthers, which form a compact column around the style in the bud, begin to separate from one another and to move away from the style. When dehiscence is completed, by noon of the second day, the anthers will be widely separated at their distal ends. The corolla drops between the third and fifth days following anthesis.*

The majority of the flowers are open within the first two hours after sunrise. Erwin (1932) concluded that temperature and sunlight were important factors in anthesis. Most authors agree that light is more important than temperature. Low humidity was also found to be a favorable factor.

Pollination and fertilization: With dehiscence the pollen becomes available; however, it remains on the anthers and becomes dislodged only when the flowers are moved by the wind or other means. Insects are attracted to the nectar in pepper flowers and a variety of bees, butterflies, aphids, and ants are known to transfer the pollen.

Before pollination can take place the stigma must become receptive by secreting a shiny, mucilaginous substance on its surface. This secretion remains "sticky" about twenty-four hours; however, in most instances the stigma has not lost its receptivity a day after anthesis (Paul 1940, [4]: 199). Cochran (1938*b*) observed that the pollen remains inactive for a short time after it is deposited on the stigma no matter what the conditions are. The period between pollination and fertilization varies with the humidity and temperature. Cap-

---

*This schedule of opening and closing of the flower was very important in my efforts to draw the blooms. Unfortunately, I did not locate the information in the literature until after many frustrating efforts to catch the bloom at the needed stage. Although there is some variation, I can vouch for the almost clocklike behavior of the pepper flower.

sicums are usually self-pollinating; however, studies show there is enough natural crossing in cultivated peppers to necessitate a certain amount of isolation in the plant beds (Cochran 1938b, 408). The exact distance of isolation or the amount of protection required has not been determined (Odland & Porter 1941, 585). Wind can account for only a small part of cross pollination. Bees are the most active pollinators but they are spasmodic, working only on warm, bright days. For aphids and thrips to transfer pollen the leaves of the plants must touch.

Flowering and setting of the fruit: Flower buds are generally initiated on pepper plants for the first time after nine to ten vegetative nodes are formed (but often it is earlier) and from there on after every second node (Dorland & Went 1947, 397). The number of flowers is quite large in proportion to the number that set fruit. At the onset of flowering the fruit-set is greater than it is as the plant grows older, with further flowering being dependent on climatic conditions. Temperature has been found to be the prime factor affecting fruit-set, with night temperature being the most critical (Cochran 1936). At Texas A&M University it has been determined that the optimum night temperatures are 18°–27°C (64.4°–80.6°F) (Longbrake et al. 1976). There is no fruit-set above 30°C (86°F) (Dorland & Went 1947). Excess transpiration at the higher temperatures is the culprit adversely affecting fruit-set. Quagliotti (1979, 408) reports that, if the night temperature could be reduced to 10°C (50°F) at the anthesis of the first flower and held through several successive flowerings, one would get the highest rate of fruit-set. The lower the night temperatures the more buds actually develop into open flowers, with the optimum range being about 15.5°–20.5°C (59.9°–68.9°F). Older plants require lower night temperatures for flowering. Daytime temperatures do not affect the flowering (Dorland & Went 1947, 397).

Development of the fruit and seed: Although the size and shape of the fruit are genetically determined, growth is affected by environmental conditions, such as temperature, moisture, light, nutrients, and so on. The length of time required for the fruit to ripen varies with the different cultivars. It can range from sixty to seventy-five days from anthesis depending on environmental factors.

The Fruit and Differentiating Characters

Fruit morphology was the principal means employed by early taxonomists to classify the domesti-cated capsicums (Paul 1940, [4]: 202). However, recent studies show that morphology alone will not produce valid taxa. Smith and Heiser (1951, 363) have found that fruit shape, color, and position are of little taxonomic value because of parallel variation that occurs with the different species.

Commercially, the fruits are used in various stages of development. Some are used only in the unripe state (e.g., Pepperoncini), others when fresh ripe but still green or yellow (e.g., Bell, Floral Gem), fully ripe with maximum color (e.g., Cayenne, Cherry), or in the dry state (e.g., Pasilla, Anaheim).

The size, shape, and position of the fruit: Within a given domesticated species the size and shape of the fruit are used to distinguish the different cultivars. Those that would use this characteristic are faced with every intergrade of size and shape from the tiny ovoid Chiltecpin (0.9 cm) to the long, flattened Anaheim (33.02 cm). To compound this problem breeders are continually creating new cultivars through selection and hybridization.

Size and shape are inherited, as are most quantitative characters, and are governed by the action of multiple factors. Kaiser (1935) found that "size is genetically determined by the interaction of a number of size genes, but is subject to considerable modification by environmental factors." These "size genes" have affected the size of all organ systems as the fruit has been selected for larger and larger types (Eshbaugh 1982, personal communication). The ultimate configuration of the mature fruit is genetically determined by the interaction between (a) factors governing relative dimensional growth rates and (b) factors governing the size of the fruit. There is a decrease in the size of the pods on the same plant as the season advances and the plants pass their optimum growth phase.

The apex of the fruit may be pointed, blunt, or lobed/sunken with a depression. The pod may have a bulged or a nonbulged base where it attaches to the peduncle; the nonbulged base is either acute or obtuse with a cup-shaped calyx. The bulged base may be truncate, cordate, or lobate and is generally associated with a pateriform calyx. The base of some fruits has a definite neck. The cross section of the fruit can be either smooth, slightly corrugated, intermediately corrugated, or very corrugated (F.A.O., in press). The fruit attachment position is another inherited character, with the pendent position being dominant over the erect position (Miller & Fineman 1937). Both the pendent and erect positions occur among the cultivars of *C. annuum* var. *annuum* and *C. chinense*. However, *C. baccatum* var. *pendulum* and *C. pubescens* have only

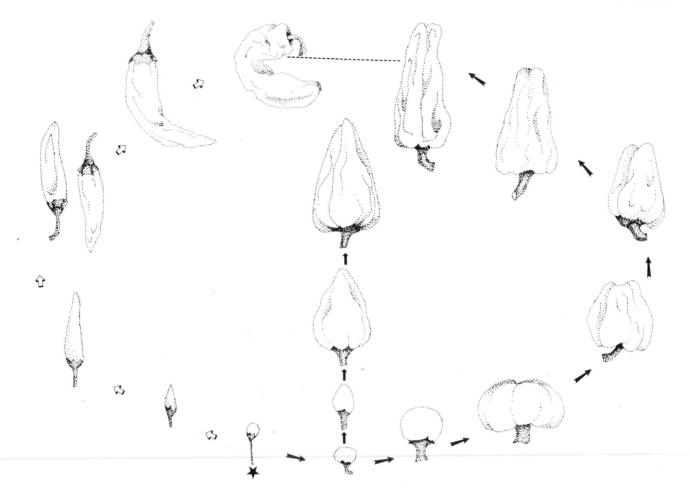

14. Evolution of fruit form. Beginning with the tiny wild *C. annuum aviculare* on the left, the elongate conical forms have evolved into the elongate flattened forms; in the cen- ter the conical cultivars are produced; and to the right the globose forms move toward the tomato type into the large blocky forms. (After Terpo 1966)

pendent fruit, and the erect position prevails with *C. frutescens*.

Pericarp: The pericarp, or fruit wall, varies in thickness with different cultivars. This inherited characteristic manifests itself as thick, medium, or thin. Those fruits with a thin pericarp are readily dried and used in the dehydrated form, while those with medium or thick pericarps must be preserved by smoking, pickling, or canning. The dried pericarps of certain cultivars, for example, Guajillo, are translucent, but it is more common for them to be opaque. The flavor of the fruit wall was found to be inherited, with the mild flavor being dominant over the pungent (Miller & Fineman 1937, 549).

Color and luster: The majority of cultivars produce green fruit in the immature form because of the chlo-

rophyll in the outer layer of the pericarp. However, some forms have "white" (ivory or very pale yellow), greenish-yellow, yellow, orange, purple, or purplish-black immature fruits. In the mature state the fruits are either red, yellow, orange, or brownish-red, red fruits being the most common. The brown fruits result from the retention of the chlorophyll so that the green pigment underlies or mixes with the red to produce brown, just as it would on the painter's palette. The usual pattern of ripening is by stages from green to red, yellow, orange, or brown, but some types show a variety of shades from green to yellow, purple to red, orange to red, or several of these colors on the fruit at the same time.

Peduncle: A persistent peduncle is a genetic character with the easily detached peduncle dominant over the persistent type. Wild capsicums have deciduous peduncles but selection has caused this character to be reversed in the cultivated forms. A firmly attached peduncle is desirable in certain dry commercial types so that their seeds will remain intact. Those peppers with a high percentage of pods with their peduncles intact have better storage qualities; therefore, they command a better price in the Far East (Paul 1940, [4]: 200). However, breeders in America are attempting to return to the easily detached peduncle in certain cultivars to facilitate machine harvesting and to eliminate waste in dried products.

Short peduncles cause loss of shape when the fruits compete for space on the stalk, making them unmarketable. Upright peduncles are preferred; however, a long erect peduncle will become pendent from the weight of the fruit as it matures.

Factors Affecting Growth, Fruiting, and Maturation

Such factors as nutrition, temperature, soil, light, and moisture, aside from inherent factors, are responsible for differences in growth and fruiting of the pepper plant. In this section we will examine the effect of these factors on flower production and fruit-set.

Nutrition: Most writers indicate the importance of nitrogen in the nutrition of the pepper plant. Studies have shown (Cochran 1936) that high nitrogen significantly increased the number of blossoms formed and the number that set fruit, the increase being greater at temperatures of 21°–27°C (69.8°–80.6°F) than at 15.5°–21°C (59.9°–69.8°F). However, this depends on the species; C. pubescens does better at lower, but above freezing, temperatures. Vegetative growth was improved by nitrogen but there was little effect on the earliness of bud formation or anthesis. Nitrogenous fertilizers and ammonium sulphate show a tendency to induce early bearing and increased yield. Texas A&M University recommends that, at planting, phosphate should be banded two to three inches below the seed (Longbrake et al. 1976). When the plants reach six to eight inches tall, a side-dressing of a balanced fertilizer should be applied followed by two or three additional nitrogen side-dressings during the growing season to maintain vigorous growth and to promote continuous blooming.

Temperature: Most authors are in agreement that the environmental factor that plays the predominant role in reducing fruit-set is temperature. During germination and while the plant is young the optimal

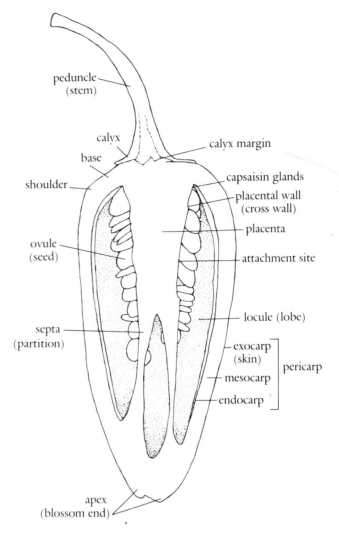

15. Cross section of a *Capsicum* fruit.

night temperature is at least as high as 30°C (86°F); however, as the plant becomes older, the optimal night temperature progressively decreases. Maximum growth occurs at the 21°–26.5°C (69.8°–79.7°F) temperature range. Early flowering and fruit maturity are augmented by high temperatures, but from the standpoint of fruit-set, with the exception of the lowest temperature range (10°–15.5°C; 50°–59.9°F), the higher the temperature, the lower the setting of fruit. No fruit-set occurs when night temperatures are above 30°C (86°F). High temperatures cause abnormalities in both the flower and the fruit. Best yields occur when temperatures range between 18°C and 27°C (64.4°–80.6°F) during fruit-setting. While certain South American species (e.g., *C. pubescens* and *C. eximium*) tolerate the cold, plants indigenous to the North American continent are highly susceptible to freezing temperatures and for the most part are grown as annuals.

Moisture: The moisture content of the soil has an important effect on the growth and yield of capsicums. Peppers are not suitable for dry farming conditions. Texas A&M University estimates that 32 to 40 inches of water are required to start peppers from direct seeding in March and growing into September for harvest. Rainfall during this period may be beneficial if the rain falls inbetween irrigations. All types of peppers respond positively to a constantly moist soil condition of 60 to 80 percent of soil moisture-holding capacity. Light, frequent irrigations of about 2 to 3 inches of water or rainfall per week provide optimum conditions. The peak moisture requirements for capsicums occur during the blooming and fruit-setting period, or forty-five to sixty days after seedling emergence (Longbrake 1983, personal communication). Much higher yields are obtained under irrigated conditions. Oviedo (1526) reported Amerindians growing their peppers in irrigated plots.

If the garden is not well drained, the home gardener should plan to grow peppers in raised beds because the plants cannot stand "wet feet." Following watering, all surface moisture should disappear within an hour or two (Peavy 1983).

Soil: A deep sandy or sandy loam soil that is well drained is ideal. A liberal supply of organic matter with a pH range of 7.1 to 8.3 is the optimum for the culture of peppers.

Light: In the tropics, where days are shorter than in temperate areas, plants are extremely sensitive to small differences in day length. The capsicums are tropical short-day plants. Pepper plants grown in temperate areas are most vigorous, flower and ripen earlier, pro-ducing higher yields in eight- to twelve-hour days than in longer days (Dorland & Went 1947). Longer days cause the plants to take more time in reaching the flowering stage. During periods of shorter days, growth is more rapid and the time of flowering lasts about ten days more than in periods of longer days (Cochran 1936). A light intensity of 3,000 to 10,000 lux is considered normal, with 3,000 lux being the minimum level (Quagliotti 1979, 402). Light has little effect in inducing ripening of the fruit. Intensity of light does not seem to influence the time of flowering.

Some suggest that peppers are day neutral (not responsive to day length), that they will flower in approximately a given number of days regardless of day length (Eshbaugh 1982; Longbrake 1983, personal communication).

Pungency, Flavor, and Color

Pungency: If you were to ask someone to name the one characteristic most typical of peppers, the reply would probably be "they burn." This burning sensation is caused by a powerful pungent principle named capsaicin (pronounced: cap-say-i-sin). In 1877 this substance was crystallized and named by L. T. Thresh, an Englishman working in India, who was continuing investigations begun sixty years earlier in Germany. Experimentation by Micko (1898) improved on the isolating technique of Thresh, thereby proving capsaicin to be the pungent principle.

By 1920 Nelson had been able to synthesize capsaicin by reacting synthetic vanillyamin with decenoic acid extracted from natural capsaicin. Working with Dawson three years later (Nelson & Dawson 1923), he found the exact chemical structure of capsaicin. However, it was not until 1930 that Spath and Darling were able to completely synthesize capsaicin, without using natural products. After this, there was little work with *Capsicum* and for ninety years after its discovery it was believed that capsaicin was the only pungent principle in capsicums. During recent years improved research techniques have brought renewed interest, resulting in the discovery of other pungent compounds in capsicums. An exhaustive study of the chemistry of capsaicin conducted by Bennett and Kirby (1968) led them to conclude that naturally occurring capsaicin was composed of at least five vanillyl amides varying in acid side chains.

Few will disagree with Nelson (1910) when he states that "the enormous pungency of capsaicin can be appreciated only by those who have been brought intimately in contact with it." Continuing, he warns that "a drop of a solution containing one part in 100,000 causes a persistent burning on the tongue. A drop of a solution of 1 part to a million imparts a perceptible warmth." That amount not only is unweighable but also extremely difficult to detect with the most delicate chemical tests. Capsaicin has virtually no flavor or odor; the detection appears to be restricted to the physiological action of the compound. An oral method employing human "guinea pigs" as a taste panel, the Scoville Organoleptic Test of 1912, is still the most used means of analysis.

Heat in peppers is expressed in Scoville Heat units. For example: the Bell type has zero heat units and the Anaheim has 1,000, while the Jalapeño and Cayenne may vary in heat from 2,500 to 25,000 units (usually 2,500 to 4,000); however, the *tabasco* rages in at 60,000 to 80,000 heat units (Peavy 1983). Pungency is effected by the stimulation of pain receptors in the mouth cavity. This test has many limitations, the first being that the subject tested cannot be one who is accustomed to a diet of chili peppers.

Maga (1975) summarizes studies that came after those of Nelson. Regarding the horticultural considerations, he found that many factors, such as climatic conditions, variety, geographical location, stage of maturity, and location within the fruit, had been reported to influence capsaicin content. Results, however, showed that pungency was not influenced by season or variety (Balbaa et al. 1968). But, as Maga's study anticipated, maturity had a significant influence since pungency was not detected until the fruits were four weeks old. Mature fruits have 50 percent more pungency. In general, warm-weather crops will be hotter than cool-weather ones, as will those grown in poor soil in hot, dry climates. High night temperature is particularly favorable for high capsaicin content (Lippert et al. 1966).

There are many discrepancies in the literature regarding the location of the capsaicin but most agree that the distribution of capsaicin within the fruit is uneven. There has been considerable argument as to whether or not the seed contains capsaicin, but now it is considered highly doubtful that capsaicin or its derivatives are present within the seed; however, seeds can acquire a degree of pungency through contact with the placenta. The majority, about 89 percent, of capsaicin is associated with the placental partition (cross wall) of the fruit, with the ratio of capsaicin in the cross wall to that in the pericarp and seed being 100 to 6 (Balbaa et al. 1968). The placental tissue is the only place where the capsaicin is produced and it is controlled by a single dominant genetic factor (Heiser & Smith 1953). The glands that manufacture and secrete the capsaicin are located at the juncture of the placenta and the pod wall (P. G. Smith 1978, personal communication). Some workers consider the presence of yellow pigmentation in the cross wall to indicate pungency; however, Huffman (1977) found that the presence or absence of the yellow pigmentation is not related to pungency.

The capsaicin content can vary among cultivars of the same species and with the fruit of a single cultivar. The pungency of a given cultivar varies with weather conditions, such as a heat wave that causes stress and increases the heat units (Peavy 1983). Those with a thin pericarp apparently have the higher capsaicin levels. Heiser and Smith (1953) propose that this variation in pungency is a result of modifying genes, which, when combined with the ratio of placental and dissepiment tissue to pericarp, act to modify the degree of pungency. The pungency increases from the first to the last stage in the fruit development and is influenced more by maturity than by climate (Huffman 1977).

Flavor: While walking through a plot of peppers at an experimental farm, a young man was observed as he moved from plant to plant tasting a pod from each. When asked what he was looking for, he replied, "I want to make some hot sauce, but I don't want a pepper that is just hot, it's got to have flavor too." This is a serious consideration in the selection of peppers throughout the world. Flavor is a complex of sensations through which the presence and identity of ingested substances are determined in the mouth (Huffman 1977). Three distinct senses are involved when we perceive a particular flavor: taste, smell, and touch (tactile). The difference in taste arises from small amounts of several aromatic substances affecting flavor, apart from pungency, which occur in capsicums. The flavoring principle appears to be associated with the carotenoid pigment: strong color and strong flavor are linked. When the color of dried peppers fades, they also lose their flavor.

The flavor compound of capsicums is located throughout the outer wall; very little is found in the placenta and cross wall; none is found in the seeds (Huffman 1977). It is not contained in a specialized structure but is produced by special biochemical reactions in the cells themselves rather than existing in isolated compartments.

Color: The colorful reds, purples, greens, yellows,

and oranges of peppers are as stimulating to our visual senses as the pungency of capsaicin is to our sense of pain. Color is a primary component of the total appearance of a product as well as an indicator of quality (Nagle 1977). The coloring properties of the capsicums are used in foods throughout the world.

The carotenoid capsanthin was listed by Mayer (1943, 63) as the primary coloring agent in red peppers. Capsanthin constitutes 35 percent of the red pigments, while the remainder is composed of five other coloring compounds. Thirty-one carotenoid pigments have been identified from the red Bell pepper and there is a wide range in total carotenoid content among different varieties (Curl 1962).

Green peppers do not contain capsanthin. The yellow and orange capsicums obtain their particular hue from the beta-carotene cucubitene, one of the carotenoids, which is readily found in *Capsicum*, *Daucus* (carrots), and *Sorbus* (mountain ash). Of special interest is a relationship between the carotenes and vitamin A, which was pointed out by Mayer (1943).

These polyene pigments are water-soluble lyochromes located in the wall of the fruit. Several German chemists, among them Kuhn, Zechmeister, and Karrer, have been their principal investigators (Mayer 1943). In capsicums, the red pigments not only have a higher tintorial capacity than the yellow but also are present in larger proportions. As the red pigment increases, the yellow content does also; but the red produces a masking effect and decreases the reflectance of the yellow (Nagle 1977).

Not only is the universal appeal of the color of capsicums esthetically rewarding but also the pigments responsible for the color cause them to be commercially important. The Pure Food and Drug Regulations in the United States require that food products be colored with natural dye stuffs only. The capsanthin from peppers is a powerful coloring agent, making it a desirable product in the foods industry. People in other parts of the world whose diets are largely colorless starches, such as rice or corn, use peppers not only for spice but also to add color to their bland achromatic diets.

Peppers are harvested within a few months after they begin to ripen, yet it might be many more months before the dried product reaches the homemaker or food processor, therefore making any loss of red color during the necessary storage period a matter of importance. Consequently, a desirable dry pepper would be one with a high initial color concentration that is retained well, thus giving a good total color after storage. In studies of this factor, Lease and Lease (1956) found that the temperature at which the pods were stored had more effect on color stability than did light, the kind of container, or whether the pepper was stored as whole pod or ground. Storage at 5°C (41°F) slowed the rate of discoloration but did not affect the inherent color stability of the variety or strain of pepper. They also found that if the pods were allowed to ripen and dry on the plant they had a better initial color and better color retention than pods picked when fully colored but succulent. Some species, for example, *C. pubescens*, *C. chinense*, and certain *C. annuum* var. *annuum* cultivars (e.g., Jalapeño), do not air dry satisfactorily under any circumstances.

A process using the spectophotometer has been found to be the most reliable method for evaluating the coloring matter of capsicums. Moster and Prater (1952) determined that the Gentry Method of using this instrument was the most satisfactory. Pohle and Gregory (1960) refined this procedure by calibrating the instrument using pure beta-carotene and expressing the color as micrograms of carotene per gram of sample.

Tristimulus colomitry is another means of measuring the color of foods. Based on a three-color light theory, it employs the Gardner Color Difference Meter. The readings from this instrument will vary; therefore, it is used only to measure small color differences among samples.

Subjective impressions of color are often more accurate than values obtained by instruments. Humans are able to see the total color impact of the product, whereas conventional instruments measure the individual components of color and do not measure the scattered light (Nagle 1977).

7

AGRONOMY

WHETHER you are a home gardener with a small plot, an apartment dweller with a couple of flower pots, a traditional small farmer with a few acres, a Mexican Indian with your doorstep favorite, or a big commercial grower with vast irrigated fields, the culture of peppers is basically the same. Much of this has been touched on in the section of this book that details soil, light, temperature, moisture, and other requirements for proper growth.

The old-time Hungarian peasant farmer's wife and daughters, carefully setting out small transplants by hand as they moved down a row on their knees (the transplanting was all done by women), would be astounded to see the modern pepper grower in Florida moving along the wide, plastic-mulch-covered beds, not rows, on a machine that plugged the plastic and earth with one motion and, with a second action, deposited a gel that contained not only the already germinated seeds but also fertilizer, insecticides, and fungicides. After planting, the plants are permitted to grow and are carefully irrigated at the prescribed intervals. Unlike the preseeded gel, irrigation is not new to the pepper grower, for Oviedo reported the irrigated plots maintained by the pre-Columbian Amerindian. The mature crop was and still is, for the most part, harvested by hand—pod by tedious pod—but today a great deal of experimentation is being conducted with mechanical harvesting methods both in the United States and in Israel. However, much remains to be done before present machines replace the hand picker. Plant geneticists are redesigning the typical *Capsicum* plant type to accommodate the machine harvester.

Germination, Planting, and Fertilization

Those gardeners who do not purchase their plants at the local nursery, supermarket, or feed store will need to start them from seed. After selecting the cultivar you wish to grow from among the tempting variety in seed catalogs that offer peppers (see Appendix), order the amount required for your space and needs based on 3 to 5 plants per person, which provides sufficient peppers for fresh use and storage. The per plant yield will vary according to growing season, area, and cultural practices but the average is one pound per plant (Stoner & Villalon 1977). A package contains from 50 to 100 seeds; 28.5 gm (1 oz.) has over 4,000 seeds and ¼ kg (½ lb.) provides enough for an acre.

Capsicums are slow to germinate. Soaking the seed in warm water for five or six hours does little to accelerate germination but by pregerminating them the time can be appreciably reduced. Sowing the seed directly in the garden is possible but not recommended for the home gardener. Sow the seed in greenhouse benches, hot beds, or flats at least six weeks before your last frost-free date. Germinate the seed in a sterile medium, such as a mixture using equal parts of milled sphagnum peat, pearlite, and vermiculite or one of the new soilless commercial products. Sow as thinly as possible and lightly cover, no deeper than the thickness of the seed. Carefully water by using a fine overhead mist or by gently pouring, being careful not to dislodge the seed. Watering from the bottom reduces soil temperature, resulting in a low percentage of germination at any temperature (Cochran 1935). Never permit the seed or seedlings to dry or wilt from the time they are sown until transplanted and well started.

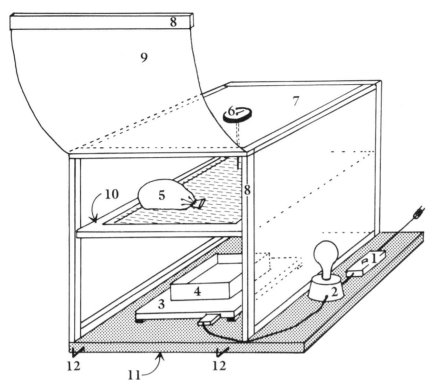

1. dimmer/on-off switch to regulate temperature

2. check light

3. food-warmer plate

4. cake pan for water

5. seed sack (more than one can be treated at a time)

6. probe thermometer

7. 4-mil or 6-mil (preferable) plastic covering for entire box

8. lath framing

9. 4-mil or 6-mil (preferable) plastic door

10. screen-wire shelf or old refrigerator shelf (more than one can be inserted)

11. single piece of plywood

12. hooks to hold door shut

16. Pregerminating seeds: 1. Suspend seeds loosely in a cheesecloth bag or tea strainer. 2. Soak in hot tap water for 2 hours (not over 50°C [122°F]). 3. Add vermiculite (3 × volume) to soaked seeds (to achieve a better distribution of seeds, to guarantee even moisture, and to guarantee aeration and prevent "drowning." 4. Place the mixture very loosely in a plastic bag; close the bag tightly. 5. Place the plastic bag in the "sweatbox" shown here (a hot water heater closet or a room not over 30°C [89°F] may be used instead). 6. Maintain 100 percent humidity. 7. Check for germination (show of radicle) after 24 hours—repeat checks every 4 hours. 8. Fill the water pan daily. 9. Most cultivars show radicles after 48–54 hours, but each cultivar and seed lot has to be tested in small amounts previous to final seeding. This method of pregermination is not limited to pepper seed. (After Muehmer & Brimner 1982)

Germination will require twelve to twenty-one days at a constant temperature of 21°C (69.8°F) for most *C. annuum* var. *annuum*, which is the most common garden variety, or longer, depending on the species and seed. At 22°–28°C (71.6°–82.4°F) irrigated seed will germinate in ten days (Cochran 1935, 478). Because temperature stress is a problem in germination, the time can be cut in half by maintaining a constant 27°C (80.6°F) during the period. Higher temperatures decrease the length of the germination period but the percentage of germination also decreases. Below 4°–10°C (39.2°–50°F) there is no germination (Cochran 1935, 478). Scarification* can also reduce the germination time, as does supplying additional oxygen to the seed (Bryan 1982). Light is apparently not a factor in the germination of the seed but it is important to have light as soon as the first leaves appear.

Storage conditions before planting greatly influence germination.* Seed viability is reduced as temperature and moisture content are increased. In most cases the fruit is harvested at a stage when the seed is too moist for storage. The mature seed should be dried in a manner that will prevent stress damage from too rapid evaporation of the moisture. For each 1 percent moisture reduction, the seed storage time is approximately doubled. Depending on the species, at least 70 percent of properly dried and stored pepper seed can be expected to germinate after one to two years of storage under favorable conditions at the latitudes of the United States (approximately 25°–48°N). The conditions will be favorable if the sum of the temperature in °F and the relative humidity does not exceed 100.

---

*Put seed in a plastic bag and roll with a rolling pin.

*The home gardener can reduce insect damage to seed being saved by spraying the seed with a household insecticide or placing a mothball or two in the container with the seed.

Comparable results can be obtained by drying seed to 5 percent moisture content or lower and storing it in sealed moisture-proof containers at temperatures up to 32°C (89.6°F); at higher temperatures refrigeration is required (Justice & Bass 1978).

Certain vegetable seeds require a period of dormancy before they can germinate satisfactorily (Paul 1940, [2]: 77). Sun-dried pepper seeds germinate much better after a six-month period of storage at low temperature than do freshly gathered seeds. The heavier and lighter-colored seeds germinate faster than light-weight, dark-colored seeds.

When direct planting, plant the seed in the moist soil on one side of the bed, near the furrow, at a depth of 12.5–19 mm (½–¾ in.). Transplanted plants bear earlier and produce a larger crop than field-planted peppers (Garcia 1908).

When the true leaves are well formed, transplant the seedlings into benches or flats containing equal parts peat, sand, and loam. Lift the seedlings by the leaves. Grow them at 21°C (69.8°F), being careful that night temperatures do not fall below 17°C (62.6°F). To prevent "leggy" stems from developing, keep flourescent lights or special grow-lights on for ten to twelve hours a day approximately 10.16 cm (4 in.) above the leaf tips from the moment the radicle appears (Bubel 1978, 71). After the plants attain a height of 12–15 cm (4¾–6 in.) and all danger of frost is past, plant them deeply in easily crumbled soil. This task should be performed in the early morning when the soil is cool but not below 13°C (55.4°F). Pepper roots will not grow and may be damaged if planted in soils having a lower temperature. If your soil thermometer reads above 13°C at the transplanting depth for three consecutive days, set out the plants (Cotner 1984, 13). Space plants 12 inches apart in rows 15 inches apart because close spacing results in more and larger fruit (Lafavore 1983). Add a cup of water to the transplant and cover with a hot cap; irrigate immediately.

Plant peppers in full sun in a fertile, well-drained soil. About a week before transplanting add 5 to 8 pounds of 5-10-5 fertilizer per 500 square feet, mixing into the soil well. A light or sandy soil will require nearly twice as much fertilizer. At the time of the first blooms apply ¼ to ½ cup of a high nitrogen fertilizer (21-0-0) as a side-dressing 35 to 40 cm (13¾–15¾ in.) from the plant's stem. Additional side-dressings should be made at about three-week intervals (Cotner 1984, 16). After the plants have set several fruits, give them a topdressing of the same fertilizer in order to maintain growth rate. A poor color and stunted growth would indicate the need for additional fertilizer (Stoner & Villalon 1977).

Transplanting can be done two to four weeks before the last killing frost in your area if the plants are placed under tunnels of white plastic. The yields will be the same as those planted after the frost-free date but the earlier date can give you peppers when others are scarce, resulting in a higher profit (Lafavore 1983).

Culture

The actual growing of the plant is so dependent on its environment that it is not possible to speak in specifics. In general it can be said that peppers are a warm-season crop that does better in a moderate climate that is not too hot to set fruit or so cold as to cause freezing. They give the best yield when temperatures range between 18.5° and 26.5°C (65°–80°F) during fruit setting. A fertile loam or sandy loam well-drained soil with a liberal supply of organic matter and moderately acid (pH 5.5–6.8) is ideal. Organic matter promotes the growth of earthworms, which loosen the soil, thus aerating it and increasing its moisture-holding qualities. Adequate moisture and good drainage are essential.

Irrigation: The number and frequency of irrigations depend on soil type, humidity, and prevailing temperature. Trench irrigation is the most common form, but in Florida a type of water-table irrigation is employed whereby the water moves up from the water table to the bed by capillary action. Irrigation water can carry diseases; therefore, it should never be allowed to touch the plant. The equivalent of a one-inch rain is required weekly. During flowering and fruit-set abundant water is essential to prevent loss of blooms and fruits. A drip irrigation system with special emitters that spray a fine mist over the leaves is recommended.

Cultivation: When the young plants are established, they should be subject to shallow cultivation. Deep cultivation results in root pruning as well as loss of moisture to the slow-growing roots. Cultivate so that the soil is thrown toward the center of the plant row. Avoid injuring the plants during cultivation because they are extremely brittle and subject to damage (Longbrake et al. 1976).

PESTS AND CONTROL

Weeds: In the past, weed control was dependent on hand labor by "hoe hands." Today this type of labor is not only costly but also difficult to come by, especially in the United States. A number of excellent chemicals have been developed to control weeds. After the determination of your particular weed problem, you would be best advised to contact your county agent or a university extension horticulturist to determine which chemicals would solve the problem.

Insects: Over thirty-five species of insects and mites are pests of peppers. These will vary depending on the region. According to the North Carolina State University Agricultural Extension Service, insects damage peppers by feeding on the foliage or fruit or by spreading virus diseases. Those feeding inside the fruit are of concern to the consumer.

Pepper insect pests can be effectively managed by incorporating such practices as these: proper field selection, growing insect-free transplants, planting early, controlling weeds and diseases, operating insect traps, examining fields periodically, timing and applying insecticides properly, and immediate destruction of crop on completion of harvest. Properly chosen insecticides can control insect pests when used as partners in crop management.

The most common insect pests are aphids, European corn borers, pepper weevils, spider mites, wireworms, flea beetles, leafminers, and pepper maggots (Sorensen 1977).

DISEASES AND CONTROL

Research horticulturists are kept busy developing disease-resistant strains of peppers. It is desirable to have disease resistance "built in" so that as little pesticide as possible will be necessary to prevent disease. There are several diseases that victimize capsicums, reducing the yields and driving up production costs. The most effective control is based on a combination of practices designed to reduce the opportunities for the diseases to become established. Diseases are difficult, if not impossible, to control once they become evident.

The diseases vary in different localities but some of the most troublesome are:

Bacterial leaf spot and leaf spot (fungus, *Cercospora capsici*): These two diseases cause more damage to sweet peppers than they do to the hot varieties. The leaves drop off, leaving the fruit unprotected from the sun so that it becomes sun scalded. Both types are seed borne and can be controlled by use of disease-free seed plus regular spraying with a combination of an antibiotic (streptomycin) and a copper fungicide.

Damping off (fungus, *Rhizoctonia*, *Pythium*): This soil-borne disease is common to moist soil, which rots the seed or kills the seedling. It can be controlled by the use of treated seed, sterilized soil, crop rotation, and chemical fungicide treatment.

Phytophora blight (fungus, *Phytophthora capsici*): This soil-borne disease is more destructive during very wet weather. Irrigation water can carry spores to several plants in a single row where they will infect both stem and fruit, girdling the plant at the soil line and causing a sudden wilt. This disease was first described in New Mexico. It moved into Mexico in 1958 and is now the biggest disease problem in that country. There is no control.

Southern blight (fungus, *Sclerotium rolfsii*): This fungus attacks the plant near the soil line, causing it to wilt and die. It can be controlled by crop rotation and deep plowing.

Ripe rot (fungus, *Altenaria calotopsicum*): This fungus causes thick-fleshed capsicums, such as pimentos, to rot in the field and in packing cases when there is a seasonal glut in the packing houses.

Mosaic (viruses): These viruses, which affect capsicums either singly or in combinations, are the main disease problem. Mottling, curling, stunting, and distortion of leaves are the symptoms. Control can be effected by removing weeds that harbor viruses, controlling disease-spreading insects, and planting away from tomatoes, cucumbers, cantaloupes, or commercial sunflowers. The aphid-borne virus can be reduced with mineral oil and the use of reflective surfaces on a paper or plastic mulch. Tobacco mosaic and tobacco etch are two typical virus diseases. Do not smoke where peppers are grown.

MISCELLANEOUS PROBLEMS

Blossom-end rot: This brown discoloration at the blossom end of the pod is not caused by a fungus, although fungi will grow on the affected areas. It is associated with extreme fluctuations in the water supply, root pruning, and heavy applications of nitrogen fertilizers. It can be controlled by even watering and careful fertilizing.

Rats and mice: These rodents frequently eat the seed and seedlings. Care must be taken to protect seedlings in the greenhouse or in the field. Transplanting larger plants will usually eliminate the problem in the field.*

---

*Rats almost terminated my efforts to do this book at one point. My paintings have been done from the living plants, which meant that I had to grow all those peppers. Some of the *Capsicums* are notorious for

Nematodes: Not a disease, nematodes are microscopic worms that live in the soil and feed on roots. Only root-knot nematode symptoms can be detected by the naked eye; others require soil examination. Crop rotation and fumigating with a nematicide prior to planting reduce damage. Shannon (1977) informs those who wish to have an effective disease control program to choose seed carefully, treat seed with a fungicide, select a desirable planting location, and rotate crops. He also states that plants should be provided with an even water supply, control of insects and weeds should be practiced, and the soil should be cultivated by throwing it toward the center of the plant row.

Harvesting

Capsicum fruit will be ready for harvesting between 70 days for the early green fruit and 130 days for some of the fully mature red pods (Stoner & Villalon 1977). Most of the peppers cultivated throughout the world are harvested today by the same method used during prehistorical times—by hand, but in mechanically advanced countries it is becoming increasingly difficult to find persons to do this type of work. To toil long hours in the summer heat, bent over, is exhausting physical labor and the hot varieties are painful to the hands.

In 1908 Garcia reported that picking in New Mexico was very slow, averaging about 18 kg (39.5 lb.) per hour. People are probably not any faster seventy-five years later. In Louisiana the usual practice was for a farmer to have a half-acre or so of peppers near his home. When it was time to harvest them his wife and children, as well as neighboring children, did the picking. During the harvest season they would make several "pickins," each one taking at least a week to work from one end of the patch to the other. A farmer near New Iberia, Louisiana, reporting this practice drawled,

"It used to be children's work in the summer but now they just want to come out and play with sticks and break down your plants. Can't get children to do anything any more." As a consequence of the labor situation, engineers are working with horticulturists to find ways to harvest the crop mechanically.

To further help the situation, plant breeders are restructuring the plant to make it easier to harvest. Some desirable new characters are concentrated fruit, set in clusters or groups, making it possible to gather a handful at one time instead of a single fruit; a shorter plant, about 45.72 cm (18 in.) tall; a compressed, bunchier plant with spaces between the nodes reduced; fewer leaves; a single stalk without lateral branches; the fruit off the ground between 15.24 cm and 45.72 cm (6–18 in.); and uniformity.

Of course it depends on the species and cultivar, but in general the pods of the commercially important types should be a uniform color when picked—those not fully mature should be either all green or yellow and those completely ripe should be totally colored, usually red. "Red" is the term used for ripe pods whether they are red, black, or other colors (Garcia 1908, 14). Green or yellow pods for home use or processing must be picked when fully grown but before further coloring develops. Harvesting peppers in the fully developed but green condition gives a much higher yield than picking all red ripe fruits. Evidently picking the green fruit stimulates the production of more flowers, therefore more fruit. The mature pods should be fully colored when picked or they will discolor while drying. Ripening on the plant, which is desirable for many products, causes a decline in fruit production. If no green fruit is picked during the summer, two different harvests of ripe pods can be made: the first when there are enough to make it worthwhile and the second just before it freezes.

Although the crop generally begins to ripen early in July in the southern United States, quantities sufficient to justify picking are not usually found before the middle of the month. Of course, this ripening time will vary according to the location. After the harvest season sets in it is necessary to pick about every seven days. This frequency prevents overloading the curing houses and the crop can be more conveniently handled. In some areas where the fruit is allowed to become fully mature or to dry on the stalk, the crop is defoliated before harvesting.

In New Mexico, India, Hungary, Mexico, and other places where the pods are hung in strings or spread on mats to sun dry, they are gathered with the stems at-

---

being slow to germinate. About eight weeks after planting the seed in flats and transplanting and labeling two hundred seedlings, I needed to go out of town. A friend volunteered to be my "pepper sitter" and the precious babies were transferred to her barn. When I returned ten days later, she was terrified to have to report that rats had eaten all two hundred of her wards. This amounted to a two-month setback with the possibility that the delay might keep the plants from maturing properly. I can also add floods and hurricanes to the list of dangers. During the five years that were required for me to grow the peppers and paint the illustrations for this book, in the second year all my plants were destroyed in a nine-inch September downpour. The next year I grew them in three locations to guard against this but Hurricane Allen defeated me by wiping out all three locations in mid-August, too late to begin again. Patience is the password for growing peppers.

tached. In South Carolina and other places where artificial heat is used, the stems are not needed and the fruits are picked without them (Sievers 1948). Again, the practice varies according to the needs of the area and the proposed usage.

Only a small amount of machine harvesting is practiced in the United States and in Israel at this time. It requires close planting and uniform plants. Presently the expensive equipment is so damaging to the plant that the field can only be gone over once. There is much work to be done before mechanical harvesting becomes common practice.

Curing

Curing is a process by which the fresh red ripe fruits of forms with thin pericarps are converted into dried pods so that they may be utilized within a period of 1½ years after they have been cured. The fresh pods weigh five times more than the dried ones. The process used to remove the moisture may vary to some extent according to local practices throughout the world but it is basically the same. Owing to the different climatic conditions of the various areas where peppers are produced and to the inherent characteristics of each cultivar, the curing process will take different forms. Nevertheless, it is possible to divide the methods into two main categories: those that use the heat of the sun and those that utilize artificial heat.

SUN DRYING

A number of sun-drying systems are used throughout the major world production areas. Several of the most frequently used ones will be described.

Drying on the plant: This method is probably the earliest and most primitive method in use today. The fully developed and ripened pods are left on the plant until they begin to dry or, in colder areas, until the first frost. At that time irrigation is suspended; before the plant is completely dry it is pulled up by the roots and put in piles where it is left until all of the fruits have dried. The fruit is then separated from the plant, packed, and taken to market (Laborde & Pozo 1982). Pods dried in this manner are light and bulky and will not withstand any pressure without breaking.

Drying on *paseras* (there is no English equivalent for this word): This method is used in Mexico primarily for preparing the dried Anchos, Mulatos, and Pasillas. The fruit is gathered when it is completely mature. The pods are spread immediately on the *paseras*, which are raised soil beds about 1 × 40–50 m in size and are slanted so that rain water will run off. This slant is oriented to receive the maximum rays of the sun. Over the clean and even bed is spread a layer of straw or dry grass, which permits circulation of air and water drainage, thus preventing rotting. The fruit is turned daily so that it will dry uniformly without sun scorching.

The process usually takes twenty to thirty days depending on the cloudiness, intensity of the sun, temperature, and humidity. This method is also used to produce seed. Because so much hand work is involved it is only economically feasible on small family-operated farms (Laborde & Pozo 1982).

Modified *pasera*: In the modified *pasera* system the inclined platforms are covered with sheets of clear plastic; then stones are arranged on the plastic. The pods are gathered and placed on the *pasera* as previously described but they are not turned as often. During the eight to ten days required for drying, each side of the pod is exposed twice. This method is quicker and requires less hand labor than the previous method, giving the fruits better color and flavor for which buyers are willing to pay a 5–10 percent premium (Laborde & Pozo 1982).

Miscellaneous methods: Spreading the fruit on various flat surfaces, such as clean sand, concrete, wooden floors, flat roof tops, or woven straw mats, and turning it daily during the drying period is a universal practice. In some cases, the fruit is trampled or rolled to flatten it on about the third day of drying while it is still flaccid. If partially ripe fruits are placed immediately in the sun they will develop white patches. Some growers store the pods indoors for several days before spreading them in the sun while others heap them in medium-sized piles from four to six days. In certain areas, such as New Mexico and Hungary, the pods are tied together in long festoons, or *ristras*, which are then hung from eaves or racks where they will dry.

ARTIFICIAL HEAT

Dehydration by artificial heat had its origin in southern California at the beginning of this century. It is the most used method in the United States and its use is increasing in Mexico and other countries where peppers are grown in large volume. If the farmer grows large amounts, one thousand acres or more, he may have his own dehydration facility; otherwise, he might sell his crop to a dehydrator or dehydrator-processor. Artificial dehydration is much faster than sun drying, which is not practical for drying large volumes of fruit.

Heat tunnel, kiln, or oven: Tunnel dehydration is

the classic, time-proven method. All of the drying chambers or tunnels are constructed in a similar form with variations in the type of fuel used, the length and number of tunnels, and the drying temperature.

The building containing the ovens is constructed of brick or material with the same qualities; each tunnel has an entrance and an exit, with or without doors, by which the carts or conveyor belts loaded with the ripe pods enter and leave. Heated air is circulated through the tunnel so that the fruit is evenly dried as it moves through the chamber. During the harvest season the dehydrating plant will operate twenty-four hours a day, seven days a week. The drying time can range from fifteen hours in a plant in New Mexico to sixty-four hours in one in Mexico. Thre are many variables. More color is retained by slow drying.

In the United States the dried fruit usually moves on to a mill to be ground. The seeds are generally ground with the pods but that product which has had the seeds removed is at a premium because the color is richer. It is a different story in Mexico where the principal pepper buyer is the housewife. There is nothing comparable to USDA standards in Mexico, and much of the public, especially in rural areas, does not trust a ground product or powder. They demand that the calyx, stem, and seed be intact when they take it home to grind it themselves. However, more recently the powder is sold in city markets.

Drying by smoking: In some cases the flesh of the fruit is too thick to dry by any of the previous methods. These pods are dried by a smoking process that was in practice when Cortez arrived more than 460 years ago. The peppers dried by smoking still bear the Nahuatl name—*chipotle*. It is thought that this is one of the first artificial means by which the indigenous Amerindian farmers preserved their produce (Laborde & Poza 1982).

The ripe pods, usually the Jalapeño, are dried by smoking with much the same principle as in a Chinese smoke oven. The pit containing the source of heat is below ground level with a tunnel leading to an inverted pyramidically shaped compartment or upside-down "bell" on top of which a latticework of bamboo is placed to hold the pods. Drafts of air serve to pull the smoke through the tunnel, up through the "bell," and over the pods. The fruit is smoked either with or without the seeds. Those without seeds are called *capones*, which is translated as "castrated ones." The *capones* bring a much higher price than do the *chipotles* with seed.

Table 5. Countries That Produce Peppers and Powdered Paprika

Peppers	Powdered Paprika
Chile	Bulgaria*
China	Chile
Ethiopia*	Czechoslovakia
Fiji	Egypt
Greece	Hungary*
Haiti	Mexico
India*	Morocco*
Indonesia	Portugal*
Israel	Romania
Japan*	Spain*
Kenya*	Turkey
Malaysia	USA
Mexico*	USSR
Nigeria*	Yugoslavia*
Pakistan*	
Sierra Leone	
Sudan	
Taiwan	
Tanzania*	
Turkey	
Uganda	
USA*	

Source: *Encyclopaedia Britannica*, 15th ed. (1981), 17:505.
 *Major source.

Production and Yield

Peppers may not be one of the world's major economic crops but they are the major spice crop, with the result that they are economically significant for individual countries or localized geographic regions (McLeod et al. 1979a, 701).

Obtaining up-to-date data regarding the production of peppers in the Western Hemisphere has been difficult and for the most part disappointing. There are several reasons for this. Large commercial plantings are the exception, not the rule, in Latin American countries where the home garden is the principal source of peppers. Mexico, the largest consumer and producer of peppers, keeps good records; Canadian production is negligible on a world scale but has increased considerably during the last decade (Muehmer 1982); but I was unable to locate data on Central and South America through sources available at this time. Even in the United States, the Department of Agriculture does not maintain detailed production figures on peppers (J. J. Pickle 1982, personal communication). Statistical data available through the official U.S. Department of Agriculture, Bureau of Census, Department of Commerce, or any of the state agriculture departments is limited and has been reduced in recent years. As a matter of fact, the *Federal Register*, March 17, 1982, includes, among other items, reporting service program cuts and the elimination of "green peppers" from the official series of estimates.

A United Nations Report (F.A.O., in press) tells us that chili-peppers are among the most important commercially grown vegetables in the tropics and are probably the most important after the tomato. They are also exported to temperate countries in a dried form for use as a spice in flavoring sauces and processed foods. India and Thailand are the most important exporters of the extractable oleoresin of *Capsicum*. Nevertheless, the largest part is produced for home consumption. Sweet or Bell peppers are more popular than chili-peppers in the temperate regions, but they are also grown in some tropical and subtropical areas, such as Mexico, Senegal, Kenya, and North Africa, during the winter months for export to Western Europe and the United States (F.A.O., in press). Some recent production figures are presented in Table 6.

In my survey of leading pepper-producing states in the United States I found few of the state agriculture departments keeping data on "pepper" production. I was told that these figures are hard for the states to get because competition between the growers, particularly

Table 6.   World *Capsicum* Production

	Average per Year (1,000 MT)	
	1969–1971	1978–1980
World total	5,027	6,757
Developed countries	2,059	2,610
Centrally planned countries	1,598	2,082
Developing countries	2,968	4,147

Source: F.A.O. Production Yearbook 1980, vol. 34.

of the hot varieties, is so heated that the farmers will not divulge the acreage they have planted (B. Villalon 1983, personal communication). The high value of a Jalapeño crop makes growers of that cultivar especially secretive. The Cayennes, Bells, Cubanelles, Anaheims, and perhaps a few others are planted only on a contract basis and it is not recommended to do otherwise. Consequently, there is considerable fluctuation in the acreage planted from one season to the next.

According to Villalon (1983, personal communication), yield is figured on the basis of one pound of fruit per plant; however, the number of plants per acre varies between ten thousand and twenty thousand, depending on the variety and growing conditions; as a result, no accurate yield average is possible.

Table 7.   Peppers Harvested for Sale, 1978

Leading States	Sweet Peppers		Pimento		Chili-Peppers		Total Acres
	Farms	Acres	Farms	Acres	Farms	Acres	
Alabama	171	512	33	249	34	39	800
Arizona	12	497			56	1,448	1,945
California	350	12,344	4	121	198	6,615	19,080
Colorado	98	671			61	170	841
Delaware	57	869			33	102	971
Florida	388	15,229			81	799	16,028
Georgia	164	1,153	7	112	28	31	1,296
Louisiana	103	505			56	200	705
Michigan	479	862			151	422	1,284
Mississippi	108	239	23	97	58	68	404
New Jersey	1,055	6,138			199	871	7,009
New Mexico	39	1,631			267	7,380	9,011
New York	741	1,228			169	109	1,337
North Carolina	654	6,105			75	1,556	7,661
Pennsylvania	610	722			91	51	773
South Carolina	91	198			40	32	230
Tennessee	367	784	79	427	46	16	1,227
Texas	252	6,929			126	2,831	9,760

Source: U.S. 1978 Census of Agriculture, State Summary Data, U.S. Department of Commerce, Bureau of the Census, July, 1981.
    Total acreage of these three types for 1978 in U.S. = 88,270.

The unofficial 1976 estimates prepared by Dale Marshall of the USDA Research Service at Michigan State University, which were prepared at the request of the Pickle Packers International, are the most complete statistics available, yet he does not stand by their accuracy at this time (Marshall 1983, personal communication). This study takes into account fifteen pepper types as opposed to three types reported by the Department of Commerce (1978) and one by the Department of Agriculture (1981). According to the Department of Commerce's data, by acreage planted, California leads, with Florida, Texas, New Mexico, North Carolina, and New Jersey following in that order.

With the exception of a few acres of *C. frutescens* var. *tabasco*, all the pepper production in the United States is made up of cultivars of *C. annuum* var. *annuum*. In Mexico this is also the major species cultivated, with some *C. chinense*, *C. frutescens*, and the recently introduced *C. pubescens*. Also in Central America, *C. annuum* var. *annuum* takes the lead, with a little *C. pubescens* and a recent introduction of *C. frutescens* var. *tabasco* by the McIlhenny Company of Louisiana. In South America *C. annuum* var. *annuum* falls behind the more popular *C. pubescens*, *C. chinense*, and *C. baccatum* var. *pendulum*, with some *C. frutescens*.

In the United States the four leading cultivars produced are Bell types (64.7%), Anaheim types (14.4%), pimento (5.3%), and Jalapeño (4.4%). All others are lumped together as "other" (11.2%). In Mexico the leaders are Ancho (20%), Jalapeño (19%), Serrano (18.5%), and Mirasol (17.1%). One percent is export types not consumed in Mexico and the remaining 24.5% is not broken down by cultivar. In Canada the Bell accounts for the largest part of the production. In Central America a large sweet Bell type and various hot *C. annuum* var. *annuum* are the most commonly found, along with the devilish *C. pubescens*. As stated previously, South America is an unknown quantity.

In the United States peppery Mexican foods are the fastest-growing ethnic food. Consumption has increased fivefold in the past ten years and the forecast is for an annual increase of 18 percent. Sales have increased from $60 million in 1970 to $300 million for 1980. Besides ethnic foods, the consumption of fresh fruits and vegetables by all income groups has doubled in the same period (Mountain Pass Canning Co. 1980).*

Although the United States raises between 88,270 and 110,683 acres of peppers of every type, yielding in

---

*Taco Bell has invaded London, Amsterdam supports at least a dozen Mexican restaurants, and even Paris offers a booming new dining experience—authentic Mexican food.

Table 8. Peppers Grown in Mexico, 1981 (estimated)

Type	Area Planted (ha.)	Average Yield (ton/ha.)	Volume of Production (ton)
Jalapeño	15,500	7.60v	117,800
Serrano	15,130	11.12v	168,246
Bell, Fresno, Caribe, Anaheim (for export)	8,700	16.00v	139,200
Habañero	500	3.00v	1,500
Ancho	16,400	10.00v	164,000
		1.30s	21,320
Mirasol	14,000	1.40s	19,600
Mulato	4,480	1.30s	5,824
Pasilla	3,080	1.10s	3,388
Costeño	2,000	1.00s	2,000
Cora, De Arbol	700	1.50s	1,050
Others*	1,000	Variable	No estimate
Total	81,490		590,746v
			53,182s

Source: Laborde Cancino and Pozo Compodonico, 1982, 20.
Ha. = hectacre; v = yield green; s = yield dry.
Piquín, perón, serranito, pico de paloma, bolita, chile de agua, carricillo, etc.

Table 9.   Peppers Grown in the United States, 1976 (estimated)

Type	% of U.S. Ac.	Harvested Acreage	Tons/ Acre	Production (tons)	$/Ton	Value ($1,000)	% of U.S. $
Bell	61.6	68,167	6.09	415,215	263	109,409	64.7
Long Chili	14.4	15,940	9.00	143,475	169	24,310	14.4
Pimento	11.7	12,900	3.28	42,270	211	8,935	5.3
Jalapeño	2.6	2,880	11.29	32,525	226	7,357	4.4
Cayenne	1.6	1,786	3.74	6,685	426	2,850	1.7
Small Yellow Pickling	1.5	1,685	8.86	14,935	404	6,040	3.6
Cherry	1.5	1,640	4.73	7,750	368	2,855	1.7
Cubanelle	1.3	1,405	5.87	8,250	247	2,040	1.2
Banana, Hot	1.1	1,255	5.93	7,440	229	1,710	1.0
Tabasco	1.0	1,200	2.28	2,740	625	1,715	1.0
Small Chili	0.7	760	1.99	1,515	290	440	0.3
Banana, Sweet	0.5	565	4.09	2,315	218	505	0.3
Pepperoncini, Italian	0.2	235	2.28	535	682	365	0.2
Mexican, Ancho	0.2	170	2.06	350	500	175	0.1
Serrano, Chili	0.1	95	6.00	570	535	305	0.2
Total all U.S. peppers		110,683	6.20	686,570	246	169,011	

Source: Dale E. Marshall, 1977. Estimates of harvested acreage, production, and grower value of peppers grown in the United States, 1976. Pickle Packers Int'l, St. Charles, IL 7 p.

the vicinity of 686,570 tons each year, the demand is such that an additional 5 to 6 tons are imported, primarily from Mexico, Spain, Portugal, North Africa, and Asia. To that can be added $6.3 million of imported oleoresin of paprika to flavor processed foods (USDA 1982).

Per acre, peppers are a better cash crop than either cotton or wheat.* Based on Marshall's (1976) figures, an acre of Bells would yield about $1,601, which is a little more than the value of Anaheims, but about 2.3 times more than an acre of pimento would bring the grower. However, the real money makers are Jalapeños, 1.5 times greater; Serranos, twice as rewarding; and the yellow pickling, almost yellow gold, being 2.2 times more valuable. It is small wonder that the producers of these types keep quiet about their acreage in order to keep the market price as high as possible;

ten acres of Jalapeños bringing $24,000 is a lot of money for such a small area.

Many factors act to bring about changes in production throughout the world, including politics. Until the last decade both Ethiopia and Hungary produced much of the best *Capsicum* for extractable color but inefficiency resulting from the centralized system of government ruined production (S. Kebede 1982, personal communication). North Carolina growers used to produce 1,500 acres of Bohemian Chili for the extremely high capsaisin content of the oleoresin but they have stopped because China now exports them in large quantities (D. Sanders 1983, personal communication). At times suppliers will default on contracts because crops were smaller than expected, causing prices to increase sharply and preventing shipment at the per pound range for which contracts were made. In addition, insect infestations of dried peppers can lower the yield. Even with the many variables, production of peppers throughout the Western Hemisphere is growing.

---

*The national average yield per acre of cotton is 542 pounds; an acre of 55¢ cotton would bring $298.10. Wheat averages 35.8 bushels per acre; at $3.67 a bushel, the value of an acre of wheat is $131.39.

8

ECONOMIC AND OTHER USES

PROBABLY no cultivated plant with such a great variety of fruit types has so many different uses over such a wide area of the world as does *Capsicum*. The majority of the capsicums grown in the Western Hemisphere that are used in the spice trade come from Louisiana, New Mexico, California, Texas, Florida, and Mexico.

Use As a Condiment, Spice, and Vegetable

Peppers have many uses and their popularity as a comestible—condiment, spice, and vegetable—is growing rapidly. There are several reasons for the phenomenal growth in consumption since World War II. Large producers of processed pepper products report that their biggest foreign customers are Japan, Germany, and the Arabic countries. They theorize that the growth in consumption is directly related to the American occupation after the war. The GI's favorite condiments, catsup and hot sauce, were poured freely on his mainstay—hamburgers with french fries. Local people employed at the American military bases observed this ritual and tried the new "taste sensation." If present sales are an indication of what went on, that American rite was readily adopted by the native populace. Although the Japanese have a history of pepper usage, the American-style condiments are more recent additions.

The producers can thank American oil field workers, who are primarily from Texas and Louisiana, for the new Arabian market. The American crews sent over to the desert oil fields carried hot sauce and Jalapeños with their personal gear. In recent years an influx of immigrants to the United States and Canada from all over the world has created a market for "ethnic foods," with Mexican food and the hot, spicy Szechuan Chinese foods among those topping the list.

Ten years ago who could have dreamed that a plastic container of nachos* dripping with melted cheese and piled with burning Jalapeños would have supplanted the traditional hot dog and peanuts at sports events as it has at the University of Texas. Corpus Christi, Texas, has a school system that is typical of those found throughout the Southwest. The lunchrooms serve a daily Mexican fare, including enchiladas, chalupas, and chili con carne alongside the ubiquitous hamburger.

Most readers will agree that a vegetable is the edible part of any herbaceous plant but there might be less accord when we speak of condiments, spices, and herbs. All are used as seasonings; however, herbs and spices are usually added during the cooking or preparation, while condiments are added at the table to already prepared food. A spice is an aromatic, fragrant vegetable substance while a condiment (L. *condire*, to pickle) is a sauce or relish combining vegetables and/or spices with other ingredients. Rosengarten (1969) explains that when the aromatic, fragrant vegetable product is from a herbaceous, temperate plant it is an herb; but if it is from a tropical shrub or tree it is a spice. Determining where an herb ends and a spice begins is difficult. Actually herbs are one group of spices.

---

*A nacho is a bite-sized piece of crisply fried tortilla topped with melted yellow cheese and a big slice of pickled Jalapeño served as a *botaña*, or appetizer. It was invented by Ignacio "Nacho" Anaya at the Victory Club in Piedras Negras, Mexico (*Corpus Christi Caller*, October 22, 1978, sec. E, p. 1).

Confusion arises because the terms are used interchangeably. Peppers can serve in all categories.

All substances used as condiments, with the exception of salt and saltpeter, are of vegetable origin and the people of the earth's hot, tropical regions, whose diet is mainly vegetarian, use many strong seasonings. During the middle ages there was a craze for exotic tropical spices in Europe that drove adventurous men to the far reaches of the earth in search of them. European tastes gradually changed and today much less spice is used for seasoning; however, the aromatic qualities are still favored by the perfume industry.

In the Western Hemisphere the per capita consumption of spices is greater in Mexico than in any of the other countries. The use in food by inhabitants of Central America gradually decreases as one moves southward.

In a typical Mexican village virtually all members of a family over five to six years in age eat pungent chili-peppers in some form at each meal. They are usually consumed ground with tomatoes and seasonings into a *salsa*, cooked in stews or soups, or served whole or in slices on foods. *Chile* flavors nearly all nonsweet food but it is seldom used with sweet foods or in beverages (Rozin & Schiller 1980).

Curry powder: This condiment, originating in India, is a combination of spices, principally chili-pepper, thoroughly dried and ground into a fine powder. It may consist of a mixture of as few as five or as many as fifty ingredients; already prepared curry powder usually contains fifteen or twenty spices, herbs, and seeds. The pungency is dependent on the amount of chili-pepper used. It is prepared by grinding slightly roasted, dried chili-peppers to a powder and mixing it with ground turmeric (*Curcuma longa*) for color and adding coriander (*Coriandrum sativum*) along with other spices, which may be one or more of the following: allspice, anise, bay leaves, caraway, cardamon, celery seed, cinnamon, cloves, curry leaves, dill, fennel, fenugreek (seeds and leaves), garlic, ginger, mace, mustard, nutmeg, pepper (white and black), poppy seeds, saffron, mint, cubeb berries, sumach seeds, juniper berries, zeodary root, and salt (Montagne 1968, 336).

Cayenne pepper: This product is not necessarily made from the cultivar Cayenne although it may contain some of it as well as other spices. The more pungent, small red varieties grown in India, Africa, Japan, Mexico, and Louisiana are ground to produce this powder. The name came from Cayenne, French Guiana, but no cayenne pepper is manufactured there.

The African varieties are known by the name of the region in which they are grown—Mombassa, Zanzibar, and so on. Cayenne is very hot and varies in color from orange-red to a deep red; consequently, it is sometimes labeled simply "Red Pepper."

Red pepper: Although cayenne pepper is sometimes referred to as red pepper, the term usually identifies a product that is less pungent than cayenne. Dried pods of one or more milder varieties grown in Louisiana, the Carolinas, California, and Turkey are ground in its preparation. Both flavor and color are enhanced by its addition to soups, stews, and Cajun, Creole, or Mexican dishes.

Crushed red pepper: In recent years this product has gained in popularity along with the pizza. "Pizza pepper" is made of several hot varieties that are dried and crushed whole, including the seeds.

Dried whole peppers: A number of different varieties are sold in packages or in bulk as dried whole pods. It is popular to buy the whole fruit in Mexico, Central and South America, and the American Southwest. The types most frequently sold this way are Ancho, Mulato, Chiltecpin, Chilipiquin, Pasilla, Cascabel, Guajillo, Catarina, New Mexico, Anaheim, De Arbol, Cusqueño in Peru, and others, including an unidentified red type that is sold in U.S. markets as "Japones," which could be a corruption of *capones* or in reference to a Japanese type. (See pp. 128–129 for preparation.)

Fresh whole peppers: Fresh pods are used as a vegetable when they are stuffed, sautéed, sliced into a salad, or chopped or pureed in sauces. In the United States and Canada the most readily available commercially are the various Bell types, long green/red chile types, and yellow Santa Fe Grande types. At times the Mexican favorites are also available, such as, Serrano, Jalapeño, Chile Chilaca, De Agua, *habañero*, and several *guëros* and *poblanos*. In South America the *rocoto* is preferred. Other types, including Hungarian Wax or Banana and Cubanelle, are also used fresh as vegetables, in sauce, and as seasoning. Another favorite is the tiny, fiery Chiltecpin, which grows wild from the American Southwest to South America.

Chili powder: This seasoning is a blend of several peppers and other spices, depending on the desired characteristics. Dried pods of Anaheim-type fruit are the principal ingredient. Garlic powder, oregano, comino (cumin), cayenne, and paprika are used in the preparation of chili powder. It was invented by a Texas German, Willie Gebhardt, in New Braunfels in 1892 and is the basis of fabled chili con carne.* So much has already been written concerning that maligned and enshrined dish that it will suffice to refer those desiring more information to J. E. Cooper's *With or Without Beans* and Frank X. Tolbert's *A Bowl of Red* or the Fischer's *Chili-Lover's Cook Book*, a compendium of more than 130 recipes for the pungent *guisado*.† A purist would never dream of using a commercially prepared powder when he or she put the chili pot on the fire. Chili powder cannot be substituted for powdered Ancho, Mulato, or Pasilla if the authenticity of a native dish is desired.

Paprika: Paprika always refers to a ground product prepared of highly colored, mild red pods of one or more varieties of capsicums used to flavor and color foods. The sweet paprika is mostly pericarp with more than half of the seeds removed, while hot paprika contains some seeds, placenta, calyces, and stalks, depending on the grade.

Paprika originated in Hungary after peppers were introduced during a Turkish invasion. An interesting book, *Hungarian Paprika through the Ages* by Halasz (1963), tells more than anyone ever wanted to know about paprika. The Hungarian powder is ground from dried pods of the long type and is more pungent than the Spanish paprika, which uses a tomato-shaped pepper. Paprika is also produced in Yugoslavia, Bulgaria, and Morocco.

World War II drove a number of Balkan growers from their homeland. One such group from Zagreb, Yugoslavia, brought their seed and settled in Dillon, South Carolina, to produce paprika. There are reports that the paprika industry in communist bloc countries has fallen far below its previous levels. That decline has given impetus to the development of a relatively new industry in the United States. California is taking the lead, producing a paprika that is more standardized and more uniformly available than the European growers offer.

Pepper sauce: There are two basic types of pepper sauce: (*a*) that made from whole pods of very pungent varieties preserved in vinegar or brine (vegetables, especially cooked greens, are doused with the hot liquid and then the bottle is replenished with fresh liquid one or more times) and (*b*) puree or mash of chili-peppers that may or may not have been fermented. Some are mixed with vinegars and spices. The three recognized grades of pepper sauce are determined according to the amount of additives, condition of pods, aging period, and amount of calyx and seeds in the liquid. These sauces are often put up in small bottles designed to dispense only a drop at a time—cautiously. "Shots" of hot pepper sauce are added to soups, stews, eggs, bloody Marys, and oysters, among other things.

The chili-peppers used in making American pepper sauce are largely imported because most of the fruit used is the small podded type requiring hand picking and that labor is no longer available here. No one in the United States wants to pick a peck of pickled peppers.

Pickled and processed products: One of the fastest growing markets in America is that for canned and pickled peppers in the form of sauces, dips, pickled whole or sliced, canned whole or sliced, and used to season Mexican, Italian, or other ethnic foods. The Spanish term for pickle is *en escabeche*. These products are used in place of the fresh or dried fruit to add zest to any recipe or to prepare traditional recipes requiring them. The companies that produce them are usually located in the areas where the peppers are grown. They require a bite-sized fruit in order to prevent "spurting" when bitten into, which causes temporary blindness in anyone unfortunate enough to catch the spray. They also want to be able to pack more than five or six into a jar. Nearly every trip to the grocery store reveals yet another product laced with chili-peppers—tomatoes, bean dip, canned okra, black-eyed peas, cheese, sausage, peanuts, breads, jelly, candy, and what-have-you.

A visit to a chili-pepper processing plant is an unforgetable experience. A mask is recommended. How anyone can work there is difficult to imagine; the visitor, with tears streaming from burning eyes, coughs and chokes as he or she blindly rushes for an exit. Processing capsicums can be classified as an occupational hazard.

Pimento: Pimento is the anglicized Spanish *pimiento* and is the name adopted by the Associated Pimento Canners of Georgia for the sweet, thick-fleshed, bright red *Capsicum* that is usually canned. The first pimento pepper variety grown in the United States

---

*Chili con carne originated in Texas, not Mexico, as a "poor man's treat" in the first part of the nineteenth century. Its earliest recorded appearance in San Antonio was during the 1880s, when it was served in homes (Tolbert 1972). The first Mexican restaurant opened there in 1889. Later "Chili Queens" sold it from chili stands on Military Plaza (Cooper 1952). A booklet from the American Spice Trade Association gives 1835 as the date of the invention of chili powder, but that date is too early.

†See Appendix for addresses of chili societies and chili cookoffs.

was introduced into Georgia from Spain out of New World material in 1911 (Greenleaf et al. 1969). The heart-shaped fruit is very aromatic.

Salsa picante or Mexican sauce: The newest chili-pepper product on the market is a standard Mexican table sauce. Now bottled, this once humble product is a mixture of chopped tomatoes, onions, and chili-peppers with a few spices, mainly cilantro, garlic, and salt. Picante sauce, or *salsa picante*, used to dip toasted tortilla chips in and on all Mexican dishes, as well as eggs and hamburgers, has a market that is growing at a rate of 15 to 20 percent annually.

Novelties: Several producers are capitalizing on the popularity of the chili-peppers, especially the Jalapeño. Sam Lewis of San Angelo, Texas, is responsible for most of these "gourmet grotesqueries": Jalapeño jelly, lollipops flavored with Jalapeño, Jalapeño jelly beans, and olives stuffed with Jalapeño. He suggests that the martini made with those olives be called a "Martínez." Jelly can be made with any of the hot varieties but is especially tasty when the Chiltecpin is used (see p. 136 for recipe).

In Texas, where there have been movements to have the armadillo elevated to the rank of state animal, armadillo eggs are to be found on menus. Close inspection reveals a deep-fried Jalapeño stuffed with Italian sausage dressing—"Mama Mia Dillo Eggs."

Mandram: A West Indian recipe designed to "strengthen" the stomach (a stomachic) is made from ground bird peppers or Chiltecpins mixed with thinly sliced, unpeeled cucumber, shallots, chives or onions, lemon or lime juice, and Madeira.

Use in Medicine, Pharmacy, and Health Care

Long before the arrival of Europeans the indigenes of the Western Hemisphere had used capsicums medicinally. This value was not lost on others, who adopted the pleasant pod. Wherever the pepper became entrenched in its global wanderings, its "curative" powers were soon discovered. Many early herbalists were doctors of medicine or apothecaries, who studied new plant introductions from a medical aspect first and a culinary viewpoint second. The pepper became accepted on five continents as a healing agent as well as a seasoning. It is not only a folk remedy; although limited, its medical value has been proven scientifically.

Pungency is apparently the only pharmacologic property required of capsicums as a medicine; hence, it is desirable that medicinal capsicums be of the highest pungency and of uniformity in this property (Gathercoal & Terry 1921). In the United States the Pure Food and Drug regulations attempt to ensure this. But we are still awaiting the official minimum standard. Latin American countries do not have any food and drug regulations.

According to the *United States Dispensatory* (Osol et al. 1973, 223), the actions and uses of *Capsicum* are as follows:

Capsicum is a powerful local stimulant; when swallowed it produces a sensation of warmth and, with greater concentration, eventually almost intolerable burning. Capsicum differs from other local irritants in producing practically no reddening of the skin even when there is a very severe subjective sensation; while it has a pronounced irritant effect on the endings of sensory nerves, it has little action upon capillary or other blood vessels. Therefore it does not cause blistering, even in high concentration. It is not proper to call capsicum a rubefacient since it does not produce reddening of the skin.

Preparations of capsicum, particularly *Capsicum oleoresin* obtained by extracting capsicum with acetone or ether and distilling off the solvent, have been used in a variety of counterirritant formulations for topical application.

Capsicum is no longer included in a U.S. official compendium.

It is easy to scoff at folk medicine and much of it is deserving of that derision, but modern scientists have found that some has sound medical basis. Pre-Columbian Amerindians did not have a dispensatory providing technical information but we have seen in early New World documents, such as those of Sahagún, Hernández, and Acosta, that they used peppers for many of the same medical purposes as those outlined by the *Dispensatory*.

PHYSIOLOGICAL EFFECTS

Some of the first research on the effects of peppers on the human organism took place in Hungary where *Capsicum* is extensively cultivated and consumed. Halasz (1963) presents interesting summaries of several of the more important experiments. In 1878, Endre Hogyes found that capsaicin stimulates the mucous membrane of the mouth and stomach, causing strong peristalsis. Thus, by intensifying secretion and by stimulating the movement of the bowels, peppers aid digestion. He found that they could be used as a condiment without any adverse effects.

At Szeged University, Professor Berkessy (Halasz 1963) undertook a study of the reaction of the acids in the human stomach, finding that acid secretion was intensified by the consumption of peppers. The stimulation of saliva and gastric juices acts to increase appetite and aid digestion (Jacobs 1944). However, observations of the histaminelike effect on gastric secretion suggest that peppers should be withheld from the diet of individuals with gastric ulcers or gastritis (Sanchez-Palomera 1951; Viranuvatti et al. 1972; Ellis 1948).

In developing countries, where bland diets are almost universal—in Mexico, corn and beans; in India and Indonesia, rice and vegetables; in Venezuela, manioc and beans—the use of peppers is extensive. This has been explained on the grounds that capsicums add color and flavor to vary bland diets, thus relieving their monotony, and they increase salivation, thereby facilitating the mastication of a mealy, starch-based diet (Rozin & Schiller 1980).

In an interesting study, Rozin and Schiller (1980) made the first attempt to account for the acquisition of a positive affective response to chili-peppers or, in plain English, why some people like them. Working with populations in the United States and Mexico, they noted a desensitization effect in chili-pepper eaters, but most of their evidence demonstrated that those who liked chili-peppers liked the burn. The pain receptors send the same message to the brain of the chili-pepper lover that goes to the brain of the chili-pepper hater; but the lover has come to prefer the identical sensation that the hater, the infant, and animals find repugnant. An American company tried to market a nonpungent, pepper-flavored corn snack in Mexico; it was a failure. If Mexicans cannot get chili-peppers during a meal they will not accept a substitute, while Americans will accept another chemical irritant, such as black pepper, curry, onion, or mustard.

The chili-pepper lover has come to enjoy a perception innately aversive—opposed because it stimulates a receptor system designed to keep animals from eating a particular class of substances. Some people have come to prefer other innately rejected substances that are bitter or irritants, such as alcohol, tobacco, coffee, strong cheeses, quinine, and strong spices. They also choose to climb a mountain, make a parachute drop, go to a horror movie, take a scalding bath or an icy plunge, ride a loop-the-loop, and other similar type activities. "These benignly masochistic activities are uniquely human" (Rozin & Schiller 1980).

Continuing, they report that the chili-pepper lover receives pleasure from experiencing a "constrained risk"; in other words, the pleasure comes from the discovery that the negative stimuli and defensive responses are not actually dangerous or life-threatening. As the consumers realize this they experience a pleasant thrill.

Eating capsicums takes the chili-pepper lovers' minds away from their troubles and mundane things by heightening their awareness of a given moment—that moment when the capsaicin hits the pain receptors in their lips and mouths, thereby disrupting their normal functions and span of attention. Their attention becomes focused by a sudden rush of sensations, on the mouth, on the heat, and on food. It has briefly altered their state of consciousness as do members of certain other genera of New World plants known to pre-Columbians, such as *Datura*, *Psilocybe* (mushroom), *Nicotiani* (tobacco), *Erythroxylon* (coca), or *Lophophora* (peyote); however, the effects are briefer, less disruptive, nonaddictive, nonhallucinogenic, and not dangerous (Kloss 1971, 217).

Weil (1980), a physician who studies the effects of psychotropic plants, informs us that this "rush" is what the chili-pepper lovers are after. They know the pain can be transferred to a friendly sensation that makes them high. Those familiar with this sensation are able to eat chili-peppers at a rate that keeps the intensity constant. Having learned this, one is able to "glide along on the strong stimulation, experiencing it as something between pleasure and pain that enforces concentration and brings on a high state of consciousness." Weil calls this technique "mouth-surfing" and tells us anyone can learn it by a change in mental attitude, perseverance, and openness to a new experience that permits something which had once seemed painful and injurious to become pleasureful and beneficial.

Rozin and Schiller (1980) concluded that the multiple factors involved in developing a liking for chili-peppers, such as salivation, thrill component, heightening of awareness, and flavor enhancement, are difficult to test, leaving us with the question of "how do tens of millions of little chili haters become chili lovers each year."

Many have asked, "Why is it that people in hot climates eat such peppery foods?" An explanation of the phenomenon of gustatory sweating may offer a solution. Two studies, by Haxton (1948) and Lee (1954), explain how *physiological gustatory sweating* differs from ordinary sweating. According to Lee, gustatory sweating is sweating in response to certain foods, especially those that are spicy, and acids. It is quite different from the two commoner types of sweating, emotional and thermoregulatory. The *only* normal people who sweat in this manner are those eating highly spiced foods in hot climates (Haxton 1948). Gustatory sweating has absolutely no effect on normal people eating that type of food in cool climates, such as Mexico City or Cuzco, Peru.

The subjects in Lee's study were required to chew

chili-peppers for five minutes. In each subject there was marked salivation accompanied by varying degrees of crying and nasal discharge along with the sweating, which is always confined to the face and scalp (Lee 1954, 530). Lee's evidence finds that "the sensory receptors mediating gustatory sweating are pain fibres. Substances which stimulate the taste fibres without causing pain do not give rise to gustatory sweating. . . . Warming the body facilitates, while cooling the body inhibits or abolishes gustatory sweating." It is seldom seen in temperate climates. In hot climates the evaporation of perspiration has a cooling effect. It could be that this cooling effect is a reason people eat spicy foods in a hot climate, therefore giving added incentive to the usual reasons people eat chili-peppers throughout the world. However, Rozin and Schiller (1980) do not think that the thermal effect of gustatory sweating is critical, pointing out that the moderate climate of the high plateau of Mexico is a part of the "original home of the chili-pepper."

Lee's study and others more directly related to pain perception found that prolonged eating of chili-peppers desensitized the sensory nerve endings associated with pain. They were made insensitive to chemical stimuli although no reduction was noted in the ability to detect physical stimuli (Maga 1975, 182). This explains why people accustomed to eating capsaicin-rich chili-peppers become inured to the pain and no longer consider them hot.

The relationship of chili-peppers and other spicy foods to lung disease is the subject of research conducted by Irwin Ziment, M.D. (n.d.), at the University of California's Los Angeles School of Medicine. The Mayans (Roys 1931) used *chiles* for asthma, coughs, sore throats, and other respiratory disorders without knowing the basis for their effectiveness. Today Ziment routinely prescribes hot spices—such as chili-peppers, curry, mustard, black pepper—to patients suffering from bronchitis, asthma, and other chronic respiratory tract ailments with hard-to-dislodge mucous congestion (Zucker 1981).

Physicians have long known that emetic drugs, which act through the vagal reflex to cause vomiting, also cause increased production of sputum and thus act as expectorants. Expectoration is stimulated by a nervous reflex that is very similar to the one involved in vomiting. Secretions in the eyes, nose, and mouth can be induced by such stimulants as ammonia, powdered chili-peppers, and onions, which not only stimulate nasal, lacrimal, and salivary secretions but also cause gagging, coughing and retching, and, perhaps, expectoration.

Hot spicy foods not only cause secretion of the nose, eyes, and sinuses but may also cause gagging or even vomiting. Therefore, all these agents when used in moderate concentration can improve expectoration; whereas, if they are used in high concentration they can cause vomiting.

Another important value of eating "hot" foodstuffs is that they create a natural desire to drink more liquids, with the resulting hydration helping to loosen sticky respiratory secretions. To be effective, the food should be hot enough to cause tingling of the tongue and cheeks and to cause some running of the nose or sneezing. Bartenders have apparently caught on to this as a means of increasing patronage.

When it is impossible for a patient to cope with eating hot foods, Ziment continues, another lesson may be taken from the known physiology of the vomiting reflex. Thus, vomiting can be induced by stimulating the back of the throat rather than by swallowing an emetic. Similarly, expectoration can be improved by stimulating the throat. This can readily be achieved by gargling with a glass of warm water containing ten drops of Tabasco Pepper Sauce (increase amount as tolerance develops). For those who cannot gargle, he suggests sucking a Throat Disc, manufactured by Parke, Davis & Co., which contains a small amount of capsaicin from chili-peppers.

Ziment cautions those who have gastric problems to use chili-pepper as a remedy for respiratory problems under the supervision of a physician. With that in mind he concludes that, by adding chili-pepper to food, "it may be possible to improve both life and breath."

Yet another medical report suggests *Capsicum* as protection against blood clots by causing an increase in fibrinolytic activity (FA). Researchers in Thailand found the enhanced FA to be of short duration but that, if a second dose was given as little as thirty minutes after the first one, stimulation would continue. This repeated effect is an important point for those people who eat chili-peppers with each meal. This daily stimulation of FA is perhaps sufficient to prevent thromboembolism among the majority of such consumers (Visudhiphan et al. 1982).

In addition, we might caution those who would overindulge in Jalapeños (overindulgence varies with the individual; it can be from 3 to 13). A report from the University of Texas Health Science Center at San Antonio (Diehl & Bauer 1978) has found that this might result in a syndrome of burning defecation that could be appropriately termed "jalaproctitis."

When Acosta (1970) spoke of the chili-pepper, saying, "it provokes to lust," he made reference to the rumored aphrodisiac property of capsicums. As yet there is no medical verification of such rumors. However, a study that examined the mechanism of the action of capsaicin on the crustacean *Daphnia magna*, a water flea, discovered that capsaicin "caused pronounced and continued excitatory movements of the male genital organ" (Viehoever & Cohen 1938).

Experiments in capsaicin desensitization on animals find a relationship between the degree of desensitization and thermoregulation, the effects of which have not been studied in human beings.

What studies like these point out amid the plethora of tables and data is that the widespread use of *Capsicum* has resulted in certain changes in bodily functions that could be nutritionally, medicinally, and emotionally significant, especially among the growing populace of developing nations (Maga 1975).

The fact that chili-peppers stimulate the appetite and aid digestion has been recognized for a long time, but until the second quarter of this century the scientific world only smiled when primitive people throughout the world of the pepper used it as a medicine against a great variety of illnesses—then came the discovery of vitamins! Capsicums are not only a rich source of certain vitamins; they also played a major role in their isolation.

NUTRITIONAL VALUE

Peppers are extremely good sources of many essential nutrients and are richer in vitamins C and A than the usual recommended sources; unfortunately, they are seldom consumed in large enough amounts to be considered an important nutritional factor in the diet (see Tables 10 and 11).

The *Capsicum* has the distinction of being one of the few plants, if not the only one, that played a leading role in winning a Nobel Prize. Scientific history has recorded that the discovery of vitamin C involved the pepper. The first pure vitamin C was produced in 1928 by the Hungarian Albert Szent-Györgyi, M.D., Ph.D., who was awarded the Nobel Prize for physiology and medicine in 1937 (Pauling 1977).

When Szent-Györgyi first found the mysterious chemical, he called it *ignose* (because he was so ignorant about it), and then he called it *God-knows* (because neither he nor anyone else could really tell what it was good for). Finally, he had to settle for calling it ascorbic acid—which has since become more and more famous as vitamin C (Szent-Györgyi 1978). During a year in America Szent-Györgyi tried to extract enough ascorbic acid from the adrenal glands of cattle slaugh-

tered for market to use in his studies. He managed to collect barely fifteen grams in a year of work in Minnesota, which was not sufficient for anything.

He likes to tell a story of what happened after he returned to Hungary and went to the University of Szeged, located in the center of Hungary's paprika-growing district. While there his wife prepared a dinner dish of sweet peppers; of that dinner he recalls: "I didn't like the paprika, so I told my wife, I'll take it to the lab. By midnight that night I knew I had found a treasure trove" (Szent-Györgyi 1978).

The paprika peppers, he discovered, were a bountiful source of ascorbic acid, and within a month he had prepared more than three pounds of it to ship to scientific colleagues all over the world. Within a year the chemical structure of ascorbic acid was ascertained, and ascorbic acid was produced by artificial means.

Vitamin C, the lack of which causes a horrible disease—scurvy—can be found only in fresh fruit. It has been ascertained that peppers contain 21 to 34 mg of vitamin C in 1 ml while lemon or orange juice contains 0.5 mg in 1 ml. Vitamin C is readily destroyed by contact with oxygen and heat. The ascorbic acid content of peppers is highly variable, being affected by the type of soil, weather conditions, and maturity of the pod (White & Godderd 1948). Gorde (1967) found the maximum vitamin C to be in green fruit and the minimum in ripe fruit. He concluded that, as the proportion of capsaicin increases, the vitamin C content decreases.

In spite of this peppers are an excellent source—more than twice that of citrus. Even cooked they are superior because the loss will not exceed one-third the original content. In canning, all the carotene and two-thirds of the ascorbic acid are retained with a slight loss in storage; however, in drying the ripe pods nearly all the vitamin C is destroyed with little reduction in carotene (Lantz 1946).

There is a voluminous literature on vitamin C from which additional information regarding the essential nutritive element may be obtained. I will digress from the subject, *Capsicum*, to express Szent-Györgyi's sentiments on that vital vitamin, so abundant in peppers. In 1978 he wrote:

I strongly believe that *a proper use of ascorbic acid can profoundly change our vital statistics, including those for cancer. For this, ascorbic acid would have to cease to be looked upon as a medicine, sold in milligram pills by the druggist.* It would have to become a household article, like sugar and salt and flour, sold in the supermarket in powder form by the pound.

Ascorbic acid is a vitamin which has to be taken as food because mankind grew up in the tropical jungle where there was plenty of it and there was no need to make it. I suspect that the lost paradise of the old biblical story was actually the tropical jungle with its ample supply of ascorbic acid.

In the early days of vitamin C research the exact quantity needed to promote good health was unknown. All that had been determined was the amount that would prevent scurvy, which is 45 mg per day, and, as Szent-Györgyi (1939) remarked, "Is no scurvy the same as health?"

Since then the need for vitamin C is better understood. The human body is unable to produce vitamin C, as are all mammals that originated in the tropics. Therefore, as Lewin (1976, section 7.4.1) reports: "The daily dose of ascorbate intake is dictated by the need to maintain an ascorbate reservoir in the body at a level which can readily meet the demands made upon it. The demands under 'normal' conditions and those when the body is exposed to attack differ considerably." Continuing, he emphasizes, "The daily requirement varies enormously because of biochemical individuality. Individuals normally not subject to mental stresses such as harrassment, worry, fear, excitement, and the 'rat-race,' should need far less ascorbate than those subject to the full rigours of modern technological/administrative life."*

Ages before information regarding the function of vitamin C had been compiled, the ancient Mayans of Mesoamerica held ascorbic acid rich peppers in their mouths to cure infected gums (Roys 1931). Dr. Millicent Goldschmidt (1983), University of Texas Health Science Center at Houston, Dental Science Institute, gave credence to that practice when she found that increasing the amount of vitamin C consumed might help the body fight peridontal (gum) disease. She reiterates that the body uses more of this vitamin during stressful situations.

The pre-Columbian Indian consumed vitamin C rich peppers with every meal. After the Conquest, the Spaniards used them on almost the same scale. Cobo, writing in 1653, recorded that Spanish sailors took "*ají en escabeche*" to sea with them. He gives no reason for this but we wonder if they had discovered that peppers, with their high vitamin C content, would prove as effective in preventing scurvy as the English sailors' limes were to do later.

---

*An explanation for the emphasis on vitamins: I majored in Home Economics at the University of Texas at Austin. In a dietetics class I was responsible for the control rat in a major vitamin experiment. The trauma of the experience and memories of the vivid results have never faded.

Table 10.　Nutritive Value of Peppers

			Water		Food Energy	
		Grams	Per-cent		Cal-ories	G
Peppers, hot, red, without seeds, dried (ground chili powder, added seasonings)	1 tsp	2	9		5	T
Peppers, sweet (about 5 per lb, whole), stem and seeds removed: Raw	1 pod	74	93		15	

Source: U.S. Department of Agriculture 1981*b*.
—: lack of reliable data for a constituent believed to be present in measu... amount.

Ripe capsicums are a rich source of not only vitamin C but also vitamins A, E, and P. Vitamin A is formed from carotene and cryptoxanthin. The name carotene comes from carrots, long held to be the food highest in vitamin A; however, it has been found that they contain no more than do peppers. The vitamin A content of food is not impaired by cooking, canning, or storage. An adult requires 4,000–5,000 International Biological Units daily. One gram of fresh, ripe Bell pepper contains about 57 International Biological Units.

Vitamin A is important for the protection of the skin, in promoting growth, and in ensuring adaptability of the eye. Garcilaso (1609) placed on record a Spaniard who ate "two roasted chili peppers after each meal" because he felt it improved the vision. During World War II night-flying aviators were fed large amounts of carrots to improve night vision; the vitamin A value of capsicums was not realized then.

Szent-Györgyi, with Istvan Rusznyak, discovered vitamin P, also called *citrin*, while working with *Capsicum* (Halasz 1963, 120). It combines with a protein to provide capillary resistance (Jacobs 1944). *Capsicum* is also a good source of the B vitamin complex.

Value As a Natural Coloring Agent

Capsicum is used throughout the world as a coloring agent. In most cases these products serve an esthetic purpose by enhancing the appeal of a bland, colorless

Fat	Fatty Acids			Carbo-hydrate	Calcium	Phos-phorus	Iron	Potas-sium	Vitamin A Value	Thiamin	Ribo-flavin	Niacin	Ascorbic Acid
	Satu-rated (total)	Unsaturated											
		Oleic	Lino-leic										
Grams	Grams	Grams	Grams	Grams	Milli-grams	Milli-grams	Milli-grams	Milli-grams	Inter-national units	Milli-grams	Milli-grams	Milli-grams	Milli-grams
Trace	—	—	—	1	5	4	.3	20	1,300	Trace	.02	.2	Trace
Trace	—	—	—	4	7	16	.5	157	310	.06	.06	.4	94

diet. They are also used to replace or enrich red color that is lost or altered in food preparation. On May 3, 1906, the U.S. Congress passed the Pure Food and Drug Act, designed to prevent the intentional adulteration of food and drugs. It was later amended to cover cosmetics. This has been a windfall to the pepper industry because carotenoids from capsicums are utilized for the specific purpose of coloring processed food products, drugs, and cosmetics, since only natural coloring agents may be employed. Of course, the appearance of a product is of value to the food industry in relation to consumer acceptance.

The extractable colors in capsicums are used extensively in the food processing industry to color a wide range of products, such as sausages and other meat products, cheeses, salad dressings, condiment mixtures, gelatin desserts, and a wide variety of processed foods. This readily available natural colorant is stable when prepared under current food technological practices (Bauernfeind 1975).

Few are aware of its application in the poultry and dairy industries. The considerable waste from processing the brilliant red pimento peppers was tried as livestock feed. The high water content of the pimento makes it rather poor as either fertilizer or livestock feed but during the trial period an unusual observation was made. Hens having access to the pimento waste produced eggs with dark reddish-yellow yolks. The consumer prefers a deep yellow color in dried and frozen egg products but not in fresh eggs for table use (Mackay et al. 1963). In the past these highly colored egg

yolks occurred only in the spring when the hens ate enough fresh grass. After some experimentation it was found that the color of the egg yolks could be controlled by feeding waste pimento to hens without affecting either the white of the egg or the shell (Morgan & Woodroof 1927). When pimento is present in a hen's ration, the red coloring factor, capsanthin (Mayer 1943), is deposited in the egg yolk (Brown 1938).

The American market prefers a yellow skin color in dressed chickens. Pimento in the ration will ensure a rich yellow color in the shanks, skin, fat, and so on, the amount of color depending on the amount of pimento fed (Brown 1930). Brown also found that hens fed on pimento laid eggs with a higher percentage of hatchability than those fed regular feed; the chicks were stronger and there was no pepper flavor in the chicken meat.

Table 11. Comparison of Sources of Vitamins C and A (equal amounts by weight, 74 grams each)

Source	Vitamin C	Vitamin A
Pepper	94 mm	310 mm
Orange	37 mm	146 mm
Grapefruit	13.5 mm	166 mm
Lemon	39 mm	10 mm
Avocado	10 mm	216 mm

Pimento waste was added to the fodder of dairy cows to study the effect of capsanthin on milk and butter. The addition had no effect on the odor, flavor, or color of the milk. The odor and flavor of the butter were also unchanged; however, the color was changed to an unnatural pinkish hue considered to be undesirable (Georgia Agr. Exp. Sta. 1927).

Another study concerned the coloring of the feathers of caged birds, such as canaries and parrots. Völker (1955) reports that the capsanthin in commercially available pepper pods added to the bird feed deepens the color of the yellow feathers to an intense yellow-orange.* Experiments with grosbeaks, canaries, goldfinches, and siskins all resulted in the yellow-orange; at no time did the feathers become orange-red or red.† Recently ingested carotenoids in peppers will restore the color in faded flamingos (Bates et al. 1970). Try it on a pet fish—it is known to improve the coloration of hatchery-reared trout (Jones 1949).

Miscellaneous Uses

In the reports of the early writers many uses for peppers were recounted: external and internal medicine for a wide array of symptoms, ritual, punishment, food, condiment, aphrodisiac, tribute, money, or exchange, to name a few. Let's review some of the more unusual present-day uses.

At any one of the biennial National Pepper Conferences there will be horticulturists, geneticists, botanists, growers, representatives of mechanical harvesters, processors, spice extractors and blenders, virologists, seed suppliers, dehydrators, nursery operators, pickle packers, anthropologists, canners, professors, and graduate students as well as Connoisseurs of Green and Red Chile, who each have their own special usage of peppers. For example, the pepper is used as a flavoring agent for comestibles not ordinarily considered to be

hot, such as ginger ale (Nelson 1910), and the extractable oleoresin paprika is approved as both a natural flavor and a color that is available in various concentrations, which are blended to order. In highly concentrated form the pepper serves as a repellent in aerosol sprays, such as Mace used by mail carriers, delivery persons, and little old ladies to ward off both dog and man. It is employed in predatory animal control by ranchers who use compounds containing capsaicin on the neck hair of sheep to keep down wolf and coyote attacks (KALSEC 1982).

Few athletes at the University of Texas make it through a season without a rubdown with a deep-heat type of liniment, such as Cramer's-Atomic Balm and Cramer's Gesic containing oleoresin of *Capsicum*. Another commercial product, Nothum, is used to prevent thumb-sucking; however, it is a lot less expensive to rub the offender's thumb with mashed Chiltecpins or other hot types as is the practice in South Texas. This also works on nail-biters.

Organic gardeners may profit from one of the homemade insect sprays that take advantage of the pepper's prowess. *Plant's Alive* (1977) directs one to place in an electric blender the following:

Tansy (*Tanacetum vulgare*, a compositae)
Garlic
Onion
Chili-peppers

Blend thoroughly and dilute with water. Strain and spray on plants. Put the mash around the base of the plants.

The *New York Times* (March 27, 1983, p. 39) also uses a blender into which are placed:

2 tablespoons cayenne powder
2 garlic cloves
4 onions
1 quart water

Blend thoroughly; strain; and dilute in 2 gallons of water with 2 tablespoons of Ivory soap flakes. Spray on plants.

The same newspaper suggests a heavy application of powdered chili-pepper around spring bulbs in flower to discourage squirrels. Other animals can be repulsed also, if we are to believe reports, such as that of Schweid (1980, 122), who recommends his peppery Dog-Gone to keep dogs out of garbage cans. The *Albuquerque Journal* (June 6, 1979) contends that cats will not dig in flower beds sprinkled with a heavy application of chili

---

*This is nothing new. In an 1897 report on Zanzibar "chillies" it was related that the most cayenne pepper was sold in English commerce, apart from medicinal purposes, to feed to birds in order to heighten the color of feathers (Kew Bot. Gard. 1897, 173).

†During the spring of 1983, Clare Smith Freeman, Austin, Texas, fed white Zebra Finches ¼ teaspoon of paprika in 4 tablespoons of finch feed daily. Within three weeks a noticeable intensification of color in beaks, legs, and stripes on the tail feathers had occurred. This suggests that the natural coloration can be intensified by introducing paprika to the normal bird diet; however, if there is no pigmentation to begin with, as in the white feathers, the addition will have no effect on coloration.

powder; while the *Austin American-Statesman* of May 24, 1983, adds armadillos to the list of animals it will control.*

Farther afield we learn that the Java Indians of the Brazilian Amazon prepare curare using plants other than *Strychnos* in the mixture, including "the juice of a few fruits of a red pepper" (Krukoff & Smith 1937). Duke (n.d.) informs us that nearby, on the San Blas Islands off Panama, the native Kuna Indians string chili-peppers behind their seagoing dugouts as shark repellents. On the other side of the world we find Indonesians hastening the performance of a slowpoke by inserting bird chili in a particular anatomical location (Riks 1975).

W. H. Eshbaugh (1982, personal communication) found the Indians of Colombia, South America, still mixing chili powder with snuff and coca powder (from the dried leaves of *Erythoxylon*, which yields cocaine and other alkaloids). The mucous membrane, which has become inflamed by the chili powder, takes up the coca faster.

Another *Austin American-Statesman* report (March 9, 1983) was of New York transit officials putting chili powder in token slots in an attempt to curtail the practice by teenage hoodlums of sucking the subway tokens out of the turnstiles.

In some chili-pepper-eating cultures, the juice from the mashed fruit is placed on the mother's breasts to facilitate weaning (Rozin & Schiller 1980; Latorre 1977).

Magic, Ritual, and Folklore Uses

Prehistoric people depended on plants in a multiplicity of ways. Ancient and contemporary folklore, superstitions, traditions, various magic rituals, and other tribal practices throughout the world bear ample proof of the vast influence witch doctors, herbal medicines, cure-dieties, amulets, and herbal charms exerted, and still exert, over both illiterate and civilized men and women. Many people still believe that illness

and injury can be cured not only through medical treatment or social reforms but also, in great part, through magical practices (Mehra 1979, 162).

Nature and nature worship were and are intimate parts of the life of primitive people. Even before they had learned to cultivate plants, they used them in many ways. The solanaceous plants have long been employed in magic, charms, rituals, ceremonies, therapeutical practices, divination, and other customs and one of that group, the *Capsicum*, is no exception. The family Solanaceae has been much more important in the New World than in the Old World in yielding cultivated plants (Sauer 1950). The Amerindians had a remarkable knowledge of plants; in fact no country in the world has domesticated more native vegetable species of such high nutritive value than Peru (Baudin 1962).

Although the pepper was employed in medicine and magic by those early primitive peoples, it must have been to a much less extent than other plants because such references as Baudin's *Daily Life in Peru*; Lewis' (1960) *Tepoztlan*, which covers the daily life in a Mexican village; Schendel's (1968) *Medicine in Mexico: From Aztec Herbs to Betatrons*, and University of Texas Press' great *Handbook of Middle American Indians* (Wauchope 1964) refer to peppers only as the most used spice or condiment but make virtually no mention of any other uses for the *Capsicum*. Schendel's list of the pharmaceuticals given to humanity by the ancient Middle Americans does *not* include *Capsicum*. Although peppers have had only limited use in the realm of magic-medicine-ritual, there have been significant instances reported.

Garcilaso (1966, 48) speaks of the Inca idea of creation in which there were four brothers who emerged at the inception of the world, beginning with Manco Cápac, who became the first Inca; followed by Ayar Cachi, *cachi* = salt; Ayar Uchu, *uchu* = pepper; and Ayar Sauca, *sauca* = rejoicing. The allegorical interpretation given by Garcilaso is that "salt . . . they declare to mean the teaching the Inca gave them about the natural life. The pepper is the relish they took in it, and the word 'rejoicing' shows the joy and contentment in which they afterwards lived."

Even today, the Mexican of Indian descent, whether in Mexico or the United States, sometimes looks upon illness as a punishment. To atone for wrongs that brought it on he or she goes to the gods with offerings, mutilations, and fastings; these are combined with traditional folk medicine based on herbs and

---

*A neighbor's pet Siamese cat regularly stalked birds at my feeder and birdbath. I caught the culprit in a "Have-a-Heart" trap. Before turning the feline loose I doused its head with a copious quantity of Habañero pepper sauce, which it immediately tried to wipe and lick off. The frenzied cat was last seen in a long run toward home. It has never returned to hunt my birds.

I tried putting ground chili-peppers on flower beds to keep armadillos out. It worked for one night—the next night they returned and rooted up my plants.

roots. The sick one might even call on a *curandero* for help. The *curandero* is a lay healer who tries to do good for a fee, using herbs, magic words, fixed looks, amulets, and superstition.

Presumably, today's *curanderos* are still using some of the ancient remedies that the scientific-minded Aztec physicians, or *tepati*, used before the Conquest. Nevertheless, it is certain that the knowledge and standards of the present-day Mexican *curandero* are decidedly inferior to those of the *tepati* (Schendel 1968).

According to Sahagún (1963), the pre-Columbian Indians used peppers mixed with other things for sore throats, ear infections, coughs, injuries to the tongue, diseases in which spitting blood is a symptom, as an aid to digestion, and to expedite childbirth.* I will not enumerate all the cures that primitive people thought eating *Capsicum* would ensure, for some have been mentioned in the reports of the early writers and herbalists. There we read of the role capsicums played in fasting, tributes, punishments, and many other customs that are little practiced today; however, peppers are still one of the herbs used in amulets worn by the Indians or placed in the home to ward off evils.

Some of the accounts of chili-peppers having been used in warfare and as torture or punishment by Amerindians were related by Heiser (1969*b*), such as burning chili-pepper smoke used as a gas by South American Indians against Spaniards. Cannibalistic Carib Indians are said to have burned and cut captives, then rubbed chili-pepper into the wounds before cooking and eating them; also, the Caribs supposedly prepared boys to be warriors in rites wherein chili-pepper was rubbed into their wounds. Another report notes that a Mayan maiden caught flirting had *chiles* rubbed into her eyes, and if she was unchaste it was

rubbed into her offending parts. The Codex Mendocino pictures a boy being held in the asphyxiating smoke from burning *chiles* as punishment. Today, a Popolocán Indian group near Oaxaca still punishes disobedient children in this manner (Hoppe et al. 1969).

Madsen (1960) brings us accounts of *chile* usage by descendants of the Aztecs who live in a Nahuatl Indian village in the Valley of Mexico where they grow their peppers and tomatoes in fields separated from their beans and corn. When a man is working in those fields his wife must not carry food seasoned with *chiles* to him if she is pregnant "lest the rain dwarfs hit her, grab the food, and put large quantities of water in her womb." After the baby is born the family can protect it from contagious persons by placing a piece of *chile* and a pepper-tree twig in the form of a cross underneath the *petate* on which the mother and baby will lie. If someone makes the child ill by giving it the evil eye, the parents must beg a *chile* from each of four grocery stores located in positions that form a cross before a *curandera* will begin treatment. There follows a long, drawn-out treatment involving saliva, eggs, herbs, and *chiles* designed to rid the child of the illness.

Pepper was so highly valued in ancient Peru that the pods were employed as a medium of exchange. In fact, until the middle of the twentieth century one could purchase things in the plaza of Cuzco with a handful of pepper pods (about 6), known as *rantii* (Yancovleff & Herrera (1934, 279).

Dangers and Precautions

The technical data sheet of a producer of chili-pepper extracts carries this message: "WARNING! Capsicums must be handled with extreme caution as they are highly irritant. When placing an order, request a Material Safety Data sheet for more specific information" (KALSEC, Inc. 1982).

Anyone handling chili-peppers is advised to wear disposable plastic or rubber gloves and to take special precautions against touching the eyes, lips, or other sensitive parts of the anatomy. The antidotes are not specific, but greasy substances might give temporary relief. (See p. 127 for an accidently discovered remedy.) Whatever you do, don't touch your contact lenses.*

While living in Snyder, Texas, during the fifties, my late first husband, then a practitioner of family medicine, was called to assist a local midwife. When he arrived, the young woman in labor was stretched out on the floor with a rope around her middle. A corn cob was being employed as a turnbuckle. Except for him, all parties present were of Mexican origin. He was dubious but did not want to reveal his ignorance among those assembled by asking, "¿Que pasa?*"

As the labor progressed he observed that with each labor pain the midwife tightened the rope, working with her patient to expedite the delivery. Standing just behind the *partera* (midwife), in unexpressed amazement, he noticed that birth was finally imminent. At this point the busy *partera* looked to him and inquired, "Shall I snuff her now doctor?" Not comprehending but loath to remain silent, although fearful of what would follow, he replied in his most sagacious voice, "Yes, go ahead and snuff her."

Immediately, thereon, she threw a handful of snuff mixed with chili powder into the face of her patient. Hastily stepping to one side of his vantage point at the foot of the mother-to-be, he gazed in astonishment as the patient gave a violent sneeze, the *partera* gave the corn cob a turn, and a bouncing, brown-skinned baby boy shot forth. At the least, this practice has to be pre-Columbian in origin.

*The contact lens warning is from personal experience; however, Eshbaugh added that he was called by an ophthalmologist with a patient who had touched her soft contacts after cutting chili-peppers. It took twenty-four hours to wash the capsaicin from the soft lenses.

17. The codices are ancient pre-Columbian manuscripts or copies of them made soon after the Conquest. Most of these elaborately illustrated books documenting the lives of the native peoples of Mexico were destroyed by the Spanish conquerors. Five hundred of the Mexican codices have survived, sixteen of them pre-Conquest. Other pictures in this codex refer to *chiles* as part of the pre-Columbian system of tribute from the villages to the imperial government. (From the Benson Latin American Collection, University of Texas at Austin)

A note in the *Medical Journal of Australia* reads: ". . . a child suffering from bad burns on the face and hands had been attended by a member of Queensland Ambulance and Transport Brigade after picking and eating chillies, with the note that these bushes grow profusely around Cairns, and wherever one is noted it should be eradicated. However, it appears that the victim was not attended by a medical man, and it seems that this isolated record scarcely justifies the extermination of this common bush in North Queensland. The effect of eating the fruit of this useful and ornamental plant is well known and most children will surely avoid it after the first taste" (Flecker 1947).

Botulism is a deadly but fairly rare disease caused by the toxin produced by the bacillus *Clostridium botulinum*, which grows only in an anaerobic nonacid medium, such as canned peppers. In the United States botulism is caused primarily by improperly processed home-canned vegetables. The toxin can be destroyed by boiling the canned food for fifteen minutes before eating it. There is an antitoxin, which, if given within fifteen hours of eating the contaminated food, provides a chance of recovery (Wylder 1948).

Entertainment

Peppers are a food with a following—the superstar of the garden, with organized fans (aficionados), fan clubs, T-shirts, mascots, slogans—the works, not just casual admirers. They have been called a good-time food, one you look forward to eating. Just thinking about them is exciting!

They not only add color and zest to your diet but also are good for you: stimulating your appetite, aiding your digestion, easing a sore throat, soothing tired muscles, raising your passions, filling you with life-giving vitamins and minerals, keeping your fingers out of your orifices, spiking your martini, making you laugh while keeping dogs and wolves at bay. Who could expect more of such a pleasant pungent pod? Old Peter Piper knew what he was doing; besides all this, look what that peck of pickled peppers would bring him at today's prices.

Can you imagine a carrot with such camaraderie? The black-eyed pea tries, but it's so colorless; who would want a wreath of black-eyed peas on the door at Christmas?

The executive secretary of the Pickle Packers International sits behind a desk at One Pickle and Pepper Plaza in St. Charles, Illinois, wearing a bright button proclaiming *Pepper Power* and passing out cards with a message that reads:

> Pepper power is the potent power of perfectly
> piquant pickled peppers to particularly
> and pleasantly pixilate and
> palpitate the public's palate.
> The producers of pickled peppers,
> ever cognizant that
> variety is the spice of life,
> have dug deep into
> their pickled pepper portfolio
> to provide a pickled pepper
> to appeal to every taste and eye.
> Pickled pepper packers proudly
> present to their
> pickled pepper–hungry populace
> the cherry pepper, the banana pepper,
> the chili pepper, the jalapeño
> pepper, the pepperoncini,
> and the bell pepper, too.
> Long may they provide zing and zest, tra la, tra la,
> in flavors from very mild to very hot-cha-cha-cha.
> Since pickled peppers are popular with
> peoples all over the world,
> let all international political
> flare-ups be well peppered
> with pickled peppers instead of
> words and actions in anger.
> Let pickled peppers preserve the
> peace. Viva la
> pickled pepper power.

Las Cruces, New Mexico, is world headquarters for an organization formed in 1973 to promote the long green/red chile (New Mexico spelling), the International Connoisseurs of Green and Red Chile. What was begun in a rather tongue-in-cheek manner has grown beyond expectations. There are now eleven pods (chapters) in the United States and one foreign country, with three thousand members scattered around the world. It has a full-time executive secretary, publishes a quarterly bulletin entitled *Chile Connoisseurs News* and computer printouts of Fellows of the Pod, by location; and serves as a clearing house for chile information.

The organization encourages long green/red chile research through grants and stipends; spreads the chile mystique and culture through "Chile Gourmet" cooking classes and "Chile Cookery" demonstrations on TV; publishes cookbooks; distributes long green/red chile seeds; and so on. As a public relations device it has been a sensation (*Chile Connoisseurs News* 1978, nos. 13–14).

Would you believe that the title of a chapter president is Pod Father. The rallying cry is, "You can keep your dear old Boston, home of beans and cods, we've opted for New Mexico and CHILE, THE FIRE OF THE GODS!" An affiliate in Utah is the Latter-Day Pod; a Pod Humos award is sought after by the Pod Fellows; a smiling chile pod wearing a chef's hat is the mascot, Chilito, who is reminiscent of Jancsi Paprika, the hero of Hungarian Punch and Judy shows. The official drink is a Chile Copita, guaranteed to light your fire:

2 shots tequilla
6 ounces Bloody Mary mix
1 whole canned long green/red chile
Put all ingredients in blender and liquify. Serve over ice.

The darling of the pod set is an unassuming horticulture professor, long green/red chile breeder, and World War II hero of Japanese descent from New Mexico named Roy Nakayama, who is reputed to be the "Hottest Pod in the West." Every journalist who gets caught up in the pepper scene pays him homage. A Texas Aggie horticultural virologist, Benigio Villalon, a younger heir apparent, is known as "Dr. Pepper" by pepper buffs. He is a founder of the very serious National Pepper Conference, which holds a scholarly session every two years. The pepper cheering section until early 1984 was led by the late well-known *Dallas Morning News* columnist Frank Xavier Tolbert, the Queso Grande (Big Cheese) of all Chili Heads. Tolberto's place in history is assured since he, under the auspices of the Chili Appreciation Society, helped found (perpetrate) the original chili cookoff—The Wick Fowler Memorial World Championship Chili Cookoff—at Terlingua, Texas, in 1967. At last count some 8,000 hardy souls dragged their bedrolls and paper rolls to that wasteland more than fifty miles from the nearest "facilities" to knock heads in the desert. A rival event at the Tropico gold mine, near Rosamond, California, northeast of Los Angeles, sponsored by the International Chile Society, brings out between 25,000 and 40,000 chili buffs. This is where the winners of all those local cookoffs meet to stir it out for the coveted title. The patron saint of the pod worshipers is Professor Fabian Garcia, who gave the world the New Mexico No. 9 in 1917. His birthday, January 19, is the occasion for fiestas and fireworks.

Several enterprises have adopted the Jalapeño as a symbol. *Texas Monthly*, a slick, trend-setting magazine, is so enamored by the potent pod that it now sells pickled Jalapeños under its own label. A South Texas broadcasting station that serves up "*musica caliente*" calls itself "Jalapeño Radio." The rugby team members at New Mexico State University style themselves the Chiles. An Associated Press correspondent has even suggested that a chili-pepper should be the symbol of the state of Texas, with pods prominently displayed at the Alamo, on the battleship *Texas*, and at the Johnson Space Center.

If you have never attended a jalapeño eating contest, a chili cookoff, the Hatch Valley Chile Festival Celebration, the World Green Chile Cookoff or a Louisiana hot pepper eating contest, you haven't lived. On the other hand, perhaps you'd live longer if you didn't. What happened at Woodstock is nothing by comparison. Having never seen a Roman orgy, I can't offer an analogy but I'll wager the only thing different is the substitution of peppers for grapes. (See the Appendix for addresses of these events.)

A headline over a newspaper story following a Jalapeño eating contest read: "THE WINNER LOSES ALL!" —and that is the understatement of the year. An untalkative character called "Smoky Joe" broke the world record by slowly and deliberately munching 115 of the corrosive culprits. These are not uncommon events; watch your local paper. It's fun, sorta like a night out to watch someone being burned at the stake.

Esthetic Value

The use of plants as ornamentals is not a universal trait. Devoted plant care and emotional identification with certain plants are strong motivating forces in some cultures, trades, and castes, but not in others. A love for flowers and decorative plants is strong in Latin American countries. In one of them, Costa Rica, all classes of society evidence this devotion to ornamental plants of many kinds, including people living just barely above the subsistence level who receive no income from the ornamentals they cultivate so skillfully. Anderson (1960, 80) asks us to take a world look at floral versus nonfloral agricultures. He points out that "they are concentrically arranged around two poles. The pole of non-floral, seed-crop agriculture is in central Africa." Continuing, he says, "The pole of floral agriculture is in Indonesia, radiating outward to Oceania, to the flowery kingdoms of China and Japan, to India, and even to rocky Afghanistan."

When the native American pepper was introduced into Europe in the fifteenth century it was held in higher esteem there as an ornamental than as a food or condiment. After the Ottoman Turk invasion during the sixteenth century, emphasis was reversed. Today there is a renewed interest in its ornamental value.

The current trend in interior and landscape design is toward naturalism. Beauty in our natural environment is being recognized and appreciated. The variform, multihued fruits of the attractive podded plant have assumed considerable decorative importance and are growing in popularity. The living plants are used both in the home and in the flower garden; no longer are they relegated to the vegetable garden. Seed catalogs offer about two dozen cultivars for ornamental use along with about seven times that number of sweet and hot varieties to eat (see Appendix). Being labeled "ornamental" does not mean that the fruit is not edible; it only means that the primary use is not as a food. Most ornamentals are of the pungent type.

Commercial florists and other flower arrangers have discovered that the smooth texture, shiny surface, and interesting shapes of pepper pods offer delightful contrasts to blossoms and foliage in table arrangements for the home, especially in designs for summer and fall. Their long-lasting qualities enhance their value as distinctive additions in arrangements.

At Christmas the bright red cones and spheres are a fresh approach to decorating with or without the traditional holly and poinsettias. Clusters of brilliant green and red pods tied with yarn and ribbons often bedeck the Yule tree. Such a fanciful tree can be found in the Albuquerque International Airport in New Mexico.

The *ristras*, or strings of dried long red pods, from New Mexico and Arizona have evolved into wreaths and swags that are used both inside and out at Halloween, Thanksgiving, and Christmas, when they are at their colorful best. What vegetable, fruit, or flower offers so many shapes and colors to enchant the creative eye as does our precious pod.

The use of pepper plants in landscape design is becoming widespread as their value in the flower garden as well as the vegetable garden is recognized. A bed of flashy *Capsicums* lends color to the landscape when summer heat has overcome flowers. Their vivid hues will prevail throughout the fall until the first frost. Many cultivars of various heights are available for borders, massing, or specimen planting. Not only are they an inexpensive means of adding brightness to the landscape but they also attract birds and provide spice for the table.

In the fall, the garden at Zilker Park in Austin, Texas, sports masses of these glowing plants in an impressive array. Not only in the Southwest but also in the National Botanical Garden and National Arboretum in Washington, D.C., *Capsicums* are making noteworthy appearances.

9

THIRTY-TWO CULTIVARS

THE THIRTY-TWO *Capsicum* cultivars presented here represent the five domesticated species of that genus plus one wild species. After the decision was made to illustrate a genus of plants that provides the world with its most used spice and condiment because it had not been adequately illustrated, the major problem was which of the hundreds of capsicums to depict and how to do it.

Consulting the literature and the experts enabled me to determine the five domesticated species. I wanted to portray the leading cultivars of each with at least two examples; however, it was quickly apparent that one species provided the world with the majority of the peppers consumed and that the others were little known outside Latin America. Since most of the peppers familiar to our tables belong to *Capsicum annuum* var. *annuum*, providing only two examples would be an injustice.

As I read the literature of peppers, I kept a tabulation of the occurrence of each cultivar. I chose those that either occurred most frequently or were the most used or are most representative of a particular type—attempting to get an example of each form. Not only scientific papers were used but also seed catalogs, recipe books, periodicals, and visits to market places. Let's say the result is a subjective attempt to be objective.

Before I started, I consulted a number of "pepper experts" to get their opinions as to whether paintings or photographs would be preferable. Paintings won hands down. A painting can be more selective than a photograph, thereby bringing out significant characteristics. These paintings are of composite branches that show the full gamut of development from bud to fully mature fruit. Although I do not show the entire plant, it is possible to get a feeling of the total growth pattern. The pepper plant is very leafy; therefore, I chose to play down the leaves so that they would not detract from the fruit and flower. The leaves are drawn as in life but have not been painted. Some have been removed in order to get a better view of the pepper; that's where the artist has an advantage over the photographer. The medium is primarily casein, an opaque watercolor, and prisma-color pencils on Strathmore 3-ply paper.

Although a complete series of photographs of each cultivar was made as a matter of record, no painting was done from the photographs. In every instance the work was done from the living plant or cut pieces of that plant. A living plant is in a constant state of change as it matures and dies. That change takes place over a very short period of time: a bloom lasts only hours, not days, and a fruit turns from green to red overnight. This creates a sense of urgency that is very stressful to the artist.

Many of the cultivars that are native to foreign lands would not produce typical fruits in Texas gardens, most being smaller than those found in their native land. It is my hope that this will not be too distracting since in all cases the basic conformation of the fruit is typical.

The paintings were done over a period of five growing seasons and each required more than forty hours at the drawing board exclusive of the time consumed in collecting seed, propagation, cultivation, and protecting the precious plants. To make botanical drawings aesthetically pleasing while keeping them scientifically accurate is a real challenge. One is not permitted "artistic license" for fear of creating a new species through unintentional alteration of a diagnostic characteristic.

Outlines of the fruit with calyxes, latitudinal cross sections showing the lobes, and outlines of the leaves, all of which have been reduced to 50 percent of life size, are included for those who wish to make comparisons of the shapes of the fruits, calyxes, and leaves or the number of locules in the fruit. It has been found (Cochran 1940) that the capsicum fruit falls into two basic shapes: those that are blocky to almost spherical and those with long fruits of various shapes. The shape of the fruit may be affected by the environment to some degree, but the final configuration is dependent on the interplay between the genes that control shape development and those that determine size. There is a positive correlation between leaf size and fruit size but little if any relationship between leaf shape and fruit shape. Small leaves are associated with pungent fruit and large leaves with the mild-flavored cultivars. Wild types have only two locules; however, the number may be increased to as many as five in the highly domesticated cultivars.

The most typical usage of each cultivar is presented. If that use is as a food, a recipe representative of the "most typical" culinary usage has been included in Chapter 10, even though it may not be my favorite way of using that pepper.

I realize that there will be those who will criticize my selection and think other cultivars should have been included. No slight was intended. There are hundreds of varieties of peppers to select from; at one time I had eighty-eight different ones in my garden. These thirty-two are only an introduction to the colorful, variform world of peppers.

ANAHEIM
(Long Green/Red Chile)

(see Plate 1)

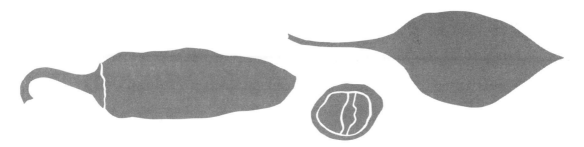

Legend has it that Captain General Don Juan de Oñate (1554–ca. 1617) brought the first peppers to New Mexico from Mexico in 1597. This is a very likely story because Oñate was the colonizer of New Mexico and the founder of Santa Fe, where he governed for twenty years. Many Spaniards had gone there before him but none had stayed. This millionaire gentleman farmer enrolled 130 men with families to make the arduous trek into the new territory to form a colony for Spain. They made the journey in eighty-three wagons while herding seven thousand head of cattle into unknown lands (Horgan 1939). Since we have been told by the early writers that the Spaniards adopted red peppers immediately upon arrival in the New World and used them as much as the Indians, we can feel secure in the belief that dried peppers were among the provisions carried in those wagons.

A California rancher, Emilio Ortega (1857–1941), went to New Mexico in 1889 to try raising cattle. During the six years that he lived in New Mexico, he became interested in the local peppers and when he returned to Oxnard in 1896 he took the seeds with him. He started a long green/red chile* cannery in Anaheim, California, in 1900. The seeds released in 1903 as Anaheim were developed by H. L. Musser (Villa 1978).

Meanwhile, back in New Mexico the type of long green/red chile produced was very mixed. Fabian Garcia, a New Mexico State University horticulturist, initiated the process of selection for larger, smoother pods that were fleshier with more tapering shoulders because the infant New Mexican canning industry (1908) found the native pods very difficult to peel. Beginning in 1907 with fourteen strains of the Pasilla, he continued the process of selection until he arrived at the desired type. Of the fourteen strains being modified, number nine was the one finally selected. In 1917 Garcia released the Improved Variety No. 9 of native long green/red chile, which was the most important of that type in New Mexico for many years to come (Garcia 1921). Garcia voiced the opinion that the most important thing determined by his study was the absolute necessity of selecting the seed from plants in the field that have the pods showing the desired characteristics.

The International Connoisseurs of Green and Red Chile have beatified Garcia for this achievement, celebrating his birthday (January 19) as their saint's day with fiestas and *chile copita* toasts.

The immature pods of the New Mexico No. 9–Anaheim type are referred to as *chile verde*, or green chile, and the mature ones are *chile colorado*, or red chile, in the principal areas where they are grown—New Mexico, Arizona, and California; however, long green/red chile is a more appropriate designation for this type. These peppers have not been a significant part of the Mexican food bill of fare in Texas or Mexico but interest in them is growing. They are used in the preparation of chili powder and paprika. The pungency of the long green/red chile is variable from mild to hot, depending on the cultivar and the growing conditions.

---

*In a paper presented to the Texas Pepper Conference, El Paso, Texas, September 29, 1983, by Benigo Villalon, we are told that "scientists of the National Pepper Conference recommend the use of two terms—Long Green Chile and/or Long Red Chile. Long green/red chile seems more appropriate."

These are the peppers strung into such colorful *ristras* and hung to dry after the harvest each autumn. If the green pods have been roasted, peeled, and dried in the sun, they are called *chiles pasados*. The red ones are the *chiles colorados* or *chiles de las tierras*. In Mexico the *chile colorado* is known as *chilacate*. It is sometimes packaged and sold in Mexican markets in the United States as Guajillo, which is a different, much smaller, more transparent cultivar.

Some other long green/red chile types are California Chili, Chimayo, New Mexico No. 6, New Mexico No. 9, NU-MEX Big Jim, NUMEX R. NAKY, Rio Grande, Sandia, Sweet-Cal, TAM Chile, TMR-23, and TMR-24.

They may be prepared in numerous ways. The best-known dish made with this cultivar is the *chile relleno* stuffed with cheese, dipped in a batter, and fried, but these are a lot of trouble. The Connoisseurs have an easier version (see the recipe on p. 130).

ANCHO
(Poblano)
(see Plate 2)

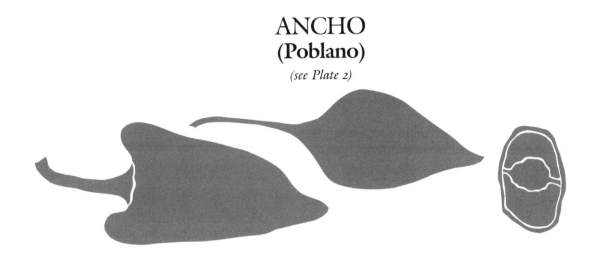

The Ancho, one of the peppers that are covered by the blanket term *poblano* when they are green, has been used in Mexico since before the arrival of the Spaniards. Some writers (Bravo 1934; Ruiz 1921; Long-Solís 1892) have considered them to be the *tzonchilli-texochilli* of Hernández, but on careful reading of his definition we see he said that "the soft flesh must be preserved by smoking" and we know that the ripe Ancho will air dry readily, thereby negating that premise. There is evidence that some Ancho peppers have been used in their present form since the past century (Laborde and Pozo 1982). The word *poblano* is derived from the name of the valley of Puebla, south of Mexico City, where these peppers were first cultivated. This term is applied to the fruit of several very similar cultivars when it is consumed in the fresh, green state. In the dried form the various cultivars are called Ancho, Mulato, Miahuateco, and Chorro. These cultivars vary from a mild to a medium pungency.

The Ancho is probably the most commonly used dried pepper in Mexico. In the central part of Mexico this cultivar is known as *chile poblano*, but farther north it becomes *chile para rellenar*. In Baja California, very confusingly, both the fresh and the dry forms are called Ancho or even Pasilla. Strangely, the people of Aguascalientes call it *chile joto, joto* being the vernacular for homosexual.

In Mexico the several Ancho-type cultivars are cultivated primarily in the semiarid valleys of the central part—the states of Guanajuato, San Luis Potosí, Durango, Zacatecas, and Aguascalientes—where the air is cool and irrigation is possible. At any given time the Ancho can be found growing somewhere in the country, thus keeping the markets supplied on a year-round basis. It furnishes one-fifth of all peppers consumed. Holiday seasons, such as Lent, All Saints' Day, and Christmas, are annual occasions for the heaviest usage. In the United States it grows in southern California. The pepper-growing areas of Texas and other parts of the United States will not produce typical fruits.

Many of the American growers and seed suppliers apply the name Ancho to the fresh green pods as well as the dry ones, disregarding the practice of calling the green form *poblano* as is the custom in the country of its origin and greatest production. The Ancho and Mulato are distinguished from each other by the color of the fully ripe fruit. The former is red when mature, turning reddish-brown when dry. The latter is reddish-brown, or *achocolatado*, when mature, turning blackish-brown when dry. It is difficult to differentiate the Mulato from the Ancho in the fresh unripe state, both having almost black-green, shiny skin and deep ridges around the base of the stem (Laborde & Pozo 1982, 36). The pungency ranges from almost mild to hot. When in the *poblano* stage the skin must be removed before using. The peeled pods are stuffed with cheese or meats for *chiles rellenos*, cut into strips (*rajas*) and used in vegetable dishes and casseroles, blended into sauces and soups, and used in other ways. If a large *poblano* is slit so that the seeds may be removed, leaving it whole, it is called a *capón*. With the seeds removed, it is said to be castrated like a capon chicken. Actually, any pepper prepared this way is a *capón*.

Approximately 50 percent of the Mexican Ancho production is used as *poblanos*. Of the remaining 50 percent, 15 percent is destined to industry for the production of chili powder and coloring agents. The dried reddish-brown color of the Ancho becomes brick-red after soaking. It is never used as a condiment and, while it is sometimes stuffed, it is mostly soaked and ground for cooked sauces (see the recipes for *enchiladas coloradas* on p. 131 and *chilaqueles con pollo* on p. 134). When dry the blackish-brown skin of the Mulato is tougher but produces a sweeter flavor. Over 90 percent of its production is used dry in cooked sauces,

the classic example being *mole poblano*. The Ancho and Mulato, as well as the Pasilla and a few others are ground and sold in a paste form, which looks like a square of chocolate. This paste is called *pisado chile* and one square is equivalent to one tablespoon of powdered *chile* (Latorre 1977, 5).

The Ancho-type cultivars are Ancho Esmeralda, Ancho Flor de Pabellon, Ancho Verdeno, Chile de Chorro, Miahuateco, Mulato Roque, and Mulato V-2.

BANANA PEPPER
(Hungarian Wax)

(see Plate 3)

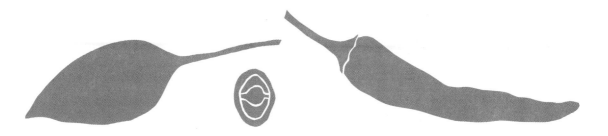

This long, shiny yellow beauty comes both sweet and hot. The sweet form is generally called the Banana pepper while the hot variety is the Hungarian Wax. Both of them are scarlet when fully mature; however, one seldom sees the red stage because they are consumed before maturity is reached. The size, shape, and color have caused it to be compared to the banana. Probably originating from Hungarian stock, it was introduced in the United States in 1932. In 1940 the Corneli Seed Co. brought out the Banana pepper.

Both the sweet and hot forms are used in the immature stage for pickles. In the fresh state they are used for salads or are filled as is stuffed celery (see the recipe for Banana pepper *botanas* on p. 131). The Hungarian Wax is almost inedible in the red state. This easily grown *Capsicum* is a garden favorite.

Some of the cultivars of this type are Early Sweet Banana, Hungarian Yellow Wax, Long Sweet Yellow, Sweet Banana, and Sweet Hungarian.

BELL

(see Plate 4)

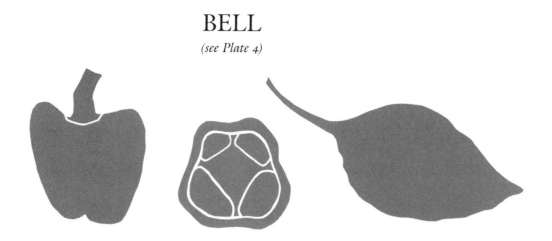

A bell-type pepper had already been developed in pre-Columbian times (A. E. Thompson 1971). The name refers to its shape but when that name was first applied is not known; however, we do find that English buccaneer Lionel Wafer handed the name down to posterity in 1681 when he spoke of the Bell as being one of the peppers he saw being grown in Panama. In catalogs from fifty-three seed houses offering *Capsicum* seed, there can be found 111 different sweet cultivars listed. Of these, 83 are various Bell-type cultivars. A list by Tracy (1902) put forth 114 pepper cultivars, half of which were Bells.

They have also been referred to as "mangoes," primarily in the midwestern United States. New cultivars are being developed continuously. They can be erect or pendent; the color can be green, red, yellow-orange, or brown; there may be two to four locules. The considerable variation is primarily a result of environmental response, with someone applying a new name to each new form. A four-lobed fruit sells better than one with two or three lobes. Calwonder, introduced in 1928, is the most popular cultivar of this vegetable, which comprises more than 60 percent of the peppers grown in the United States.

Although not commonly consumed in Latin America, it is grown in Mexico for export to U.S. markets.

In Mexico it is called *chile dulce* or *chile morrón*. In the region near Oaxaca and in Guatemala a similar large, hot form is found in the markets under the name *chile de agua*, or water chile, because it is used when succulent. The green bell is known as *pimentón* in Peru and *ají* in Argentina, while the red bell is *pimientón* in Peru and *morrón* in Argentina and Chile.

Bell peppers are sweet, thick-fleshed fruits used primarily as a vegetable. Very few are canned except as a part of prepared foods; however, the ripe red ones are occasionally processed and sold as pimento. Most of them are used in the mature green stage, although beautiful big red pods have been finding their way to the market recently. Bells are sautéed and served as a vegetable; chopped and added to flavor casserole dishes; used in ethnic dishes; served raw in salads or as a garnish; and stuffed or filled (*relleno*) in a variety of ways (see the recipe for stuffed Bell peppers on p. 131). Dehydrated flakes are available for seasoning. Bells are one of the few vegetables that can be frozen without blanching.

Some of the more popular Bell-type cultivars are Aconcagua, Bell Boy, Big Bertha, Bull Nose, California Wonder (Calwonder), Dutch Treat, Golden Bell, Keystone Resistant Giant, Midway, Staddon's, and Yolo Wonder.

CARRICILLO

(see Plate 5)

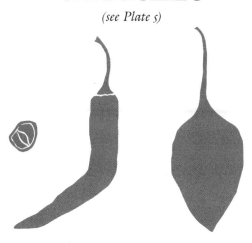

The Carricillo is a pungent pod unknown outside Mexico but there it is considered to be something special. The significance of its Spanish name is not certain but it is considered to be the *tonalchilli* reported by Hernández (1943) as being used by the indigenous Amerindians. The Nahuatl word *tonal* means the sun. The fruit ripens only in the summer and is a delicate yellow gradually diffusing into vermillion. It is used in the yellow stage, which suggests the color of the sun. It is also known as *chile güero, chile largo, chile cristal*, and, in Yucatan, *x-cat-ik*.

It is used pickled and is highly esteemed with fish dishes, especially a Basque dish introduced by the Spanish, *bacalao-a-la-Vizcaíno*, a traditional Easter and Christmas dish among those Mexicans of Spanish descent (see the recipe on p. 132). It appears to have the same climatic requirements as the *poblano*-Ancho, growing in higher elevations where it is cooler. It is well adapted to the climatic conditions of Chapingo, where it fruits abundantly each summer (Muñoz & Pinto 1967).

CASCABEL

(see Plate 6)

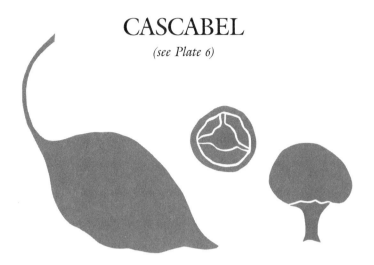

The very pungent Mexican Cascabel looks a lot like the Cherry pepper when it is growing. It is used in the fresh green stage but is most popular as a dried pepper (see the recipe for *carne a la Jacaranda* on p. 132). In the dry state the skin becomes translucent and the seeds are loose so that they rattle, hence *Cascabel*, which means sleigh or jingle bells. Another cultivar, the elongate Catarina, is often called Cascabel because its dry seeds also make a noise within its translucent dry skin. Cascabel should not be confused with the U.S. Cascabella, a small cone-shaped yellow pod that has flesh too thick to dry in the same way. The word *cascabella* refers to the husk or peel and literally means pretty skinned pepper and not a small bell as does *cascabel* (see Fresno and Santa Fe Grande, or Caribe, pp. 101 and 109).

The dry Cascabel is a dark reddish-brown, smooth, glossy globe. It is grown in the states of Coahuila, Durango, and San Luis Potosí (Bravo 1934). The Cascabel seed that came from the USDA Plant Introduction station in Georgia produced erect fruit, while plants grown from seed of dried Cascabel pods purchased in Mexico City produced pendent fruit; however, the shape was the same in both cases.

A second, smaller round form occurs in Mexico, the *chile bola*. A *bola* is a ball or marble. There are two types of *bola*, one green and the other yellow when immature, but both are red when ripe. A still smaller version is called *bolita*, little ball. These are smaller than Cascabel and are used fresh or pickled. They are grown in the Bajio and Aguascalientes, Mexico. In Guatemala we find Cascabel being referred to as *coban*.

Bancroft was not speaking of the Cascabel in particular but of hot *chiles* in general when he told this tale: "This pungent condiment is at present day as omnipresent in Spanish American dishes as it was at the time of the conquest; and I am seriously informed by a Spanish gentleman who resided for many years in Mexico and was an officer in Maximillian's army, that while the wolves would feed upon the dead bodies of the French that lay all night upon the battlefield, they never touched the bodies of the Mexicans, because the flesh was completely impregnated with chile. Which, if true, may be thought to show that wolves do not object to a diet seasoned with garlic" (1882, 175).

CATARINA

(see Plate 7)

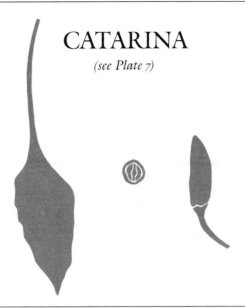

The Catarina is not found outside Mexico except along the Texas border. It is not grown extensively in Mexico but it has a following. Catarina is one of several cultivars whose skin becomes translucent when it is dry and the seeds become loose inside so that they shake around as in a rattle. It is sometimes called Cascabelillo (a tiny bell) which may confuse it with the round Cascabel. It is grown primarily in the state of Aguascalientes and can be found packaged in the *super-mercados* or in bulk in the market places.

There are small parakeets in Mexico called *catarinita*. It could be that the shape of the pod of this blistering berry appeared to someone to look like the beak of the *catarinita*, hence its name. At least that sounds logical even if it may not be the correct derivation. Catarina is used interchangeably with Cascabel in the dry form, but when green it is used in sauces as one would use Serrano.

This is one of the many small *chiles* that could have been used to make the concoction described by Miller in 1768 when he gave the recipe for cayan butter or pepper pots: "Dry ripe peppers in the sun. Put in earthen or stone pot. Layer flour and peppers. Put in oven after baking bread to thoroughly dry. Clean flour off. Remove any stalks. Beat pods, or grind to a fine powder; to each ounce add 1 pound wheat flour and as much leaven as is sufficient for quantity intended; mix thoroughly and make into cakes and bake as common cakes of the same size. Cut into small parts. Bake again to dry and harden the biscuit. Beat into powder and sift. Keep for use" (unpaginated).

CAYENNE

(see Plate 8)

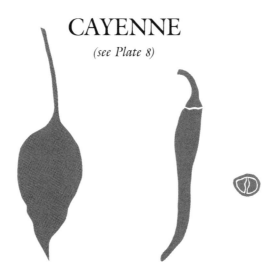

Cayenne is an enigma. The prepared condiment cayenne pepper may or may not contain Cayenne peppers and it is not manufactured in Cayenne, French Guiana. This pre-Columbian cultivar, which was first referred to in 1542, probably originated in the South American country of French Guiana and was named after the Cayenne River, which flows through that tropical land. From that area it spread throughout the hemisphere to India and to the Orient; yet, today, it is not cultivated in Latin America. This is probably the type described by Hernández (1943, 432) as *milchilli*, which he records as being "long, narrow, ending in a sharp point. Red when ripe and sown and reaped in corn season."

Cayenne pepper is made from very pungent, small red varieties grown in Africa, India, Japan, Mexico, and Louisiana and ground to produce a powder. The whole fresh or dried Cayenne, which varies in size from 10.16 cm (4 in.) up to 30.48 cm (12 in.) in some of the newer stock, is the favored spice used by Creole and Cajun cooks to give their gumbos, shrimp creoles, and crayfish dishes special zest (see the recipe on p. 132). It is used dry, fresh, or processed but its primary use is in a hot sauce. Its pungency is so great that the removal of veins and seeds is suggested. This cultivar is easily grown in the home garden and may be substituted in any recipe calling for Jalapeños, *habañeros*, or Serranos. When grown potted, it will produce fresh pods all winter if provided with a warm, sunny location in the home or greenhouse.

The Cayenne group, often called chili or finger peppers, is characterized by long curved pods ranging from 4 to 12 inches in length. In some cultivars, for ex-

ample, Cayenne, the pods are slender; in others the base is enlarged, forming an elongated conical shape. They may be highly pungent or only mildly so. The dried fruit of this cultivar are known in commerce as "Ginnie peppers."

The Mexican De Arbol is considered to be a Cayenne type with close affinity to Mirasol/Guajillo, which is also a Cayenne type. This very pungent pepper, said to be "*bravo,*" is used dried, in which state it is translucent. The slender, curved shape occasions the names *pico de pájaro* (bird's beak) and *cola de rata* (rat tail). The *quauhchilli* that Hernández (1943, 430) called *chilli árbol* in no way fits the description of the contemporary cultivar called "Chile-de-árbol." He was referring to the woody, treelike character of the branches of his plant. De Arbol is grown in the states of Jalisco, Nayarit, Sinaloa, Zacatecas, and Aguascalientes.

Cayenne can be cultivated over a wide range. In the United States it is grown commercially in Louisiana and in home gardens throughout the country. The ground pods constitute an important article of commerce in the pharmaceutical trade. Early varieties of Cayenne were long, slender pods; however, in recent years a shorter and more blocky type has been introduced.

Some Cayenne-type cultivars are Cayenne Langer, Cayenne Pickling, Come d'Orient, Dwarf Chili, Du Chili (smallest), Japanese Fuschin, Jaune Long, Large Red Chili, Large Thick Cayenne, Long Cayenne, Long Narrow Cayenne, Long Red, Mammoth Cayenne, New Giant Cayenne, New Quality, Prolific, Rainbow, Red Chili, Red Dawn, Rouge Long Ordinaire, Trompe d'Elephant, and True Red Chili.

CHERRY

(see Plate 9)

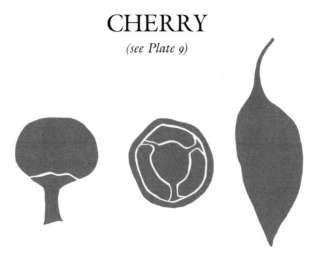

The Cherry pepper, so named because its shape is similar to that of a cherry, is another pre-Columbian cultivar. It was referred to in literature as early as 1586 and was illustrated in Besler's *Celeberrimi eystettensis horti icones plantarum autumnalium*, which was published in 1613. There were fifteen peppers illustrated in this handsome herbal. Six engravers were required to prepare the plates for the drawings, which had taken sixteen years to complete. In some volumes the plates were hand colored.

The Cherry name is often applied to a type or group that has pods which are cherry shaped or globose. The fruits are borne on long, slender, upright pedicels, which carry the fruit more or less above the foliage. The berries are orange to a deep red in color, solitary, three celled, pungent or sweet, large or small. They are grown as ornamentals or are pickled and used as a condiment. They will not air dry satisfactorily.

The Jerusalem cherry, *Solanum pseudo-capsicum*, which is not a *Capsicum*, is often confused with this group.

Some Cherry-type cultivars are Bird Cherry, Bird's Eye, Bolita, Cascabel, Cerise, Cherry (hot and sweet), Cherry Jubilee, Christmas Cherry, Creole, Holiday Cheer, Japanese Miniature, Red Giant, and Tom Thumb.

18. Besler, *Celeberrimi eystettensis*. (From the Rare Books and Manuscripts Library, Harry Ransom Humanities Research Center, University of Texas at Austin)

CUBANELLE

(see Plate 10)

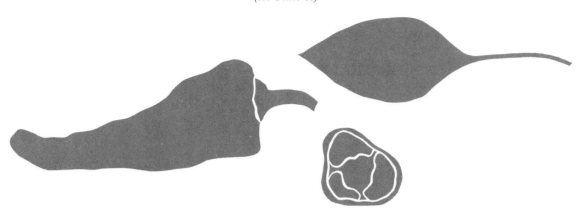

This colorful sweet pepper, rivaling a macaw in vibrancy, is referred to in the trade as one of the "ethnic" types. Others falling into this category are the Romanian, Sweet Hungarian, Gypsy, Shepherd, and Szegedi. These large-fruited cultivars are grown in the United States and Canada where they are gaining in general popularity while continuing to be favorites of people of Italian and Slavic descent. They are characterized by a thick, sweet flesh that is much more flavorful than those of the Bell type. Most of these are not available on a regular basis in the American markets because it is difficult to persuade the pepper-buying public to accept a new product. However, among home gardeners who have grown these cultivars in place of the Bell, many will buy Bell peppers only in the seasons when their gardens are not producing.

Cubanelle (Cuban, Cubanella) was introduced in 1958 (A. E. Thompson 1971) and is thought to be of Italian origin. Regardless of where it originated, it is delicious when used for the same dishes as the Bell (see the recipe for *pepperonata* on p. 133).

FIPS

(see Plate 11)

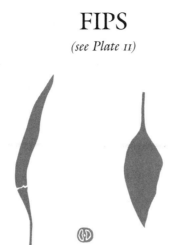

When Columbus returned to Spain with a shipload of seeds and cuttings from exotic plants native to the new lands of the "Indies," much of the first planting was carried out by monks in monastery gardens. Many of these new plants that served as staples in the diets of the Amerindians were grown only as ornamentals in the Old World. Peppers were among those that offered bright spots of color in containers and gardens. It was only after invading Turks reintroduced peppers to Europe through the Balkan countries as a spice and condiment that they gained acceptance as a food. Today there is renewed interest in the *Capsicum* as an ornamental.

One of the most delightful peppers to be used as a decorative plant in both pot and garden is a cultivar known as Fips. Short nodes produce clusters of dazzling, rocketlike pods that are held erect above a compact, dwarf plant. The clusters change color from green to yellow, orange, and red in an order that presents a mixture of all the colors in a bright display. They can be eaten but are extremely hot and are not particularly flavorful. It is best to use them only as an ornamental. They are easily grown and make beautiful pot plants to give to friends.

Fips has been offered by the Geo. W. Park Seed Co. since 1965 but they do not have an exclusive on it. They first obtained it from the House of Venay in Germany but its origin is not known to them. The seeds are now supplied by Sabat Seeds of Japan. At Christmas time Fips can be found in florist shops and nurseries.

There are several other ornamentals from Park worthy of special mention, especially Black Prince and Variegata. The first has fruit much like those of the Chiltecpin, except that they become black before turning red. The second lives up to its name, for it produces beautiful green, white, and purple variegated foliage, with purple and white blooms that become small eggplantlike fruits. Both are edible but not recommended; there are so many better.

Under ornamental pepper listings in seed catalogs one can find several members of the family Solanaceae that look like capsicums but are members of other genera. One of these, the Jerusalem cherry, is well known; however, there is another, *Solanum mammosum* Linné, that should bear a warning. This native of Central and South America is poisonous and should be avoided. The natives of its homelands show it great respect and are quick to point out its dangers.

FLORAL GEM

(see Plate 12)

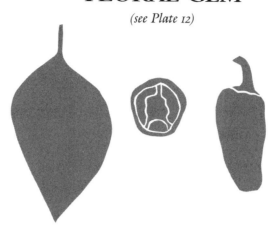

The delicate, spreading habit of the Floral Gem plant belies the pungency of its pods; however, it accounts for the name of the cultivar. The erect plant tends to spread, giving a vinelike appearance. This is one of the peppers referred to as a yellow wax type even though it is a rich red on reaching maturity.

It was released in 1921, but the originator is unknown. In order to introduce the gene for tobacco mosaic resistance into a good wax type, Paul G. Smith of the University of California, Davis, crossed Floral Gem, which was highly susceptible, with the resistant Fresno Chili. The result of this cross was then crossed by Dr. Smith with the Hungarian Yellow Wax to produce Caloro in 1966.

Floral Gem is used commercially in the yellow state. This medium-sized, three-lobed fruit is processed into pickles. Trappey's of Louisiana puts it up as Torrido Chili Peppers but it is not always on the grocery shelves because they are not available from growers in sufficient amounts for pickling on a regular basis. The peppers may be used in salads or chopped and cooked with meats, gravies, or beans.

Other cultivars of the Floral Gem type are Floral Gem Jumbo (origin unknown) and Floral Grande (Peto Seed Co., 1963).

FRESNO

(see Plate 13)

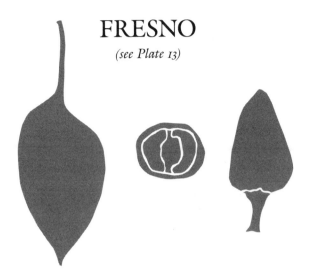

The name of the Fresno pepper honors the city of Fresno, California. That cultivar was apparently developed and released by the Clarence Brown Seed Company in 1952. This one-man operation went out of business during the 1950s and Brown died soon thereafter (P. G. Smith 1982, personal communication). It is a medium-sized wax-type fruit, which holds itself erect on a sturdy peduncle, is tobacco mosaic resistant, and was used by Paul G. Smith to develop Caloro in 1966. The Petoseed Company developed the Fresno Grande from Caloro stock and released it in 1970. Recently plant breeders at Heublein, Inc., in Oxnard, California, have developed a pendent-type Fresno designed to facilitate harvesting.

Although the pungent Fresno turns a bright red when mature, it is used primarily in the green stage for seasoning, sauces, and pickling (see the recipe for *salsa cruda* on p. 133). The pods look very much like those of the Santa Fe Grande type; however, they are never yellow or orange, maturing from light green directly to red. It is sometimes called simply Hot Chili in the southwestern United States where it is grown. It makes a beautiful ornamental, while at the same time keeping the table supplied with pungent pickles.

A similar but smaller cultivar is the closely related Cascabella. The plant is bushier than that of the Fresno and the fruit is yellow at first, turning orange and be-coming red upon maturity. It was also developed by Brown in the late 1940s or early 1950s (P. G. Smith 1982, personal communication). The Spanish *cascabella* is formed from two words—*casca* (skin, husk), referring to the waxy outer covering, and *bella* (beautiful). The name is similar to another Spanish word, *cascabel*, which is used as the name of a round, red Mexican *chile*. *Cascabel* means jingle bells and is used in reference to the rattling sound the seeds make within the dried pod. Even though it has a Spanish name, the Cascabella is unknown in Mexico, and in the United States only residents of the Mexican-American border have ever heard of Cascabel.

Cascabella is generally used in the yellow state for hot pickled *chiles*. Its small size makes it highly desired by pickle packers. The processed products usually do not carry the name of the cultivar on the label but the Cascabella can be distinguished from the small, yellow Floral Gem by the difference in apexes: the latter is lobed, whereas the former is acute.

Although the principal use for the conical, yellow Cascabella is as a condiment, its ornamental potential should not be overlooked. The gleaming yellow, orange, and red pods standing at attention in close formation along the branches are highly decorative as are those of the equally brilliant but sturdier Fresno.

JALAPEÑO

(see Plate 14)

It is a safe bet to wager that the Jalapeño is the best known pepper of them all. Its fame and popularity are growing day by day. In Costa Rica, which is evidencing a revival of interest in the piquant pod, one can hear market vendors calling any type of *Capsicum* a Jalapeño. The true Jalapeño originated in Mexico and was named for the town of Jalapa in the state of Veracruz. A short, fat version is called *chile gordo* (fat chile) in the coastal area of Mexico. The fresh green pod is known as *cuaresmeño* (Lenten chile) in Mexico; only the pickled form is called Jalapeño there. When fully ripened and smoked it becomes a *chipotle*, except in Oaxaca, where it is a *chile huauchinango*. A pickled *chipotle* is called a *mora* or *morita*. In the United States it is known as the Jalapeño no matter whether it is fresh or pickled.

A pepper similar to the Jalapeño was probably the *tzonchilli* or *texochilli* of Hernández (1943), even though he described that variety as "sweet" not with "a smooth bitterness." The Jalapeño, which we consider to be hot, could have been considered to be sweet four hundred years ago when he wrote. Tastes may have been different then; also that is plenty of time for selection to have altered the degree of pungency. The fact that both the ancient *tzonchilli* and the contemporary Jalapeño can only be dried by smoking weighs in favor of the Jalapeño-*tzonchilli* analogy. Sahagún noted that a "*chile ahumado*" (smoked chile) called "*pochilli*" could be found in the market at Tlateloco during the sixteenth century.

There are three principal zones of Jalapeño production in Mexico: the valley below the Papaloapan River in the states of Veracruz and Oaxaca, the northern part of the state of Veracruz near the town of Papantla, and the region of Delicias in Chihuahua, which produces a type exported to the United States. In Costa Rica the area around Turrialba produces and processes the Jalapeño, while in the United States it is a minor crop grown mainly in Texas and the Southwest.

Near Weslaco, Texas, Texas A&M University has an active research program being led by virologist Benigio Villalon. Texas A&M has developed a completely nonpungent Jalapeño that could be used by processors to produce a product with controlled capsaisin content. Starting with the neutral pods, measured amounts of the pungent principle, capsaisin, could be added, thereby enabling the product to be accurately labeled "mild," "hot," or "extra hot" according to the specific quantity of the "hot stuff" that had been introduced. So far this mild Jalapeño has not caught on; evidently, the Jalapeño-eating public still likes an element of chance . . . a Jalapeño roulette. However, a mild Aggie Jalapeño, TAM Mild Jalapeño-1, is gaining acceptance.

In 1978, one of the big national pizza franchises used almost two million dollars' worth of hot *chiles*, primarily Jalapeños. Large suppliers have found that the Jalapeño customer wants safety—no contaminated fruits and a pod that will not burst and spray juice into the eyes when bitten. The desired appearance is a broad-shouldered fruit with blunt ends and the typical corky cracks of the Veracruz type. They desire a flavor representative of the variety, but not too hot. The color must be a good, clear, dark green, not brown (Brummett 1978). Make this observation for yourself: when Jalapeños are put on the counter in a bowl, a customer will pick through the batch until he or she finds the one with those characteristics.

The Jalapeño is a fun food. A cult has been built

around this torrid terror of the tropics. Hardly a day passes that one cannot read a periodical with a story about Jalapeño-eating contests, Jalapeño lollipops, Jalapeño jelly, Jalapeño music, et cetera, et cetera, et cetera. The sprightly Jalapeño has outdistanced all the rest by becoming the first *Capsicum* in space when a bag full of the fresh pods accompanied astronaut Bill Lenoir on the spaceship *Columbia* in November 1982, thereby becoming the world's first astropod.

Many look upon Jalapeño lovers as masochists. This is not altogether true; most enthusiasts know how to eat their favored fruit and have developed a tolerance. If a less pungent fruit is desired, select immature pods, then slit and remove the veins and seed before processing, taking care to wear some type of waterproof gloves while performing the operation. This procedure is what makes the mild canned Jalapeños more expensive than hot whole ones.

The green Jalapeño is used fresh in sauces, salads, or meat and vegetable dishes. When it is canned Mexican style (*en escabeche*) with oil, vinegar, and spices or American style in water, the fruit may be served as a condiment sliced or whole (see the recipe for pickled Jalapeños on p. 134). The pod may be slit, deveined, and stuffed with meats or cheeses and served cold, or the stuffed pod may be dipped in batter and fried for a hot appetizer. The processed product is eaten sliced on nachos, in salads, on hamburgers and pizzas, and in casserole dishes. When chopped, it adds zip to cheeses, cold meat products, mustards, and sundry things. The smoked *chipotle* is an essential ingredient in certain sauces or floated in steaming bowls of *tlalpeño* soup.

Some Jalapeño cultivars and subtypes are Early Jalapeño, Espinalteco (*pinalteco*), Jalapeño M. Americano (Jalapeño M.), Jarocho, Meco, Morita (*bolita*), Papaloapan, Peludo (*candelaria, cuaresmeño*), Rayada (ideal for *chipotles*), San Andres, 76104 Jumbo-Jal, TAM Mild Jalapeño-1, and Típico.

MIRASOL/GUAJILLO

(see Plate 15)

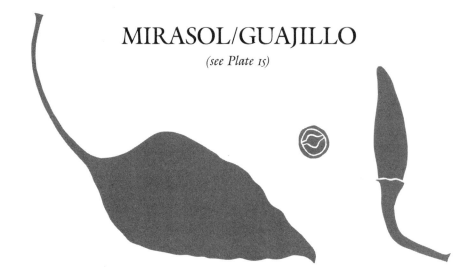

The erect attachment position of this medium-sized hot *chile* from Mexico has caused it to be called Mirasol, which means "looking at the sun." In some localities the green Mirasol is known as *puya* or *pullia*. However, when the fruits are dried they are given different names, the most common being Guajillo and, less frequently, Cascabel. Both of these names have reference to the rattling sound that the seeds make in the dried pod; the first means "little gourd" and the second means "jingle bells." When ordering Cascabels you must specify whether you want the round ones (see Cascabel, p. 94) or the long Guajillos. The Mirasol is sometimes called *chile travieso*, or "naughty" chile, in reference to its devilish bite. Others may call it *chile trompa*, "elephant's trunk," alluding to the curved shape. The Mirasol/Guajillo is one of the favorite cultivars grown in Mexico and is pre-Columbian in origin. Most likely it is the cultivar that Hernández (1943) found the Nahuatl-speaking Indians calling *chilcoztli*, referring to the yellow color that it imparts to foods cooked with it. The flavor is very distinctive, and surprisingly small amounts of the dried pods are required to both flavor and color the dishes prepared with them.

There is considerable variation in the size of the fruit. Much of that grown in Mexico is larger than those pictured in Plate 15. The plant is also quite variable but in general is erect and compact. The leaves are smooth and no pubescence is exhibited in either leaf or stem. In most cases the fruit is erect, although it may become horizontal as it ripens. The green pods turn a brownish-red when mature, becoming raisin colored when dry.

The pungent Mirasol/Guajillo is cultivated primarily in the Mexican states of Aguascalientes, Durango, and San Luis Potosí. It serves the same culinary function as the Serrano when used in the green stage. Generally, it is consumed dry in stews, *chilaqueles*, and soups and as a condiment with chicken dishes (see the recipe for *chilaqueles con pollo* on p. 134).

There are several cultivars of the Mirasol type: La Blanca 74, Loreto 74, and Real Mirasol.

Another narrow-shouldered, elongate, cylinder-type chili-pepper is hardly distinguishable from the Mirasol/Guajillo. This one, called Costeño, is only grown in the state of Guerrero, Mexico. It is one of the many *criollos* to be found throughout Mexico. The shape and color of the Costeño are more varied than those of the Mirasol and the immature pods are a lighter green. When a shopper locates the variform Costeño he or she will be sold the longer and wider dried pods by volume (liter) and the small, narrow pods by weight. The Costeño is used in the same manner as the Mirasol/Guajillo.

The Chilhuacqui is yet another Mexican pepper that may or may not be a Mirasol type. Some say it is more like the *poblano*-Ancho; however, the pods sold as Chilhuacqui are so varied that the assignment of type is difficult. This cultivar is used in the dried state. You will be offered almost black pods from red fruit called *chilhuacqui negro* or the paler, narrow-shouldered *chilhuacqui amarillo* from yellow fruit. The dark one does resemble the color of an Ancho but the yellow one has no resemblance.

The name comes from the Spanish *huacqui* used as "old dried thing," which is from *huaca*, "ancient Indian tomb." Other names are *chihuaque, chilhuaque, shihuac, chilquacle,* and *chilhuache*. In parts of Mexico it is known as *siete caldos* (seven soups) because one pod is enough for seven bowls of soup. It is found principally in Chiapas and bordering Guatemala.

PASILLA

(see Plate 16)

The dark brown color and extremely long, narrow curving shape of a ripe undried fruit make this cultivar unique among the capsicums. In Mexico this brownish-black color is referred to as *achocolatado*, or chocolate colored, a reddish-brown. When dry, the wrinkled pod is the color of a raisin, hence the name Pasilla, which is the diminutive form of *pasa*, or raisin, in Spanish. When used in the fresh state this cultivar is called Chile Chilaca. There is some regional confusion over the usage of the name Pasilla and to just which cultivar it actually applies. It is the correct name for the readily recognizable form illustrated in Plate 16, but in California and the Mexican states along the U.S. border, the much wider Ancho and Mulato, which are the same color when dry, are mistakenly referred to as Pasillas. Along the west coast of Mexico and in Baja California, the true Pasilla is known as *chile negro*, or black chile. In Guatemala it is called simply *pasa*.

The brown color, which distinguishes this long slender pod, results from the retention of chlorophyll during the ripe stage. The green of the chlorophyll and the red pigment, capsanthin, are present at the same time, a condition that produces the chocolate color just as if an artist had mixed the two pigments. The Pasilla is said to be the parent stock giving rise to the long green/red chile that hangs in brilliant red *ristras* in the fall throughout the southwestern United States (Garcia 1921). In the region around Oaxaca, Mexico, there is a cultivar known as Pasilla that is unlike the widely recognized very long Pasilla. The Oaxaca Pasilla is *achocolatado* but its conformation is more like that of a small long green/red chile of New Mexico.

The gentle-flavored pods of the Pasilla are common in Mexican markets and in those along the border with the United States but are rarely found elsewhere. The Pasilla has the same cultural requirements as the *poblano*-Ancho and most of it is produced in the Mexican states of Aguascalientes, Jalisco, Guanajuato, Zacatecas, and, in lesser amounts, Nayarit. The production is almost entirely used in the dry form; only a small amount reaches the markets to be used fresh as *chilacas*. It is used in making sauces and *moles* (see the recipe for *chalupas de chile pasilla* on p. 135).

The grades of Pasilla are:

No. 1. *pasilla bueno:* shiny black
       colorado bueno: no spots
No. 2. *pinto bueno:* spotted
No. 3. *pinto jicote:* bumpy, spotted
No. 4. *shuri bueno:* spotted
No. 5. *shuri malo:* smaller, spotted, bumpy
No. 6. cholote, *sholote,* or *xolote:* not used

The two principal cultivars are Apaseo and Pabellón 1.

There is a hot pepper Pasilla,
One taste and it just might kill ya,
It's a culinary surprise;
Keep it away from your eyes.
We're sure you won't try it . . .
or will ya?
—Anonymous

PEPPERONCINI

(see Plate 17)

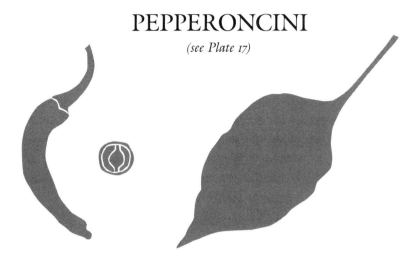

The Pepperoncini is a sweet, red cultivar from which only the green fruits are used to make a popular pickled pepper that is one of the typical accompaniments of an Italian salad (see the recipe on p. 135). Little is known of its origin. The name comes from the Italian word for pepper, *peperone*, and it was probably developed from stock of Italian origin, but there is no record providing this information. A yellow form known as the Golden Greek occurs in Greece and is available in the United States.

It is grown in Louisiana and other southern states in limited quantities.

PETER PEPPER
(Penis Pepper)

(see Plate 18)

19. Peter Pepper.

Once upon a time this curious *Capsicum* made print in a column of the *Dallas Morning News* called "Tolbert's Texas." Within the confines of that vehicle, the late Frank X. Tolbert, Sr., of the Terlingua Chili Cookoff fame, brought to light little-known facts about little-known things that occur in little-known places in Texas. Given those restrictions, the Peter Pepper certainly qualified to be honored by his pen.

Surely any pepper with the dubious distinction of receiving such a sobriquet should be included in this study. But . . . where to get the seed? Naturally, when I started this study, Tolbert no longer had any verifiable seed—having seen it once was verification enough for him. The word was put out among pepper enthusiasts of the need for seed of that pulsating pod. A friend with the highway department, Dick Roberts, recalling having passed some during his travels over the endless roads of Texas, placed an urgent call. Lo and behold, a burning packet arrived from Waskon in deep East Texas bearing a supply of that ferocious fruit from a compadre of his, Ted A. Hays. Next season the seeds were grown and the resulting pods naturally and consistently contorted themselves into a miniature replica of the circumcised male organ. Of the two color variations, one red (pictured in Plate 18) and the other a golden yellow, the latter is truer in form to its namesake.

The red type is a hobby of James Fontenot, a horticulture professor at Louisiana State University in Baton Rouge, who furnished the plant illustrated here. Neither Hays nor Fontenot was able to supply any information as to its origin. This blistering berry is too hot to eat; therefore, it is classed as an ornamen-

tal, or should we say as a conversation piece for the gardener who has everything?

At this time you will not find Peter Pepper among the valid cultivars listed by seed suppliers. It awaits official recognition. However, voucher material can be found in the herbarium of the University of Texas at Austin.

PIMENTO

(see Plate 19)

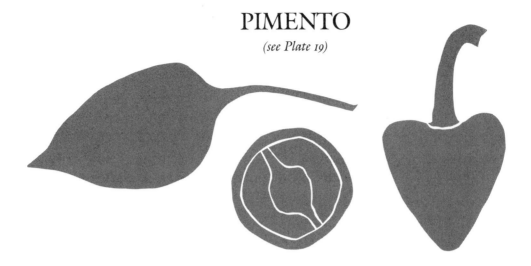

The state of Georgia was the site of the first pimento cultivation in America. The pimento was introduced in 1911 from Spain out of New World material. That large, sweet cultivar, which had pointed, heart-shaped fruits with a distinctive aromatic flavor, was to be the nucleus of the pimento industry in the United States. At the time, all the canned red pimento was being imported from Spain. The word *pimento* has been adopted by the Georgia Pimento Growers Association to designate the canned product or one of several cultivars with pimento-type fruits derived from the original Spanish introduction. The word comes from the Spanish *pimiento*, which means pepper.

The American canned pimento industry followed the invention of a roasting machine in 1914 by Mark Riegel of Experiment, Georgia. This machine facilitated the peeling of the fruit, but there is still much waste from the production of canned pimento. Studies have shown that this waste can be fed to poultry and livestock with beneficial results. Dried, ripe pimento waste can intensify the color of the yolks of eggs during the winter months when fed to hens in quantities of from 0.4 to 0.5 grams per hen each day. The hen deposits the coloring agent, capsanthin, in the egg yolk. Outside of their value as a coloring agent, the ripe pimento pods have a rather low feeding and fertilizer value, largely due to the high water content.

When fed to dairy cattle pimento waste was found to have no effect on the color, flavor, or odor of the milk. This was also true of the flavor and odor of the butter but its color was noticeably affected. The pimento waste in the cows' diet imparted an undesirable pink color to the butter.

Most of the pimentos are grown in the southern United States; however, some large California Bell types are also canned as pimento. The canned Bell and Tomato flesh is recognized by its true crimson color, while the pimento exhibits a tomatolike color when processed. The pimento is delicious fresh in salads and vegetable dishes, but its primary use is canned to add color and flavor to casserole dishes, garnishes, and cheese dishes and to stuff olives (see the recipes for *bacalao-a-la-Vizcaíno* on p. 132 and pimento cheese spread on p. 135).

Some pimento-type cultivars are Bighart, Mississippi Nemaheart, Perfection, Pimiento-L, Pimento Select, Truhart Perfection, and Truhart Perfection-D.

SANTA FE GRANDE

(see Plate 20)

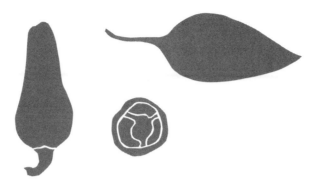

In Mexico any yellow pepper is called a *güero*, which is the Spanish term for a blonde. The Santa Fe Grande would be considered to be a *güero*, although it is red when fully ripe, because it is used in the mature yellow phase. According to most authorities, the Santa Fe Grande, Caloro, and Caribe are virtually one and the same cultivar. Paul G. Smith of the University of California, Davis, developed and released the Caloro in 1966. It happened that he had loaned some Caloro stock to the Petoseed Company of Saticoy, California, for observation. Shortly thereafter, from that Caloro parent stock, the company released the Santa Fe Grande. The Caloro–Santa Fe Grande type is grown throughout the southwestern United States. In Mexico the same cultivar was renamed Caribe and is being grown for export to markets in the United States. The Caribe is not consumed in Mexico; moreover, seed suppliers in the United States do not sell a cultivar by that name. The name was probably given to it when it recently came to Mexico to be grown as a new agricultural export (J. A. Laborde Cancino 1982, personal communication). The fiercely hot Caribe takes its title from a tribe of cannibalistic Indians that inhabited the West Indies at the time of Columbus. Their name was also given to the area that was their range, the Caribbean.

In addition to the above-named cultivars, there is a fourth that differs only in size from them, the much smaller fruited Cascabella. Cascabella is discussed with the Fresno (p. 101).

These *güeros* are used fresh in sauces or for seasoning and are processed as pickles or hot vinegar sauce. Although the principal use for this conical, yellow *güero* is as a condiment, its ornamental potential should not be overlooked. The gleaming yellow and red pods were the featured attraction on the banquet tables at the 1982 National Pepper Conference in Las Cruces, New Mexico. You can be assured that if you pick up these "blondes," they would be hot. Gentlemen might prefer blondes but it takes a real "macho" to handle a *güero*.

Santa Fe Grande–type cultivars are Caloro, Caribe, and Hybrid Gold Spike.

SERRANO

(see plate 21)

The Serrano is more widely used in Mexico and the southwestern United States than any of the fresh chili-peppers, despite the popularity of the Jalapeño. It is assumed that the Serrano originated on the mountain ridges (*serranías*) north of Puebla and Hidalgo in Mexico from which it acquired its name. However, a chili-pepper bearing the same characteristics but of a smaller size grows on the Gulf coast of Mexico. This little form, called *serranito*, is thought to be a possible ancestor of the commercial type that is grown today. It is very adaptable and grows in all regions of the country: in tropical as well as temperate zones, in semiarid to humid regions, and in altitudes that vary from sea level to 2,000 meters on the central mesa. The states of Veracruz, Tamaulipas, Sinaloa, and Nayarit, where it is called *cora*, are the biggest producers of the Serrano in Mexico. Other than a small amount in South Texas, Serranos are not grown commercially in the United States.

There is considerable variation in both the plant and the fruit within the different regions where it is cultivated. More than 90 percent of the national production is used in the fresh green state and is often called *chile verde*, although it in no way resembles the *chile verde* (long green/red chile) of New Mexico. Most of it is eaten fresh and mixed with food on the plate or is made into an uncooked sauce (see the recipes for tomato sauce on p. 133 and *guacamole* on p. 135). The remaining 10 percent is canned as pickles. Very little is used in the dried state. The three-alarm pods can be frozen for use throughout the year if care is taken to blanch them first; otherwise, they will lose their flavor and pungency.

Dry, small red chili-peppers can be found in American stores labeled "Japones" that are said to be dried Serranos, but close examination reveals little resemblance. The narrow, long, pointed pod of the dry Japones simply does not fit the Serrano silhouette. Whether this name came from a reference to a Japanese cultivar or whether it is a distortion of the word *capones*, which is applied to any peppers that have had the veins and seeds removed (*capón* = castrated), is not known. Whatever it refers to, the pods bearing that label are not Serranos.

There are three types of Serranos, all hot: the *chico*, or *balín* (small-bore bullet), which is short and fat and is preferred over the others by the canning industry; the *típico*, which has longer fruits and is most desired by the shoppers in the national market; and the *largo*, which is a longer recurved pod that has gained little acceptance among processors or the buying public. The various Serrano cultivars fall into one of these categories.

Some of the Serrano-type cultivars are Altamira, Cotaxtla Cónico, Cotaxtla Gordo, Cotaxtla Típico, Cuauhtemoc, Huasteco-74, Panuco, Tampiqueño 74, and Veracruz S69.

TEXAN

(see Plate 22)

For want of an established name, this cultivar will be identified as Texan because memories bring back a picture of this colorful plant in Grammy Smith's South Texas garden. The seed for this vivacious, erect, cherry-like pepper came from the yard at Nixon Courts in Port Aransas, Texas, where it had volunteered year after year as long as anyone could remember. This long-time resident of the Coastal Bend of Texas may not be one of those offered by seed houses at this time. It is a tall (over 60 cm), compact shrub, while most of the ornamentals to be had from seed suppliers are much smaller. Voucher material is in the herbarium of the University of Texas at Austin.

The ornamental value of the colorful plant was immediately recognized by Spanish fanciers of exotic plants when Columbus returned from the New World with the first capsicums. In Europe it was grown for its aesthetic value long before its value as a food was recognized. Modern home gardeners and flower lovers have been aware of its ornamental potential for a long time and have used the plant in pots to provide color indoors during winter months.

A number of ornamental cultivars are offered in flower seed catalogs (see Appendix). Besides their use as decorative house plants, ornamental types have great potential in landscape plans. Outdoor plantings of this heat lover can be incorporated to provide bursts of color in late summer and fall when the color from annual flowers is usually absent. The medium and dwarf types of plant with erect fruit showing above the foliage are recommended for ornamental use as borders or massed against a green background. Some plants may present a rainbow of hues ranging from white to purple, yellow, orange, and red all at the same time.

The ornamental peppers are edible; however, most of them are extremely hot and without the savor of those grown for the table. Birds will also be attracted by your vivid display; they are not deterred by the pungency of the pretty pods. Several cultivars grown for food offer additional value as ornamentals. The Fresno, Santa Fe Grande, *tabasco*, and Cascabella should not be overlooked for their use as decorative plants.

Some of the most useful ornamentals are Aurora, Ball Christmas Pepper, Black Prince, Christmas Cherry, Christmas Greetings, Christmas Ornamental (Celestial), Coral Reef, Craigi, Dwarf Variegata Jigsaw, Fiesta, Fips, Fireworks, Firey Festival, Holiday Cheer, Holiday Flame, Holiday Time, Midnight Special, Red Boy, Red Missile, Roter Schnitt, Variegata, and Variegated Flash.

TOMATO
(Squash)
(see Plate 23)

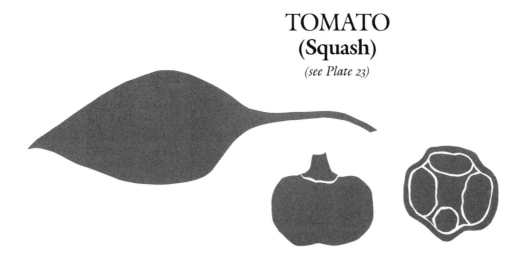

This sweet pepper with tomato- or squashlike fruits is one of the oldest forms of *Capsicum* still being cultivated today. It was first illustrated by Besler in his *Celeberrimi eystettensis* of 1613. Although it probably originated in Mesoamerica, little, if any, is grown in that area today. This thick-fleshed fruit, derived from New World stock, was widely acclaimed in Spain and nearby Morocco, where it is still the chief cultivar used in the production of high-quality paprika. Sturtevant (1885) declares that it had reached North American gardens before 1828 from the Old World. Early systematists, such as Erwin (1929), used "Tomato Pepper" to designate a group of nonpungent capsicums, which can have either red or yellow oblate fruits, scarcely longer than broad with ridges and furrows and very thick flesh. The Bell type was probably developed by selection from this early variety.

The same factor that causes the Tomato pepper to be esteemed as paprika, its high color content, also makes it valued for the extractable oleoresin, which is used as a coloring agent in food and other industries where natural pigments are required. In the southern United States the thick, sweet red flesh of this cultivar is sold to be canned, as is the true pimento.

It can be used fresh as you would use the Bell type; the pickled fruits are often served as condiments or used as garnish; canned, it serves the same purpose as pimento; and the dry processed form of paprika is frequently used to enhance the color and flavor of cooked dishes or as a garnish (see the recipe for veal paprika on p. 136).

Some Tomato-Squash–type cultivars are Canada Cheese, Early Sweet Pimento, Sunnybrook, Tomato Pimento, and Yellow Cheese Pimento (also Red).

CHILTECPIN
(see Plate 24)

Many names are used for this notorious little *chile*. We will call it Chiltecpin* (Chill-tech-péen), which is the name used by the pre-Columbian Amerindians and in the sixteenth century by Hernández when he wrote his study of the plants of New Spain. Many of the names applied today are corruptions of that word. This is the common bird pepper, which is considered to be the wild or spontaneous variety of *C. annuum* Linné. To add to the confusion, many other small-fruited capsicums have been referred to as bird peppers from the fondness that birds show for their fruits.

There are two principal variations of this species; the tiny ovoid form is called Chiltecpin or Chiltepin (Chill-tey-péen) and the longer, more acute form is labeled Chilipiquin. In the American Southwest the common form is egg-shaped, hence our choice of Chiltecpin. Originally, the Nahuatl word meaning flea was applied because of the similarity in size and bite. Other local names are *chile mosquito*; *chile de pájaro* (bird); *chile bravo* (savage, wild); *chile de perro* (dog); *chile silvestre* (wild); *chile del monte* (woodlands); *chillipiliento* (flea); *tecpintle, totocuitlatl* or *estiércol de pájaro* (bird droppings); and *tlichilli* (black). The Mayans call it *max* or *max-ic*, and in Haiti it is *huarahuao*.

Still other names for this widespread wild *chile* are *chiltepiquín*, a corruption of Chiltecpin; *chile enano*; *chilillo pequeño, chile max, chicniqui, chile amomo, pico de paloma*, and *ululte* in Yucatán; and *parado* and *chile chipas* near Oaxaca, Mexico. The green berry is known as *chile diente de tlacuache* in Tamaulipas, *gachupín* in Veracruz, and *tichushi* in Oaxaca.

This tiny pepper is considered to have a very distinct, easily recognizable flavor, as well as being "*arrebatado*," an expression that means "although it is extremely hot the sensation disappears easily and rapidly." It is sold in the markets both fresh and dry and is quite expensive in comparison to the other types. There are no large plantings of the Chiltecpin; most families have a plant or two in or near their own yard. Housewives gather their Chiltecpins by breaking off branches and letting them dry in a covered area. The branches of dried berries are shaken and the tiny pods are then collected and taken to market. It is important to gather them before the birds do. They are deciduous, making them easy prey for our feathered friends. During the time of year when they are ripe they are favored by the people of Mexico over all other types of *chiles*.

In northern Mexico, Nabhan (1978) reports that the Chiltecpin is one of the few wild plant harvests that is still economically profitable. Entire families move into the hills west of the Río San Miguel in Sonora during the harvest season. There they camp out until they get a load. The gatherers drive their pickup trucks back to riverside villages, such as Meresichic, where they sell their harvest to spice company buyers. In 1975 the peppers sold for $4.50 a pound.

In the fall, the Papago Indians of southern Arizona make pilgrimages into the desert mountain ranges to collect Chiltecpins. Even the Apaches and Pimas, who live beyond the northern limits of its range, traditionally sought the peppers out, through travel or trade. The pods are so precious to the Tarahumara

---

* *Chiltepin* is an acceptable modern adaptation of the Nahuatl word, *tecpin*, for flea.

of Chihuahua, Mexico, that stone walls are erected around wild plants in the Sierra Madre to protect them from goats and grazing animals.

The fiery spice is used fresh in both the green and the ripe forms, and also dried. The dried pods are used to season cooked dishes of every sort, from *frijoles* (beans) to stews, while fresh pods are blended into sauces, bottled with vinegar for hot vinegar sauce, mashed into almost any food on the table, and used for larding meat before roasting (see the recipe for Chiltecpin jelly on p. 136).

When I was growing up in South Texas, I knew that at almost every meal one of the "kids" would have to run to the back yard for a few Chiltecpins from the doorside bush. Some Texans are so addicted to these fiery morsels that they carry them in elaborate little cases, such as might be used for pills, in order to assure themselves of a supply when visiting outside their own territory.

Generations of Texas children have tormented one another by rubbing the burning fruit into eyes, hiding it in candy and bites of goodies, or making dogs run just for the sport. There are probably as many similar applications of the tortuous pod as there were children. While youngsters who said "dirty words" in some parts of the country got their mouths washed out with soap, many a Texan can recall having his or her mouth rubbed with a Chiltecpin for the same misdemeanor. Such punishment recalls pre-Columbian torture as shown in the Codices of Mexico (see p. 81). Every adult native Texan is certain to have his or her own recollections of that ubiquitous red berry.

Although the Chiltecpin grows wild from the southern United States to northern South America, it is very difficult to get started as a cultivated plant. The germination period is much longer than that of most other *Capsicum* cultivars. However, once the plants are established they usually continue to volunteer year after year. Birds are the principal agent in the dispersal of the seed; the plants can usually be found along fence rows or growing under bushes frequented by birds. Occasionally the perennial plant survives winters often enough to develop thick, trunklike stems. Near El Coyote, Sonora, Mexico, they grow as "saplings as tall as a man and form a dense wild Chiltecpin forest" (Nabham 1978, 32).

If you are fortunate enough to have a Chiltecpin bush, you can keep a supply year-round by collecting them, either green or red, and storing them in a plastic bag or freezer jar in the freezer to be used as needed.

TABASCO

(see Plate 25)

Capsicum frutescens var. *tabasco* is the only species other than *C. annuum* var. *annuum* cultivated commercially in the United States. This little incendiary is not merely hot; it is explosive, having been the subject in various litigations and its origin a cause célèbre.

The first documented appearance of a pepper called tabasco was in the *New Orleans Daily Delta* of January 26, 1850, crediting Maunsell White, a prominent banker and legislator, with introducing "Tobasco [*sic*] red pepper." According to a court transcript, three years later J. N. Caballero offered two hundred bags of "Tobasco [*sic*] pimenta" through a newspaper advertisement. In 1859, White was advertising "Extract of Tobasco [*sic*] Pepper." Further testimony given in that transcript implies that White gave some pods, along with his sauce recipe, to his friend Edmund McIlhenny during a visit to White's Deer Range Plantation (U.S. Circuit Court 1922). This would have been sometime before the Civil War because White had lost control of that property before his death in 1862 (*Times Picayune*, January 10, 1977). Between 1850 and the next record in 1865 was a period of legend and undocumented development that is quite sensitive to those whose ancestors were involved in the origins of this exotic variety.

In 1859, McIlhenny married the daughter of Judge D. D. Avery. After the Civil War began they moved to her family's Avery Island plantation. The couple remained on that salt dome island for several years before fleeing from invading Union forces. When they returned to their home in 1865 after that disastrous conflict, "they found ruin" (Ries 1968, 8). Amid the "wasted kitchen garden a few defiant plants still stood." These pepper plants produced the seed for an industry based on their fruit that is now international in scope

and whose product, Tabasco Pepper Sauce, has become such a part of our language as to be listed in the dictionary (Funk & Wagnall's 1959).

During the Reconstruction Period, McIlhenny experimented with his peppers at the Avery Island plantation until he arrived at his own tangy, fermented pepper sauce that satisfied his epicurean requirements. By 1869 enough of that fiery red liquid was ready for him to begin marketing it. "In 1870, letters of patent on the condiment were obtained" and the famous sauce was on its way to becoming the *número uno* pepper sauce in the world (Ries 1968, 9).

In 1888 McIlhenny gave seeds of the plant to E. Lewis Sturtevant, M.D., whose "Notes on Edible Plants" (1919) is an American botanical classic (Irish 1898, 67). These were grown out at the New York Botanical Garden and labeled *tabasco* after the McIlhenny sauce of that name. Sturtevant's plant material with the name was the basis of the first published description of the *tabasco* variety, which H. C. Irish classified as *C. annuum* var. *conoides* 'Tabasco' in his revision of the genus *Capsicum* (Irish 1898). In 1951 Smith and Heiser assigned 'Tabasco' to *C. frutescens*.

That is how the variety got its name; as to how the sauce was called Tabasco, it is best to defer to the originators who named it. In the recorded testimony of the founder's son John, we read: "It was called tabasco sauce because, when my father began putting it on the market, it was necessary to give it a name. The man who had given him the pepper originally told him that he had, just prior to giving him the pepper, been in the Republic of Mexico and in the State of Tabasco. My father, after discussing other names, decided to give the name of 'tabasco' to this sauce, be-

20. During the two hundred years of Spanish dominion in Louisiana, the inland port of Tabasco, Mexico, was second only to Veracruz in commercial importance. Goods came regularly from Central Mexico, south through the passes to the river port to avoid the impassable mountains that separate the central highlands from the coast. From Tabasco much of the merchandise went directly to American markets through New Orleans. (Disturnell map of Estados Unidos, 1847; photograph from the Cartographic History Library, the Library, University of Texas at Arlington)

cause it was a euphonious name" (U.S. District Court 1917).

There are other places McIlhenny might have heard the word *tabasco* at that time. In 1847 the inland town of Tabasco on the banks of the Tabasco River (now Grijalva) in the territory by that name south of the state of Veracruz, Mexico, was second to the port of Veracruz in commercial importance on the Gulf of Mexico (Ghigliazza 1948, 59). Commerce with Mexican ports was commonplace because the bustling port of New Orleans was a city with strong ties to Mexico dating from the period of Spanish dominion, which had lasted until 1801.

The place name Tabasco was current in New Orleans in the late 1840s, not only because of the established trade but also because New Orleans played an important role in the war with Mexico (1846–1847). It was the major staging point as well as the closest large U.S. port where the sick and injured Americans engaged in that conflict could be brought for treatment and recuperation (Bauer 1974, 388).

Com. Matthew Galbraith Perry, in command of the U.S. Home Squadron in the Gulf of Mexico, directed the second seizure of Tabasco (currently, San Juan Bautista). The first, in October of the previous year, was an action designed to break the monotony of blockade, but the second was an effort to halt the flow of arms to Santa Anna. On July 16, 1847, the tropical town was easily taken by "scarcely more than 1,100 men poorly trained for campaigning on land" (Bauer 1969). After the capture Perry decided to hold the city with a garrison of 420 marines (Ghigliazza 1948).

Illnesses that befell two-thirds of the men caused the garrison to be abandoned after several months and we can be certain they were taken to New Orleans for treatment, as was the practice in that war (Bauer 1974). For several years, immediately before the 1850 newspaper record of a pepper referred to as "Tobasco," there were a lot of men who had served in Tabasco, Mexico, in New Orleans. The toponym Tabasco was no stranger to the city.

The seed of the *tabasco* progenitor reached Avery Island before the family fled in 1863. We are told that those seeds were brought to this country by Friend Gleason, a soldier in the Mexican war, who gave some to his friend Edmund McIlhenny (E. McIlhenny, Jr., 1983, personal communication). The McIlhennys have maintained that same strain of peppers, which were later named *tabasco*, since the end of the Civil War. Each year the president of that family-owned company makes a ceremony of going into the fields and with "painstaking care" selecting the plants that will furnish the seed for future crops; "no outside pepper has contaminated the strain" (Ries 1968).

The labor situation and the demand for the sauce have forced the company to expand its growing operation to Mexico, Honduras, Colombia, and Venezuela, but the family still furnishes all seed and maintains stringent control. Ironically, the *tabasco* pepper has returned to its alleged homeland where it was unknown before its reintroduction in the mid-1960s by the McIlhenny Co. of Louisiana. A search of the current Mexican literature covering the cultivation of *chile* in that country failed to produce one reference to a *chile tabasco*. However, Roys (1931, 58) referred to *Myrtus pimienta* (allspice) as "*Pimienta de Tabasco*" when he listed the ingredients of a Mayan curative.

Not only McIlhenny but others who grow and process this cultivar in Louisiana have been forced to curtail their efforts there because the willing hands to do the painstaking handpicking necessary for a good product are no longer to be found.

In 1898 another enterprising man established a business based on the *tabasco* pepper. B. F. Trappey, the founder of B. F. Trappey and Sons, had, at one time, worked on Avery Island. He left there to go to Jeannerette, where he began growing peppers on his in-laws' sugar farm. Soon afterward he was selling a bottled pepper sauce, which he called Tabasco Sauce, made from *tabasco* peppers grown originally from Avery Island seed. This operation continued until 1929 when the McIlhennys were victorious in a suit brought against the Trappeys for infringing on their trademark. After a prolonged court battle, which had begun in 1922, it was established that the trademark came before the varietal name; therefore, no one could market a product with the name Tabasco in its title although they could list *tabasco* peppers among the ingredients. This decision forced the Trappeys and other processors to branch out into products made from different cultivars. Today Trappey markets large volumes of their varied products around the world but is among those who agree that Tabasco Pepper Sauce is the only one of its kind that the American public asks for.

The name Tabasco was the name of a territory, now a state in Mexico. The word was used by a conquistador, Hernán Cortez, in 1519 when referring to that area (Gil y Saenz, 1892). He had probably heard the Nahuatl-speaking indigenes say *tapach-co* in reply to his demands to know what the place was called. Tabasco is a Nahuatl word, and the etymology, according to Hopkins, is:

Tapachtli coral, concha o venera
(Molina 1970: 90; Karttunen 1983: 214)

The Spanish to Nahuatl states:

Coral. Tapachtli.
(Molina 1970: 30)

and:

Concha de ostia dela mar. eptli, eptapalcatl, tapachtli.
(Molina 1970: 18)

Therefore *tapachtli* is shell, including oyster shell, and the 'place of oyster shell,' formed from the stem *tapach-* and the locative suffix *-co* is the following (which could also mean 'place of coral'):

tapacho-co. Place of coral or (oyster) shell.

From *tapachco* it is no problem to get to *tabasco*, as there are many place names that go through this kind of transformation, for example,

tlachco to *Tasco* or *Taxco*
The place of the ball court.*

Previously, the word had been erroneously translated to mean "land where the soil is humid" (Griffen 1953, 20). Nicholas A. Hopkins, along with several Nahuatl scholars, considers that to be an unlikely etymology (F. Karttunen 1982 and McLeod 1982, both personal communication).†

Capsicum frutescens var. *tabasco* is highly susceptible to an "etch" wilt disease, which often causes large crop losses. At one time the somewhat similar appearing *C. annuum* var. *annuum* cultivars, Mississippi Sport and Louisiana Sport, were used as a substitute in vinegar-packed whole pods when disease threatened the crop. Neither are cultivated to any extent today. In 1970 the Greenleaf Tabasco, a tobacco etch virus resistant variety, was introduced by Auburn University of Alabama (Greenleaf et al. 1970). The fruit of the new Greenleaf Tabasco is more pungent and a deeper glossy red than those of *tabasco*.

One of the first uses of the scorching sauce was on Louisiana oysters, both raw and cooked. No self-respecting oyster bar would open its doors without a bottle of Tabasco Pepper Sauce in easy reach (see the recipe for oyster stew on p. 136). The *tabasco* pepper is not used fresh or dried.

---

*This etymology was worked out by Nicholas A. Hopkins, Ph.D., an anthropologist with the Universidad Metropolitana, Iztapalpa, Mexico, at the time, 1982. His address is Route 2, Box 1435, Del Valle, TX 78617.
†Frances Karttunen, Ph.D., the author of *An Analytical Dictionary of Nahuatl*, is with the Linguistics Research Center at the University of Texas at Austin. Barbara MacLeod, a doctoral student at the University of Texas at Austin, is fluent in Yucatec, Chol, and Chorti, having lived among Indians who speak those languages for a number of years while serving with the Peace Corps.

UVILLA GRANDE

(see Plate 26)

The beautiful *uvilla grande* is a *C. frutescens* as is its famous kin, *tabasco*. The *uvilla grande* is a good example of the type of *chile* known in Mexico as *criolla*, or creole. A creole person is born in the Americas of Spanish or French parents. When the term is applied to a *Capsicum* cultivar, it means a very local type, native to a particular land area and not widespread. In Mexico the *criolla* type of any cultivar is usually the form used to develop other cultivars of that type (J. A. Laborde Cancino 1982, personal communication).

The seed for the plant illustrated in Plate 26 was number 188-477 from the U.S. Southern Regional Plant Introduction Station in Experiment, Georgia, and was said to be *C. frutescens*. Although no description was included in the report, *uvilla grande* was one of the varieties grown by Smith and Heiser (1951, 365) in the study that determined *C. frutescens* and *C. annuum* were two distinct species. I do not know if my specimen is the same *uvilla grande* used in that work or not.

This cultivar is so hot that it could be used in the same manner as the Chiltecpin; however, I would recommend ornamental usage only.

KELLU-UCHU
(Ají Amarillo/Cusqueño)

(see Plate 27)

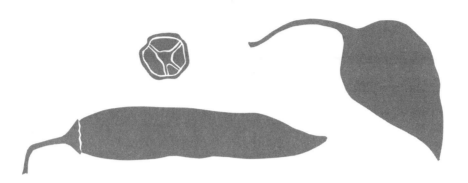

The South American peppers are little known in other parts of the hemisphere at this time, particularly those from Brazil. When botanists make collecting expeditions on that continent, they usually gather samples at market places, in gardens, or in the wild without learning the local name for the cultivar. The specimens are entered into study collections where they are known only by their plant introduction (P.I.) number and place of origin. Most of the material currently available comes from the coastal valleys of the western slopes of the Peruvian Andes; other regions of the continent have not been adequately surveyed as yet. As a consequence, the vernacular names applied here are from reliable sources but may be a variation of regional names.

The *ají* is so much a part of the diet of the natives of Peru that it must have seemed natural for the Spanish-trained Indian artist who painted the *Last Supper* for the Cathedral of Cuzco during the seventeenth century to place a dish of *ajís* on the table before the Christ and his Apostles for their last meal. After all, who can eat without *ajís*?

On a visit to Cuzco, Peru, I found the dried, large *ají amarillo*, or *cusqueño* (from Cuzco), to be the principal type offered for sale. Beside the golden heap of *cusqueños* was a bin filled with a very similar dried, large, red pod from a cultivar of a different species. Attempts to grow seed from both types resulted in very tall (over five feet) plants that had hardly matured before winter freezes set in. This fresh yellow-podded type is called *ají amarillo* and *ají verde* by the Spanish-speaking population, while those who speak Quechua call it Kellu-uchu, *uchu* being the Quechua word for pepper. It is more frequently used in its dry state, known as *cusqueño*. The *cusqueño* is the principal condiment for traditional Peruvian foods, accompanying such dishes as *cau cau*, tripe and potatoes; *cuye chactado*, a roasted whole guinea pig; and *ceviche*, raw seafood marinated in lime juice. This colorful, piquant fruit is used with the seed for very hot sauces or without for milder ones; both are made by grinding the peppers with other ingredients, such as *culantro* (*cilantro*, coriander) or other herbs (see the recipe for *anticuchos* on p. 137). The sauce is consumed by rural people, for the most part, who apply it liberally to their potatoes. The famous Irish potato had its origin in Peru, having only arrived in the Old World after the Spanish conquest.

The *ají amarillo* and the potato are very important ingredients in the primitive preparation of a popular Andean dish, *pachamanca*. A hole is dug in the earth and a fire is built in the hole. Stones are then placed in the fire. When the stones become very hot, the coals are removed and the hot stones cleaned. Meat, such as guinea pig, llama, chicken, or pig, and potatoes are wrapped in banana leaves and placed on the hot rocks, then covered with aromatic plants, such as *huacatay*, *culantro*, and *ají*. All this is covered with cloth, then earth, and allowed to cook. A *pachamanca* is a festive occasion, similar to a New England clambake or a Texas barbecue. It is the traditional dish served on June 24, Saint Juan's Day.

Most of the hot South American chili-peppers will cause the Mexican *habañero* to pale by comparison. Palates north of the Panama Canal to the Arctic Circle will need some adjusting to be ready for the blistering fruits from below the Equator. Our temperate growing season is not suited to the cultural requirements of most of them.

PUCA-UCHU

(see Plate 28)

Peru is the home of this brilliantly colored, variable chili-pepper for which we only have its Quechua name, Puca-uchu. *Uchu* (*ushu, ucha*) is the Quechua word applied to capsicums in general by Indians of Peru and Ecuador, whose mother tongue is this pre-Columbian language. The plant on which these pods hang has a vinelike habit that requires considerable space to accommodate its sprawl.

Except for the Chaucay and Huacho valleys in Peru, as in most South American countries, there are no large commercial fields of *ajís*; instead, they are grown in home gardens by rural peoples. A single plant is good for at least two years, but the gardener seldom has to replant them once they are established because volunteer plants take the place of old ones. Since the pepper plant is normally a perennial shrub in the tropical part of the world, fresh fruits are always available for use in sauces in the home or in popular-class restaurants.

Three types of sauce are made with uncooked Puca-uchus. One of them consists of chopped *ají* with herbs and onions (the Indian onion does not form a bulb, only the leaves are used). *Ají molida* is a type of sauce made with ground herbs and onions. The third is *ají molida* with water added. Recently these have been bottled commercially. Each is made fresh daily and served in bowls that are passed around, one to a table. This passing of the sauce bowl serves a social as well as a gustatory function. In the past these bowls for *salsa de ají* were ceramic but now most are plastic. In the cities, china sets include special bowls for the sauce.

On the coast, fishermen eat *ají* directly from the plant or make it into a sauce with olive oil and/or lemon juice, sometimes adding Mediterranean-type olives and chopped onion, which is served on *yuca* (manioc) and uncooked fish.

This cultivar readily adapted to my Texas garden, producing an abundant supply of very hot pods, which must be used fresh because the flesh does not air dry well enough to store (see the recipe for *ají de gallina* on p. 137).

Despite a long history of cultivation east of the Andes since before 400 B.C., the *C. baccatum* var. *pendulum*, with its distinctive spotted flower, is only cultivated in southeastern Peru, Bolivia, southwestern Brazil, and Colombia, with recent introductions to Central America. In Costa Rica members of this species are known as *cuerno de oro*, horn of plenty.

CHINCHI-UCHU

(see Plate 29)

The *chinchi-uchu*, another South American pepper, is little known outside Peru and Bolivia. Only one variety of *C. chinense*, the *habañero* of Yucatán and the Caribbean, is cultivated to any extent, except by plant geneticists, in North America. *Chinchi-uchu*, a beautiful, cherrylike berry that hangs from a delicate stem, is also known as the *comun-uchu*. When it is in the dry state it becomes *chaki-uchu* and the powdered form is *allpa*. Garcilaso referred to the *chinchi-uchu* in the early seventeenth century (1966, 505).

Dr. Ramiro Matos, an anthropologist at the University of San Marcos in Lima, Peru, informs us that this little *ají*, which is used like a tomato, is grown in coastal valleys where the required warm climate is found; it is only cultivated in home gardens. *Chinchi-uchu* is used to make a hot sauce (see the recipe for *pebre* on p. 138). "Elegant" families do not serve the *salsa picante* with every meal but do use it with everyday-type fare, such as a South American boiled dinner, or *sancochado*, which is derived from the traditional Spanish *puchero*.

On the day that an upper-class household is to have *sancochado*, the family cook will go to market early to get the freshest produce. There she selects carrots, mint, leeks, and *ají* for a soup bouquet to be boiled with a nice marrow-filled bone. To add to the broth that this will produce she purchases corn, sweet potatoes, yuca, cabbage, and some yellow potatoes. Moving to the meat section, she orders a beef brisket and some pig skin before returning to the home where she is employed. The beef and vegetables will be cleaned

and prepared to be added to the rich broth. The corn is left on the cob, which is chopped into small pieces before being added to the pot. When all is ready, the vegetables and meat are drained and the resulting broth is served as a savory soup. This is followed by a platter of the boiled vegetables and meat, which the family seasons with a pungent *ají* sauce. This sturdy meal is topped off with rice pudding. In the past, this typical boiled meal was never served when there were guests; however, since the 1950s there has been a growing interest in native customs and the acceptance of the *sancochado* has become general (L. Shofield 1982, personal communication).

This may or may not be the *ají* used to produce the powder that was described in the *Saturday Review* of September 15, 1886, but the description is worth repeating. We are told that fresh pods, seeds removed, are ground into a paste the consistency of "spring butter." The paste is then put into a small, "well-dried" gourd, especially prepared for this purpose, of the size and shape of a "well-grown" orange. After the gourd is filled, it is coated with a layer of "well-tempered" clay and placed in the sun to dry or to "ripen" as the "simple rural people" would say. When the clay is "well baked," the paste has been dried into a fine yellow powder and is ready for use. One of these *ají*-filled gourds is exhibited in London's Kew Museum. Early visitors to remote areas in South America often thought "these *ají*-laden gourds, with their exquisite flavor and refined taste, were some uncommon and little known natural fruits."

HABAÑERO

(see Plate 30)

HABAÑERO!!! This is the chili-pepper that separates the men from the boys. Until the relatively recent introduction of the South American *C. pubescens*, *C. chinense* var. *habañero* held the undisputed title of the hottest *Capsicum* in North America. It still is the most potent pod readily available because none of the *C. pubescens* are marketed widely (see *rocoto* p. 124). The *habañero* is found throughout the West Indies, Belize, and the Caribbean littoral, where its bright yellow-orange, lantern-shaped fruit is easily recognized; however, in Mexico it is limited to the Yucatán peninsula. Attempts to cultivate it in other parts of that country have had unsatisfactory results.

The Mexican origin of the *habañero* is not certain; some believe it came from South America; others, because the name means "from Havana," suggest that it came from Cuba. Two things give credence to the latter theory: until the twentieth century, the peninsula of Yucatán had major commercial ties with Cuba, and the *habañero* is the only pepper cultivar in Yucatán that has no Mayan name (Laborde & Pozo 1982). In 1768, Miller described *C. angulofum*, the bonnet pepper of the West Indies; without doubt the description fits the *habañero*. Regardless of where it originated, it is indispensable to the regional dishes of its present range.

Since it is also used in Brazil and Trinidad, this variety probably reached the Caribbean from South America, where there are many other cultivars of *C. chinense*. The unique chili-pepper is called Scotch Bonnet in Jamaica. Although there are a few fairly large plantings in Yucatán, for the most part throughout its range the typical type of cultivation is in the house yard or in separate patches in the *milpa* (cornfields) (Redfield & Villas 1962). Large amounts are not necessary because a few go a long way. Seventy-five percent of the Mexican production is consumed fresh, 22 percent is processed into sauces, and the remainder is kept for seed.

The fruit has fiery pungency and is highly aromatic with an unmistakable flavor. Even though it is blistering, we are told the burning sensation is very short-lived. It is the favorite among the West Indian blacks. The *habañero* is used daily by Caribbean folk, who generally cut the green or ripe fruit into little strips that they mix with lime juice and salt to pep up their other dishes (see the recipe for *ixni-pec* on p. 138).

For many years B. F. Trappey and Sons of New Iberia, Louisiana, sponsored a pepper eating contest at their Dulcito plantation. "Mr. Bernard," as the patriarch of the Trappey clan is fondly known, could not keep his eyes from twinkling as he recalled those renowned bouts with the pod. When the contestants were getting down to the wire, a "Secret Weapon Pepper" would be brought forth. The tight security around the plant, which had been grown and nursed for the event, was now lifted and it was unveiled as the determining factor. The twinkle almost turned to tears as he recalled how that beautiful little golden fruit, the *habañero*, made the judges' decision a simple one, for few could survive its fire, which is reported to be one thousand times that of a Jalapeño. Those infamous contests are no longer held; could it be that no one is willing to face the perils of the pod?

The germination period for this cultivar is extremely long. It needs a warm moist environment to produce the compact plant that is filled with several glowing lanterns from a single node. The results, both esthetic and gastronomic, are worth the wait.

Cultivars are INIA and Uxmal.

ROCOTILLO

(see Plate 31)

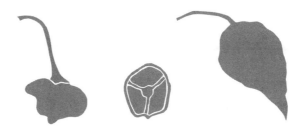

After growing and tasting peppers from all over the Western Hemisphere for five years, my hands-down favorite "eating" pepper is the *rocotillo*. This crisp textured fruit with enough pungency to be interesting but never caustic is not only delicious eaten raw but also beautiful to look at when used as a garnish. On plant introduction lists it is referred to as "red squash" because of the fruit's similarity in shape to the Pattypan squash, but in Peru it is sometimes known as *rosasuchu* and, more frequently, just *pimiento*, or sweet pepper. (Do not confuse with *C. a.* var. *annuum* Tomato or Squash.)

The *rocotillo* is only used fresh and can be found seasonally in the markets. Its primary use is as a condiment—not as a sauce—with beans or *carne asada* or it can be cooked with them. This deep carmine-red pod is employed as is the Bell in North America.

Ajís and *pimientos* are becoming expensive in South America. Until recently the shopper never paid for peppers; they were given as *propinas* or *yapas* (Quechua), little bonuses with the purchase of other vegetables.

This interesting pepper grows well in Central Texas, although the fruit does not attain the size it would in its homeland. It is a highly recommended addition to your garden, whether grown outside or in pots. The members of this species, *C. chinense*, are multishaped and varicolored, probably more so than any of the other *Capsicum* species. At the experimental farm for tropical plants, CATIA, in Costa Rica, this species comprised the largest number of the 250 cultivars being grown in April of 1982. Shapes and colors that eyes accustomed to North American peppers had seldom seen or imagined were growing profusely.

ROCOTO

(see Plate 32)

Capsicum pubescens is readily distinguishable from the other domesticated species of that genus by a quick glance at the flower and seed. Although there are a few *C. annuum* var. *annuum* that produce purple or purple-streaked blooms, the large violet corollas held erect above the foliage make *C. pubescens* unmistakable. If blooms are not available, the seeds will give the identification for they are the only rugose, blackish-brown seeds within the genus. Eshbaugh (1971, 1979) reported this species to be grown and marketed at relatively high elevations, higher than any other domesticated *Capsicum*. *C. pubescens* is cultivated as a large cash crop in only a few Peruvian (e.g., Arequipa) areas and one Mexican (Patzcuaro) area and is primarily grown as an individual plant around mid-elevational (1,200–2,000 m) homes. In some instances it has become a large shrub, taller than a man (Rick 1950).

Introduced after the Conquest, the *rocoto* has become the dominant pepper of highland Indians on either side of the Andes in western South America, which is its traditional range. Garcilaso (1966, 505) referred to *C. pubescens* as *rócot-uchu* or *locoto*. In South America it appears in myriad forms and colors, called *rocoto*, *rócot-uchu*, *ro'qote*, *lo'koti*, or *llata*. It can be yellow-orange, orange, red, or lemon-yellow but all are green when immature.

The *rocoto* was introduced to Central America and Mexico in the twentieth century. A plump, ovate, yellow-orange type seems to be the only one widespread in Central America and Mexico, although a few red forms have been observed. It is consumed exclusively as fresh, fully matured fruit in the form of sauce, condiment, or vegetable.

In Central America the *rocoto* is variously referred to as *chamburato*, *garrapato*, *cuadro-caldo*, *manzana*, *petenero* (Honduras), and, most frequently, *chile caballo*. The South American pattern of cultivation in home gardens with one or two plants along the borders prevails throughout this area (Rick 1950). However, in Mexico this newcomer has been given different names, such as *canario* in the Oaxaca region and *jalapeño* in Sierra de Chiapas, but more commonly it is known as *chile perón*. There is a limited commercial production in an area near Patzcuaro, Michoacán, Mexico. *Rocoto* requires a long growing season with day lengths of eleven to thirteen hours, making it unsuited for cultivation in the United States.

During a visit to an Indian market at Etla, northwest of Oaxaca, Mexico, I came upon a tiny highland Indian woman with a well-used gourd bowl filled with fresh *canarios*. Desiring evidence of the find, I attempted to photograph the golden fruits only to be blocked by a deft swish of her *rebosa*, which quickly covered the precious pods, thus protecting them from the evil eye of my camera. The same fate befell similar photographic efforts in Chichicastenango, Guatemala, when I came upon a Mayan vendor selling *chile caballos* on the steps of the church amid clouds of smoke from burning incense.

The gracious *ladina* woman (a non-Indian native Guatemalan) who managed a lovely inn in "Chichi" had her kitchen staff collect examples of the various chili-peppers used in cooking. When the *chile caballo* was pointed out, she informed me that only the Indians ate it because it was so very hot. However, she added, her little eight-year-old daughter, who attended the local school with the Mayan children, had developed a taste for it. The mother had learned that the nutritious, but pallid, *ladino* lunch she carefully packed each morning for the youngster to take to school was being exchanged for the skimpy fare brought by the Indian children, which was invariably tortillas enclosing strips of the fiery *chile caballo*.

Throughout Central America the eating of food highly spiced with chili-pepper is largely confined to Indian populations and is not as widespread as it is in Mexico or parts of South America.

Attesting to the murderous pungency of the *rocoto* are such Peruvian expressions as *levanta muertos*, raising the dead; and in the town of Huanta it becomes *gringo huanuchi*, will kill a gringo. Gringo is not derogatory in this expression; it is used as blonde. There is a popular dish in Arequipa, Peru, called *rocoto relleno*. The seeds are removed and the pod is filled with cheese or sausage and then baked in the same manner as American stuffed peppers (see the recipe for *papas a la huncaina* on p. 138).

At least fourteen different fruit shapes have been recognized (Rick 1950), but these various *C. pubescens* have not received individual names as have those of *Capsicum annuum* var. *annuum* to my present knowledge; they are all apparently referred to as *rocoto*.

PREPARING AND SERVING

WITHIN these pages much has been said about the New World's blistering berry, probably more than you ever wanted to know while all the while you just aspired to learn how to eat them or otherwise use them. However, before you embark on that mission let me stress that you should familiarize yourself with the methods for preparing and handling our precious pods correctly in order to ensure an enjoyable experience. Please, in your rush to become a pod fellow, take the time to follow instructions. Peppers are expensive, you don't want to waste them, but, most of all, DON'T GET BURNED.

Peeling

Some varieties—*poblano*-Ancho, long green/red chile, and, sometimes, the Jalapeño, plus a few others less commonly used—must have the tough transparent outer skin removed before preparation, unless they are to be ground or pureed. There are several ways to remove the skin after the pods have been veined and seeded.* Wear gloves.†

---

*These methods were compiled from several sources: *N.M. State Univ. Coop. Ext. Ser. Guide* E-312, 1977; *N.M. Agr. Ext. News* 38:4–5, 400E-311, 1958; *Univ. Ariz. Rural Ext. Ser. Cir.* 221, 1954; *Chile Connoisseur News* 18:5, 1980.

†The University of New Mexico's Poison, Drug Information, and Medical Crisis Center recommends immersing hands burned with chili-peppers in cold water for temporary relief. Although this agency is working on a solution to this problem, that is the only suggestion they will make at this time.

In November 1983, I gathered *habañeros* and removed the seeds in order to save them, carelessly forgetting to wear rubber gloves. Such a failure usually results in hands that burn and continue to burn every part of your body that you touch for a day or two. Earlier that day I had

BLISTER METHOD

First step: "Blistering" the skin. This may be done by any one of the following methods:

1. Burner Roasting: Place a square of hardware cloth or a small grill over:

   a. Electric stove burner set on high.

   b. Gas stove burner set at medium. Place 1 to 4 pods on the grill; turn frequently, permitting the outer skin to blister evenly. The skin will be charred but the flesh will not be burned.

2. Broiler Roasting: Place the pods on a cookie sheet or foil-covered oven rack. Place rack about 3 inches below broiler unit or flame for 6 to 8 minutes. Leave the door open. Turn frequently for even blistering of the pods.

3. Oven Roasting: Preheat the oven to 550°F (288°C). Prick the skin with a fork to prevent bursting. Place on an open rack and roast 3–7 minutes or until blistered. No turning required.

---

been cleaning seashells in a plastic container filled with a concentrated household chlorine bleach. On an impulse, I dipped my burning hands into the chlorine, then rinsed them immediately. I observed that this wash in a 5.25% aqueous solution of sodium hypochlorite, NaOCl, followed by rinsing in water, completely eliminated the irritant effect.

Dr. Tom Mabry of the Department of Botany, University of Texas at Austin, suggested that the alkaline bleach ionizes the phenolic hydroxyl group in the active ingredients, all of which are phenolic amides (e.g., dihydrocapsaicin), making the compounds water soluble; at the same time, the ionized phenolic ring in each compound would be readily oxidized by the bleach, thereby altering the structures and properties of the compounds.

It is not necessary to use the chlorine bleach full strength, a solution of one part common bleach to five parts of water works equally well.

$$HO-\bigcirc-CH_2-NH-\overset{\overset{\displaystyle O}{\|}}{C}-(CH_2)_4-CH=CH-CH(CH_3)_2$$
$$CH_3O$$

Dihydrocapsaicin

4. Oil Roasting: In a large saucepan, heat cooking oil to 400°F (204°C). Drop the pods in a few at a time; remove with tongs. This is good for a large number. The oily residue may become rancid in storage.

Second step: Remove the blistered pods from the heat and cool them in one of the following ways:

1. Place them in a cold, wet cloth; allow to steam 10–15 minutes.

2. Plunge them into ice water.

3. Place them in a plastic or paper bag for 10 to 15 minutes.

Third step: When the pods are cool, start peeling at the stem end while holding under running water. A small knife will help. If your hands are sensitive, wear rubber or disposable plastic gloves. For freezing, do not peel—more vitamins, color, and flavor will be retained.

Fourth step: Slit the pod; remove the veins and seeds by cutting and washing.

HOT PARAFFIN DIP

1. Melt 1 or 2 cakes of paraffin (enough to cover the entire pod with one dip) in a large can set in a kettle of boiling water (essential safety precaution to prevent flaming).

2. Wash and dry the pods thoroughly. Prick the skin with a fork to prevent steam forming within.

3. Heat the paraffin to 250°F (121°C) or until bubbles break the surface. Flash point of paraffin is 390°– 400°F (199°–204°C).

4. Place 2 pods at a time in the hot paraffin.

5. Allow the skin to blister and turn white all over (4 minutes).

6. Remove the pods from the hot paraffin and plunge into icy water. The paraffin hardens at once.

7. Working on newspapers to avoid a mess, peel the fruit. This method leaves the pod clean and whole, with no traces of oil or scorching; it retains more nutrients, color, and flavor than the blister method.

Freezing

Frozen peppers may be used in cooking for seasoning or as stuffed peppers. Most of the nutritive value is retained but care must be taken not to expose the peeled fruit to the air because oxygen destroys vitamin C rapidly. It is better to leave the blistered and steamed peel on the pod of *poblano*-Ancho and Anaheim types. Bell types do not need to be peeled or blanched. Jalapeños and Serranos should be blanched 3 minutes or they will lose flavor and pungency. To freeze:

1. Blister and steam in a damp cloth but do not peel.

2. Remove the stem and seeds. If ample space is available, freeze whole and do this step after thawing. The less area exposed to the air, the more nutrients are preserved.

3. Flatten the whole pods to remove air and fold once for easy packing and handling.

4. Pack in a moisture-vapor-proof package, excluding as much air as possible. Double layers of waterproof paper between the pods will facilitate removal.

5. Freeze and store at or below 0°F (−17.8°C).

6. Storage life is about nine months to one year (Morris 1954).

Drying

SUN DRYING

Sun drying is a primitive method that is very satisfactory in arid climates but impossible in humid areas.

Green pods:

1. Select full-grown pods. Wash, peel, and slit the pod and remove the seeds and stem.

2. Spread the peppers in single layers on trays or racks. Tilt to face the sun. Turn the pods occasionally. Cover with cheesecloth to exclude dust and pests. Glass covering will increase the heat. Dry for 2 to 3 days, bringing trays in at night to prevent moisture from condensing on them. The product should be crisp, brittle, medium green. To use, soak 1 part pepper in 2 parts water for an hour or more.

Red pods: Use one of the following methods:

1. Let the pods remain on the plant until deep red. Select only mature pods. Using heavy twine, string through the stem end and hang in the sun to dry.

2. Let the pods ripen and remain on the plant until deep red; place on trays or heavy papers to dry in the sun.

3. Let the fruit ripen on the plant; place the pods on a sunny windowsill to dry.

Store the whole pods in jars in the refrigerator or grind them into powder and keep in a jar in the refrigerator. To use, soak 1 part pepper in 2 parts water for 2 hours.

DEHYDRATION

Dehydration is drying with artificial heat. Studies show that not only is the job done quicker but also the product is cleaner, has better color, and retains more of the nutritive value than in sun drying.

1. Peel the fruit.

2. Place the pods in a colander and blanch over boiling water for 10 minutes to destroy the enzymes that cause changes in color and flavor, if other than the paraffin method of peeling is used. This step can be omitted with long green/red chiles but not with Jalapeños, Poblanos, or Bells.

3. Cut the pods in half.

4. Spread the pods in a single layer between two pieces of cheesecloth on racks, nylon screen, or trays. Place in a dehydrator at 130°–135°F (54°–57°C) for about 8 hours. In an arid climate they may be dried in the sun but it takes longer.

The dehydrated product can be placed in a blender and chopped into flakes or powder. Once ground it will keep better refrigerated. It may also be used whole in recipes that require a long cooking time and a large amount of water.

HOW TO USE DRIED RED PEPPERS

The method is the same for any type of dried red pepper, such as Ancho or Anaheim. Rinse the pods in cold water, tear off the stem end, and shake out the seeds. Tear the pods into pieces and soak in warm water, about 6 to 1 cup, for half an hour. If they are very dry soak longer. Puree them with the water in which they have soaked in a blender or food processor fitted with a steel blade. The pastelike puree is then ready to be cooked in hot oil with the other ingredients specified in the recipe to make the sauce.

Canned *chipotles* or Moritas are pureed right out of the can without soaking. The small hot dried red peppers are usually just crumbled with the fingers. Always wash the hands in warm soapy water after handling peppers.

Store dried peppers in plastic bags or in jars in the refrigerator (Ortiz 1979).

Pickling

This method of preservation is used for Jalapeños and many other types of small podded fruits. It is but one of several workable methods and can be added to as taste dictates.

1. Wash the fruit.

2. Prick with a fork or toothpick.

3. Soak the pods in salt water for 24 hours. Use 1 part dairy or pickling salt (do not use table salt) to 15 parts water.

4. Remove the pods, rinse them in fresh water, and place them in a mesh bag.

5. Put the bag of peppers into boiling water and boil for 3 minutes.

6. Remove the bag and rinse in cold water. Drain.

7. Sauté onion slices in olive oil. To them, add garlic cloves and bay leaves.

8. Fill hot sterile glass jars with the pods, onion slices, and spices. Add the oil used to sauté the onions. Fill the remaining space with boiling white vinegar. Seal and let cure for 3 weeks before using.

Canning

The *Capsicum* is a low-acid vegetable, which must be canned in a pressure canner for safety. Temperatures higher than that of boiling water, 212°F (100°C), are required to destroy bacteria causing spoiling and disease. Because few homes have the proper equipment for this method, it is not recommended that such vegetables as beans and peppers be home canned. Always boil home-canned peppers for 15 minutes before eating. Caution is urged in preparation and usage to prevent botulism.

1. Peel the pods; remove the stems and seeds.

2. Pack the pods loosely in hot jars, leaving 1 inch (2.54 cm) head space.

3. Add salt: ¼ teaspoon to half pints and ½ teaspoon to pints.

4. Pour in boiling water, leaving 1 inch (2.54 cm) head space.

5. Tighten the lids and place the hot containers on the rack in a pressure cooker.

6. Fasten the lid on the canner so that no steam escapes around the edge. Let steam escape from the petcock for a full 10 minutes, then close petcock.

7. As soon as the gauge registers the pounds of pressure required for your altitude, control the heat unit to keep an even pressure for the recommended processing time.

Altitude in Feet	Pressure in Pounds
2,000–4,000	12
4,000–6,000	13
6,000–8,000	14
8,000–10,000	15

Jar Size	Processing Time
½ pint	30 minutes
1 pint	35 minutes

TO FIRM PEPPERS

Canned peppers are often softer than desired when put up at home. To achieve a firmer product, the pH should be 4.0 and a shorter processing time should be used. Hoover (1960, 5) suggests the following method:

1. Cut the pod into ⅜-inch pieces.

2. Dip the pieces in 0.3% to 0.4% lime (calcium carbonate) for 1 to 2 minutes while agitating.

3. Drain the pieces for 30 minutes.

4. Rinse the pieces thoroughly with cold water.

5. Blanch the rinsed pieces for 1 to 2 minutes in boiling water.

6. Put the pieces in sterile jars.

7. Fill the jars to within ½ inch (1.27 cm) of the top with a hot solution of 2% salt (sodium chloride) and enough citric acid (0.8% to 1.0%) dissolved in water to equalize contents at a pH of 4.0 (e.g., 1 quart water, 4 teaspoons salt, and 2 teaspoons citric acid).

8. Seal the jars while hot.

9. Heat the jars for 10 minutes in boiling water.

10. Remove the jars immediately and allow to cool.

The long green/red chile can be safely canned if the acidity level is increased (lowering the pH level); however, the flavor is changed somewhat. Two recipes developed at New Mexico State University can be safely canned in a water bath (*Chile Connoisseurs News* 1978, nos. 13–14).

Long Green/Red Chile and Tomatoes

3 cups peeled and chopped tomatoes
3 cups peeled and chopped long green/red chiles
1½ teaspoons salt
1¼ cups vinegar or lemon juice

Taco Sauce with Long Green/Red Chile

3 cups peeled and chopped tomatoes
3 cups peeled and chopped long green/red chiles or Jalapeños
¾ cup chopped onion
1½ teaspoons salt
3 cloves garlic, minced
1½ cups vinegar or lemon juice

Prepare each of the recipes as follows:

Combine all ingredients. Bring to a boil, cover, and simmer 5 minutes. Pack in hot, clean jars. Use all liquid divided evenly among the jars. Adjust the lids. Process in water bath for 30 minutes. Start counting processing time when water returns to boiling.

Recipes

The following recipes were selected as being very typical, if not the most typical, of the edible cultivars pictured in this book. Lenore Schofield, a native of Peru, assisted in the selection of recipes typical of the South American cultivars. The remainder were chosen by me. All the recipes were tested by me and served to guests at a series of "guinea pig" dinners. The original recipes have been adapted to American preferences in taste and cooking method. In several instances a different recipe would have been selected if it had not been my intent to present one of the most typical uses, even though it may not have been my preferred usage. In other words, these recipes may not represent the tastiest way to prepare a particular cultivar, but they are all good.

The Latorre (1977) and Ortiz (1979) books give the reader many other choices, as do a myriad of recipe books on the market. I went to Mexico City to purchase the proper peppers and spices for the recipes; however, such exotic items are becoming more common in U.S. markets.

Caution: Before proceeding with the recipes, read how to peel peppers at the beginning of this chapter.

Easy Chile Relleno Casserole

This recipe was introduced by the International Connoisseurs of Green and Red Chile as a substitute for the tedious, fried *chile rellenos*. The rich, custardy dish is a real delicacy when served as either an entrée or a side dish.

SERVES 6 TO 8

1 10-ounce can whole long green/red chiles
⅔ pound sharp Cheddar cheese, grated
¾ cup cracker crumbs
4 eggs, slightly beaten
1½ cups milk
½ teaspoon salt
¼ teaspoon pepper
¼ cup flour

Preheat oven to 350°F

Drain chiles and remove seed clumps. Layer one-half of the chiles, opened flat, on the bottom of a greased 9 x 5–inch casserole. Cover with one-half of the cheese and repeat layers.

Combine eggs, milk, salt, pepper, and flour. Pour mixture over chiles and cheese, lifting to let egg mixture run underneath. Top with crumbs. Bake until knife inserted in center comes out clean (30 to 40 minutes).

Note: This can be gotten ready to bake ahead of time; to prevent sogginess, do not put the cracker crumbs on until just before baking. Do not bake ahead of time.

Enchiladas Coloradas
(Enchiladas with Red Sauce)

The variety of dishes called "enchiladas" (tortillas with *chiles*) is virtually unlimited but those made with a red *chile* sauce are the most common. They may be filled with cheese, beef, chicken, or whatever you care to try; these are cheese.

SERVES 6

Red Ancho Chile Sauce (Ortiz 1979, 130):
- 3 Anchos
- 1 cup boiling water
- 1 medium onion, finely chopped
- 1 clove garlic, minced
- 2 cups peeled, seeded, and chopped tomatoes
- 3 tablespoons salad oil
- 2–3 sprigs *epazote* or parsley, chopped
- ¼ teaspoon sugar
- Salt and pepper to taste
- 1 cup chicken or beef stock

Put the Anchos and the boiling water in a bowl to soak for 1 hour. Remove the seeds and veins; shred the Anchos. Put the *chiles* and *chile* water in a blender and reduce to a puree. Add the onion, garlic, and tomatoes; blend to a puree.

Heat the oil in a heavy skillet, add the puree, and cook 5 minutes over moderate heat, stirring constantly. Add the herbs, sugar, and salt and pepper to taste. Pour the mixture into a fairly large saucepan and add the cup of stock (more if needed) to thin the mixture to a souplike consistency. Simmer for 5 minutes. This can be made ahead of time and frozen; warm the sauce when ready to use.

THE ENCHILADAS:
- Vegetable oil
- 12 corn tortillas
- 1 pound longhorn or mild cheddar cheese, grated
- 1 medium onion, chopped

Heat the oil in a skillet; fry each tortilla on one side only until just soft, not stiff. Dip the fried tortilla in the warm sauce; remove and place on a flat surface. Fill the tortilla with a tablespoon each of the grated cheese and chopped onion. Roll and lay seam-side-down in a baking dish.

When all the tortillas are rolled, cover with the remaining sauce, especially the open ends. Sprinkle the rest of the cheese on top. Bake at 350° for 10 minutes or until the cheese is melted.

Banana Pepper Botanas
(In Mexico appetizers are called botanas)

SERVES 12 TO 24
- 12 fresh, sweet, yellow Banana peppers
- Roquefort Filling:
- 2 3-ounce packages cream cheese, softened
- 1 clove garlic, crushed
- 1 tablespoon mayonnaise
- ¼ cup crumbled Roquefort cheese
- Tabasco sauce, to taste
- 1 tablespoon Worchestershire sauce
- ½ cup chopped pecans (optional)
- Paprika for garnish

Wash and split peppers in half lengthwise. Remove the seeds and veins. Fill with your favorite cheese or meat filling, such as the Roquefort filling given here.

To make the filling: Place all the ingredients but the pecans in a food processor or blender. Blend until smooth. Stir in the pecans by hand.

Fill the Banana pepper halves with the cheese mixture and garnish with a dash of paprika. Serve cold. If too large, cut as desired.

Rice-and-Meat-Stuffed Bell Peppers

There are many recipes for stuffed Bell peppers; this one is presented because it can be prepared ahead of time and cooked for a short period when you come home from work.

SERVES 4
- 2 large green Bell peppers
- 2 tablespoons fat
- ½ pound ground beef
- 3 tablespoons minced onion
- 1 cup cooked rice

2 eggs, well beaten
2 canned tomatoes, mashed; reserve remainder of can
½ teaspoon salt
  Tabasco sauce, to taste
¼ teaspoon pepper
1 teaspoon Worcestershire sauce

Preheat oven to 350°

Wash, stem, halve, seed, and devein the peppers. Parboil the 4 halves for 3 minutes.

Melt fat in a large skillet. Add the meat and onion; stir until cooked.

Add the rest of the ingredients to the meat mixture; mix well. Fill the pepper halves.

Place in a 9-inch square baking dish. Pour the remainder of the can of tomatoes on and around the stuffed pods. Bake for 20 minutes.

Bacalao-a-la-Vizcaíno
(Salt Cod Biscay Style)

This is a Basque dish from northern Spain. In Mexico, families of Spanish descent serve *bacalao* prepared this way as a traditional Lenten dish using the Carricillo, a pungent yet delicately flavored *chile*. In Spain a nonpungent type would be used in its place. This is strictly for salt cod fanciers.

SERVES 10 TO 12

2 pounds *bacalao* (salt cod fish)
2 pounds fresh tomatoes
3 sprigs parsley, chopped
½ cup olive oil
5 cloves garlic, minced
1 cup chopped onion
1 small can red pimento
  Chopped Carricillo, to taste

Soak the fish overnight in cold water. Drain; add fresh water and parboil until it flakes. Drain; flake the fish.

Puree the tomatoes and parsley in a blender or processor.

In a skillet sauté the garlic and onion in oil until translucent. Add the tomato puree. Simmer until thick (about 15 minutes), stirring occasionally. Add the flaked fish, pimento, and Carricillo.

Serve over rice or in pastry shells.

Carne a la Jacaranda
(Meat Jacaranda Style)

This specialty of the Jacaranda restaurant in Muzquiz, Mexico, was the favorite dish of Dolores Latorre (1977, 55) during the twelve years she lived in that village while studying the Kickapoo Indians.

SERVES 4

1 pound lean round steak, cut into ½-inch cubes
1 tablespoon flour
  Salt to taste
  Freshly ground black pepper
2 tablespoons salad oil
1 medium onion, chopped
1 tomato, peeled, coarsely chopped
1 clove garlic, minced
½ teaspoon cumin
  Ground Cascabel or cayenne pepper to taste

Sprinkle the meat with a mixture of the flour, salt, and pepper. In a heavy iron skillet, heat the oil until it smokes. Quickly brown the meat in the oil. Mix the other ingredients in a blender and add to the meat. Cook until done. If the sauce is too thick, add beef stock or hot water.

Shrimp Creole

This is an old-time favorite adapted from the *Original Picayune Creole Cook Book* (1947, 59). It is a great party dish served over steamed rice. Most cooks tend to overcook both the shrimp and the sauce; if cooked too long it loses the fresh taste and takes on the character of spaghetti sauce.

SERVES 8

1 bunch celery and tops
1 large onion, quartered
12 bay leaves
4 cloves garlic
4 lemons, quartered
1 teaspoon cayenne pepper
4 tablespoons salt
1½−2 pounds medium shrimp
1 onion, chopped
1 tablespoon olive oil
1 No. 2½ can tomatoes or 12 large, ripe tomatoes, finely chopped
4 stalks celery, chopped
1−2 cloves garlic, minced

1 sprig fresh thyme or a pinch of dried

2 bay leaves

¼–½ teaspoon cayenne powder

Salt, to taste

Put the first seven ingredients into a 5-quart pot; cover with water. Boil for 10 minutes. Add the shrimp and boil 10 minutes more, until the shrimp are pink. Drain and peel the shrimp, leaving them whole; set aside.

In a deep skillet or Dutch oven, sauté the onion in the oil. Add the rest of the ingredients. Cook 20 minutes, stirring frequently. Add the peeled shrimp. Cook 10 minutes more. *Caution*: never pour water into stewed shrimp as the tomato juice makes gravy enough. Remove the bay leaves. Serve over steamed rice.

Pepperonata

This Italian vegetable dish is good with broiled meats or served as an antipasto. Cubanelles are very flavorful sweet peppers that can be used in any recipe that calls for Bells or any sweet pepper.

SERVES 2; 4 TO 6 AS AN ANTIPASTO

1 tablespoon olive oil

2 large Cubanelles, quartered

1 small onion, diced

Salt and pepper, to taste

1 clove garlic, minced

⅓ cup tomato sauce (recipe follows)

½ cup grated Parmesan cheese

Preheat oven to 400°F

Sauté the Cubanelles and onion in olive oil in a skillet on medium heat for 4 to 5 minutes.

Add salt and pepper and put in an ungreased baking dish. Sprinkle garlic on top of the pepper-onion mix. Pour the tomato sauce over the peppers, onion, and garlic. Sprinkle cheese on top.

Bake, uncovered, for 15 minutes.

Tomato Sauce

YIELDS ABOUT 6 CUPS

1 tablespoon olive oil

1 tablespoon butter

1 small onion, chopped

1 medium carrot, chopped

1 stalk celery, chopped

2 28-ounce cans peeled Italian tomatoes, chopped, and their liquid

2 tablespoons tomato paste

4 cloves garlic, minced

1 bay leaf

11 teaspoons oregano

½ teaspoon basil

1 Serrano, minced

1 tablespoon sugar

½ cup red wine

Salt and pepper, to taste

1 tablespoon olive oil

Sauté the onion in the fats until translucent. Add the carrot and celery; sauté on medium heat for 5 minutes.

Add tomatoes and liquid, tomato paste, garlic, bay leaf, oregano, basil, Serrano, sugar, and wine to the onion mix and bring to a boil on high heat, stirring frequently; simmer, uncovered, on low heat for 1 hour.

Season with salt and pepper; strain through a fine sieve (it should be thick).

When desired consistency is reached, remove from the heat; add oil but do not mix in. Allow sauce to cool, uncovered and unrefrigerated, for at least 4 hours.

Covered, this may be refrigerated for up to 2 weeks, or it may be frozen.

Salsa Cruda
(Hellfire and Damnation Sauce)

This is probably the most commonly used condiment in Mexico and can be found on tables there at any time of the day. This uncooked *salsa* should be made up at the last minute in order to ensure the desired crunchiness, which is lost after several hours. It goes as well on your morning eggs as it does on supper tacos or fajitas.

YIELDS ABOUT 1 TO 1½ CUPS

1 medium unskinned tomato, finely chopped

½ medium onion or 2–3 green onions, finely chopped

6 sprigs fresh cilantro (culantro, Chinese parsley), chopped

3 Fresnos, chopped (or any green chile-pepper, e.g., Serrano)

½ teaspoon salt

⅓ cup cold water or ⅓ cup lime juice or ⅙ cup water and ⅙ cup vinegar

Mix together in a bowl.

Jalapeños en Escabeche
(Pickled Jalapeños)

This recipe was given to me by an old friend and *chile* aficionado, the late Frank X. Tolbert. *Escabeche* means pickled. Any fresh green or yellow chili-pepper can be used in this recipe.

Important note: Peppers, like beans, grow much bacteria when only partially cooked; therefore, it is important to acidify the fruit with vinegar. If you plan to store them for more than a few weeks, they should be processed.

YIELDS 6 PINTS

1½–2 pounds Jalapeños
  1½ pounds pickling salt
  ¾ cup olive oil
  2 medium onions, sliced
  12 cloves garlic, peeled
1–2 bay leaves
  3 teaspoons pickling spice
  3 cups 4% white vinegar

Wash the Jalapeños with the stems on. Puncture each with a toothpick or an ice pick. Soak the *chiles* in salt water for 24 hours (1½ pounds pickling salt to 1 gallon water), making certain all the pods are under water. Take the Jalapeños out, dry them, and put them in a mesh bag. Drop the bag into boiling water; let boil about 3 minutes. Remove the *chiles* from the bag and rinse them in cold water. Drain.

Heat the oil in a heavy skillet; sauté the onions, garlic, and bay leaves until soft. Fill 6 sterile glass pint jars with the Jalapeños. Place equal portions of the oil and sautéed ingredients along with ½ teaspoon of the pickling spice in each jar. Fill up the remaining space with vinegar to within ½ inch from the top. Seal and process in a hot-water bath for 20 minutes by placing the hot filled jars in hot water to cover. After the water boils, keep boiling for 20 minutes covered. Remove from the water immediately. Let season for 3 weeks before using.

Note: Carrot slices may be sautéed and added to the jars for color.

Chilaqueles con Pollo
(Chicken Chilaqueles)

Chilaqueles, meaning *chiles* with greens or edible herbs, is a dish designed to use up stale tortillas. There are as many variations as there are cooks. This one is mine. The Guajillo not only has a distinctive flavor but also is a strong coloring agent. Anchos may be substituted for Guajillos. Chilaqueles, without chicken, are often served at breakfast.

SERVES 6 TO 8

  About 2 dozen tortillas or 1 pound dry tortilla quarters or 1 pound packaged natural *toastado* triangles
  1½ cups shredded Monterey Jack cheese
2–3 cups cooked shredded chicken
3–4 cups chicken broth
  1 cup sour cream
  1 medium onion, sliced in thin rings

Sauce:

  6 Guajillos
  2 Anchos
  1 cup boiling water
  ½ cup chicken broth
  ½ medium onion, chopped
  2 cloves garlic
  ¼ teaspoon cumin seed
    Salt to taste
  2 tablespoons olive or salad oil

Soak the *chiles* in the hot water for 1 hour. Remove the *chiles* from the water, devein, seed, and shred. Place the *chiles* and the broth in a blender with the onion, garlic, cumin seed, and salt and puree. Heat the oil and cook the puree until it is darkened.

Use a large flameproof dish or casserole. Layer the bottom with one-third of the tortilla pieces. Cover with one-third of the cheese, one-third of the sauce, and one-third of the chicken. Repeat the layers twice. Add the broth and bring to a boil. Simmer until the broth is cooked down. This can also be done in a 350° oven, but it takes longer.

When the desired consistency is reached, cover the top with sour cream and garnish with onion rings just before serving. Do not assemble this until you are ready to start cooking so that the tortillas will not disintegrate. Use your judgment when cooking the broth down. Some like this dish soupier than others.

Chalupas de Chile Pasilla
(Chalupas with Pasilla Chile Sauce)

The most traditional dish using the Pasilla is Turkey in Mole Sauce, but this is a long-drawn-out procedure that few modern cooks would care to tackle. Besides, *mole* sauce is now available in cans. The Pasilla has a rich earthy flavor. The sauce used on these chalupas is also good on eggs (Latorre 1977, 40).

SERVES 6

- 3 Pasillas
- 1 cup boiling water
- 1 medium onion, finely chopped
- 2 cloves garlic, minced
- 3 large tomatoes, peeled and chopped
- 1 teaspoon sugar
- ½ teaspoon oregano
- 4 tablespoons salad oil, divided
  Salt and freshly ground pepper to taste
- 2 dozen tortillas
- 1½ cups cooked shredded pork or chicken
- ½ cup crumbled feta cheese

Soak the Pasillas in the hot water for 1 hour; remove the seeds, devein, and shred. Put the Pasillas and the *chile* water in a blender. Add the onion, garlic, tomatoes, sugar, and oregano and puree. Heat 1 tablespoon of oil in a heavy skillet and fry the puree for 10 minutes over a moderate fire, stirring constantly. Season with salt and pepper. Set aside.

Heat 3 tablespoons of oil (add more if necessary) in a heavy skillet and fry each tortilla until crisp. Place the tortillas on a plate or on large platter. Put 1 or 2 tablespoons of meat on each, cover with hot Pasilla sauce, sprinkle with cheese, and serve immediately.

Italian Salad

The Pepperoncini is used primarily as a pickled condiment. It is also delicious when fresh and ripe red chopped in a tossed green salad. This Italian salad may be prepared ahead of time.

SERVES 6

- 1 cup diced cooked beets
- 1 cup diced cooked carrots
- 1 cup chopped celery
- ½ cup chopped cooked asparagus tips
- ½ cup cooked peas
  Mayonnaise

Garnishes:
Filets of anchovies
Pepperoncini pickles
Black olives
Capers

Prepare beets and carrots; chill several hours. Combine with celery, asparagus tips, peas, and mayonnaise. Mound on lettuce and add garnishes.

Pimento Cheese Spread

YIELDS 6 CUPS

- ½ small onion, minced
- 1 pound sharp Cheddar cheese, grated
- 1 pound Velveeta cheese, grated
- 1 7-ounce jar pimentos, chopped
- 2 teaspoons salt
- 2 tablespoons Worcestershire sauce
- 2 tablespoons vinegar
- 1 pint mayonnaise (not salad dressing)
  Cayenne pepper, to taste
  Paprika, to taste
  Garlic, onion, or celery salts to taste, if desired

Combine all ingredients. Add seasonings to taste.

Guacamole
(Avocado Salad)

YIELDS 2 CUPS

- 4 ripe avocados, peeled and mashed with a fork
- 1 small tomato, chopped
- 1 tablespoon minced onion
- 1 clove garlic, juice only
- 1 or more fresh Serranos, seeded and minced
  Lemon juice, to taste
  Salt and pepper, to taste

Mix all the ingredients in a bowl. This mixture should have some texture. If a processor is used, care must be taken to keep the mixture from becoming too smooth.

Veal Paprika with Noodles

Paprika originated in Hungary as did this rather heavy dish. It will seem fairly bland compared to the Mexican and South American dishes given here.

SERVES 4

¼ cup salad or olive oil
½ cup chopped onions
¼ cup chopped sweet green tomato pepper
 1 tablespoon paprika
 2 pounds veal, cubed
⅓ cup flour
 1 teaspoon salt
½ teaspoon black pepper
½ cup hot water

Sauce:
 1 tablespoon butter or margarine
 1 tablespoon flour
½ teaspoon paprika
½ cup milk
 1 cup sour cream
 Noodles

Heat the oil in a Dutch oven; add the onions and peppers; simmer slowly until golden. Add the paprika. Salt and pepper the veal; dredge it in the flour; add to the onions and peppers and brown slowly. Add the hot water to the meat mixture; cover and simmer. Stir frequently, adding additional hot water as necessary to keep from sticking. Cook until tender (45 to 60 minutes).

To make the sauce: In a saucepan melt the butter; stir in the flour and paprika until smooth. Remove from the heat; gradually add the milk, stirring constantly. Return to low heat; cook until thickened. Remove from the heat. Slowly add the sour cream to the white sauce.

Measure and prepare the noodles as directed on the package.

Add the sauce to the meat mixture. Cook over low heat, stirring constantly, for 3 to 5 minutes or until heated; do not boil. Serve over the boiled noodles.

Chiltecpin Jelly

This is a delightful accompaniment to meat and cheese dishes. It is a favorite served with cream cheese and club crackers as a *botana* (appetizer). It offers a snappy hot contrast to bland food, much as do the sweet and sour sauces used with Chinese dishes. Any chile-pepper can be substituted for the Chiltecpin. Many cooks use Jalapeños; however, the Chiltecpin imparts a very special flavor.

YIELDS 7 CUPS

¼ cup chopped red or green Chiltecpins
¾ cup chopped sweet peppers, any variety
6½ cups sugar
1½ cups vinegar
 6 ounces Certo liquid fruit pectin
 Red or green food coloring

Seed and devein the sweet peppers. Leave the hot Chiltecpins whole. Chop the peppers together in a processor or blender. Mix the peppers, sugar, and vinegar. Bring to a boil for 2 minutes. Cool 5 minutes. Add the pectin and one or two drops of food coloring; boil for 1 minute (do not exceed time or jelly will sugar). Pour into hot sterile jars.

For a clear jelly, strain the mixture after it has boiled for 2 minutes; return to the pan, bring to a boil, and continue as directed.

Microwave instructions:

Mix the ground peppers and their juices with the sugar and vinegar in a 5-quart casserole. Cover and bring to a boil on HIGH (100%); boil 10 to 12 minutes, stirring once. Let stand 5 minutes.

Add liquid fruit pectin and 2 or 3 drops of food coloring. Stir well. Pour into hot sterilized jars, seal with lids and store in the refrigerator.

Caution: Use the bottled pectin exactly according to the directions on the label. Overcooking results in the formation of sugar crystals, resulting in a sugared jelly.

Oyster Stew

Oyster stew or soup is a southern specialty that evolved in the antebellum period. There are many variations, some with onions and herbs, others without milk, but this is my favorite.

Tabasco Pepper Sauce was invented for oysters, or was it vice versa?

SERVES 4 TO 6

 4 dozen large oysters, sautéed in 2 tablespoons butter
 1 tablespoon butter
 1 tablespoon flour
 1 pint oyster liquor, heated
 1 pint half-and-half, heated

½ teaspoon Tabasco Pepper Sauce
  Salt and pepper, to taste

Drain the oysters in a colander. Sauté oysters, in just enough butter to keep from sticking, until their edges curl. Set aside.

In a sauce pan, melt butter and stir in flour until there is a smooth paste. Gradually add the warmed oyster liquor, stirring constantly, until thickened. Gradually stir in the warm half-and-half, taking care not to scorch. Add the seasonings. Bring to a boil once and add the sautéed oysters. After heating for 3 minutes serve in bowls. Pass the Tabasco Pepper Sauce.

Anticuchos
(Skewered Beef Heart)

Antichuchos, according to Ortiz (1979, 21), are the most famous of all Peruvian *entradas*, or appetizers. Beef heart must be ordered ahead of time or substitute a lean cut, such as round steak. If the Cusqueños are not available, use Guajillo, De Arbol, or some light-colored dried chili-pepper. The Ancho and Pasilla are much too dark and the flavor is not the same.

SERVES 8 TO 10
Marinade:
1 beef heart (about 4 pounds) or beef round, cubed
1 cup red wine vinegar
1 head garlic, about 16 cloves
1 tablespoon diced fresh chili-peppers (e.g., Serrano)
1 tablespoon ground cumin (comino)
  Salt and pepper, to taste

Sauce:
1 cup diced dried Cusqueño
1 tablespoon ground annatto or paprika
1 tablespoon vegetable oil
  Salt, to taste

To make the marinade: Remove the nerves and fat from the beef heart; cut into 1-inch cubes. Put into a large bowl and cover with vinegar and spices, adding more vinegar if necessary to cover. Refrigerate, covered, for 24 hours. Remove the meat from the marinade and set both aside.

To make the sauce: Remove the seeds from the *chile*; soak in hot water to cover for 30 minutes. Drain and put into a blender with the annatto or paprika, oil, and ¾ cup reserved marinade. Season to taste and blend until smooth. Sauce should be quite thick.

To make the anticuchos: Thread the meat on skewers. Brush with the sauce; broil, turning to cook all sides, over charcoal or under a gas or electric broiler, about 3 inches from the heat for 4 minutes. Serve with sauce on the side.

Ají de Gallina
(Chicken in Pepper Sauce)

This variation of an unusual Peruvian dish is delightful (adapted from Ortiz 1979, 175). It may be prepared ahead of time and frozen. Allow it to return to room temperature before heating.

SERVES 8 TO 10
1 3½-to-4-pound chicken, quartered
1 large onion, quartered
2 to 3 stalks celery
1 teaspoon salt
1 teaspoon pepper
  Water to cover

Sauce:
2 cups fresh bread crumbs
2 cups milk
2 medium onions, chopped
2 cloves garlic, minced
5 fresh Puca-uchus or Serranos
2 medium tomatoes

1 cup grated Parmesan cheese, divided
6 ounces walnuts, chopped
  Salt and pepper, to taste
½ cup cracker crumbs
½ cup sliced black olives
4 eggs, hardboiled, sliced lengthwise

Cook chicken, onion, celery, and seasonings in a large pot until tender. Allow to cool in the stock. Remove the skin and bones; shred the meat. Strain the stock. Set the chicken and stock aside.

To make the sauce: Soak the bread crumbs in the milk in a large mixing bowl. Sauté the onions and garlic until golden, then add to the soaked crumbs. Puree the peppers and tomatoes in a processor or blender; add to the crumb mixture. Put the sauce in a large pan; cook until it thickens.

Preheat oven to 350°

Add chicken, 1 cup chicken stock, ½ cup cheese, walnuts, and seasonings to the sauce. Cook over medium heat for about 5 minutes, stirring frequently. Pour into a greased 9 x 15 x 2-inch baking dish.

Spread ½ cup cheese and cracker crumbs over the top of the chicken and sauce. Bake until very hot and bubbly (30 to 40 minutes).

Garnish with black olives and egg slices.

Pebre
(South American Hot Sauce)

YIELDS 1 CUP

  1 medium onion, minced
  1 clove garlic, minced
  2 tablespoons finely chopped cilantro
  1 tablespoon finely chopped parsley
  2 or more *chinchi-uchus*, seeded and finely chopped
    (Serranos may be substituted)
  3 tablespoons olive oil
  1 tablespoon lemon juice
    Salt, to taste

The number of *chiles* used in this sauce is up to personal taste; more or less may be used. Combine all the ingredients in a bowl and let stand for about 1 hour before serving for the flavor to develop. Serve with any meat. (Adapted from Ortiz 1979, 311.)

Ixni-Pec
(Habañero Pepper Sauce)

The golden Habañero is the hot pepper commonly used on the Yucatán peninsula, around the Caribbean, and in Trinidad. It is very aromatic as well as flavorful . . . and hot! I like to add one or two to two pounds of pinto beans. In Yucatán the black bean is used and the number of Habañeros is increased. If you intend to cut or mash this very hot pepper, protect your hands.

YIELDS 1 CUP

  ¼ cup finely chopped onion
  ¼ cup finely chopped tomato
  ¼ cup finely chopped Habañero; rinse if pickled
  ¼ cup Seville orange juice, or use ⅔ orange juice to ⅓
    lime juice to make ¼ cup
    Salt to taste

In a bowl combine the onion, tomato, and Habañero. Add enough orange juice to make it soupy, about ¼ cup. Add salt to taste. Serve with Yucatecan or any other dishes calling for a hot sauce. Use the same day.

(Ortiz 1979, 312)

Papas a la Huncaina
(Potatoes with Cheese and Rocoto Sauce)

The potato originated in Peru; consequently, dozens of varieties are to be found there. A Peruvian friend said that this recipe used a yellow type, but when she couldn't get any she put yellow food coloring in the water the potatoes are boiled in. This dish is a little trouble, but don't omit anything—it's a real treat (adapted from Ortiz 1979, 219).

SERVES 8 TO 10

  ½ cup lemon juice
  ¼ teaspoon cayenne pepper
  1 large onion, thinly sliced
  8 medium potatoes or 16 small new potatoes

Sauce:
1 or 2 *rocotos* or 4 or 6 Serranos, seeded and chopped
  3 cups chopped Muenster cheese
  1 teaspoon *palillo* or turmeric
1½ cups heavy cream
  ⅓ cup olive oil

    Lettuce leaves
  4 eggs, hardboiled, sliced lengthwise
  3 ears corn, cooked and cut into 6 pieces each
  12 black olives, chopped

Marinate the onion slices in the lemon juice and cayenne pepper at room temperature for several hours.

Boil the potatoes unpeeled until tender; drain, peel, and keep warm.

To make the sauce: Combine the *chiles*, cheese, *palillo* or turmeric, and cream in a blender or processor; blend until smooth. Heat the oil in a skillet; pour in the cheese mixture; reduce the heat to low. Cook, stirring constantly with a wooden spoon, until creamy.

To serve: Garnish the serving platter with lettuce leaves; arrange the hot potatoes on the platter; cover with the sauce. Arrange the egg slices, corn, and olives around and between the potatoes. Drain the marinated onion rings and arrange them over the potatoes.

Note: The Ortiz recipes were adapted by permission of Alfred A. Knopf, Inc., and Collier Associates from *The Book of Latin American Cooking*, by Elisabeth Lambert Ortiz. Copyright © 1979 by Elisabeth Lambert Ortiz. The Latorre recipes were adapted by permission of Encino Press from *Cooking and Curing with Mexican Herbs*, by Dolores L. Latorre. Copyright © 1977 by Encino Press.

APPENDIX
Seed Sources
Events Featuring Peppers

Seed Sources

Seed Suppliers Offering Twelve or More Capsicum *Cultivars*

[W&R] = wholesale and retail; [W] = wholesale only

1. Blum Seeds [W&R]
   Idaho City Stage
   Boise, ID 83707
2. Brawley Seed Co. [W&R]
   1010 North Main Street
   P.O. Box 180
   Mooresville, NC 28115
3. D. V. Burrell Seed Growers [W&R]
   P.O. Box 150
   Rocky Ford, CO 81067
4. W. Atlee Burpee [W&R]
   300 Park Avenue
   Warminster, PA 18974
5. Comstock, Ferre & Co.
   263 Main Street
   Wethersfield, CT 06109
6. William Dam Seeds
   P.O. Box 7400
   Dundas, Ontario
   Canada L9H6M1
7. Dominion Seed House [Canada only]
   Georgetown, Ontario
   Canada L7G4A2
8. Exotica Seed Co.
   8033 Sunset Boulevard, Suite 125
   West Hollywood, CA 90046
9. Farmer Seed & Nursery Co.
   Faribault, MN 55021
10. Henry Fields Seed and Nursery Co.
    Shenandoah, IA 51602
11. de Giorigi Co., Inc.
    P.O. Box 413
    Council Bluffs, IA 51502
12. H. G. German Seeds, Inc.
    103 Bank Street
    Smethport, PA 16749

13. Gurney Seed & Nursery Co.
    Gurney Building
    Yankton, SD 57079
14. Joseph Harris Co., Inc. [W&R]
    Moretown Farm
    Rochester, NY 14624
15. Chas. C. Hart Seed Co. [W&R]
    304 Main Street
    P.O. Box 169
    Wethersfield, CT 06109
16. Hastings: Seedsman to the South
    434 Marietta Street, N.W.
    P.O. Box 4274
    Atlanta, GA 30302-4274
17. Horticultural Enterprises
    P.O. Box 340082
    Dallas, TX 75234
18. J. L. Hudson, Seedsman
    P.O. Box 1058
    Redwood City, CA 94064
19. Orol Ledden & Sons
    P.O. Box 7
    Sewell, NJ 08080-0007
20. Liberty Seed Co.
    P.O. Box 806
    New Philadelphia, OH 44663
21. Earl May Seed & Nursery Co.
    Shenandoah, IA 51603
22. McFadden Seeds
    P.O. Box 1800
    Brandon, Manitoba
    Canada R7A6N4
23. Meyer Seed Co.
    600 South Caroline Street
    Baltimore, MD 21231
24. L. L. Olds Seed Co. [W&R]
    P.O. Box 7790
    Madison, WI 53791
25. Geo. W. Park Seed Co.
    Cokesbury Road
    Greenwood, SC 29647

26. The Pepper Gal [lists 91 cultivars]
    10536 119th Avenue North
    Largo, FL 33543
27. Plants of the Southwest
    1570 Pacheco Street
    Santa Fe, NM 87501
28. Porter & Son, Seedsmen
    Stephenville, TX 76401
29. Redwood City Seed Co. [home growers only]
    P.O. Box 361
    Redwood City, CA 94064
30. R. H. Shumway Seedsman, Inc.
    628 Cedar Street
    P.O. Box 777
    Rockford, IL 61105
31. Stokes Seeds, Inc.
    737 Main Street
    P.O. Box 548
    Buffalo, NY 14240
32. Takii & Co. Ltd.
    P.O. Box 7
    to central
    Kyoto, Japan
33. Otis Twilley Seed Co.
    P.O. Box 65
    Trevose, PA 19047
34. Vaughn's Seed Co.
    5300 Katrine Avenue
    Downer's Grove, IL 60515
35. Vermont Bean Seed Co.
    Garden Lane
    Bomoseen, VT 05732
36. Asgrow Seed Co. [w]
    7000 Portage Road
    Kalamazoo MI 49001
37. ESCO Ltd. [w]
    Box 838
    Pharr, TX 78577
38. Petoseed Co., Inc. [w]
    P.O. Box 4206
    Saticoy, CA 93004-0206

USEFUL

The Non-Hybrid Garden Seed Inventory [a computerized inventory of all non-hybrid garden seeds available by mail order in the U.S.A. & Canada; lists 164 sweet peppers and 116 chili-peppers]

Seed Savers Exchange
RFD 2, Box 11
Princeton, MO 64673

Cultivars Offered

[*Names are those used in seed catalogs; numbers correspond to seed suppliers*]

SWEET

Ace: 4
Ace, New: 12, 30

Aconcagua: 6, 12, 15, 17, 25, 26, 37
Agronomico 10-6: 36
All American Bell Boy: 9
All Big: 12
Argo: 28, 30
Banana, Sweet: 1, 2, 3, 4, 5, 6, 11, 13, 14, 15, 16, 19, 20, 24, 25, 28, 30, 31, 33, 35, 36, 37, 38
Bell Boy: 2, 5, 6, 7, 12, 15, 16, 19, 28, 33, 35
Bell Boy Hybrid: 4, 10, 13, 22, 23, 24, 25, 31
Big Belle: 20
Big Bertha: 2, 7, 10, 13, 16, 19, 20, 23, 28, 30, 33, 34, 35
Blue Star: 36
Bountiful, Early: 11
Bull Nose, Large, Sweet: 6, 9, 11, 15, 25, 26, 29
Burpee's Fordhook: 4
Burpee's Tasty Hybrid: 4
California Wonder (Calwonder): 2, 4, 5, 6, 7, 9, 11, 12, 15, 16, 18, 19, 20, 23, 24, 25, 26, 28, 29, 30, 31, 32, 33, 34, 35, 36, 37, 38
Cal Wonder, Early: 5, 11, 12, 14, 20, 32, 34, 36, 38
Cal Wonder, Golden: 2, 4, 7, 18, 24, 31
Cal Wonder 300: 38
Canada Bell, Early: 30
Canada Cheese: 30
Canape: 11, 14, 30
Cherry, Sweet: 3, 4, 6, 7, 10, 11, 12, 13, 14, 15, 16, 17, 18, 20, 22, 24, 25, 26, 28, 30, 31, 33, 34, 37, 38
Chinense Giant: 31
Cubanelle: 1, 5, 6, 13, 15, 19, 20, 25, 26, 28, 30, 33, 34, 36, 38
Delaware Belle: 12
Dutch Treat: 2, 4, 5, 6, 7, 9, 10, 15, 25, 26, 31
Earliest Red Sweet: 30
Early California: 1
Emerald Giant: 11, 14, 20, 23, 33, 38
Express Bell: 32
Faribo Hybrid Pepper: 9
Festival: 16
Fushimi Long Green: 32
Gedeon Hybrid: 4, 26
Glory: 32
Golden Belle: 11, 23, 25, 28, 33, 34
Golden Wonder: 11, 37
Growner's Big Pack: 33
Gypsy: 2, 5, 7, 14, 15, 16, 20, 26, 28, 30, 31, 35
Gypsy Hybrid: 4, 6, 9, 10, 13, 19, 22, 24, 25, 33, 34
Harris Early Giant: 32
Hungarian Yellow Wax, Sweet: 7, 10, 11, 15, 19, 23, 26, 30, 34, 37, 38
Hybelle: 14
Italian Sweet: 12, 13, 17, 26, 28
Italian Sweet Frying: 12
Jade: 36
Keystone Giant No. 4: 36
Keystone Resistant Giant: 2, 10, 11, 12, 14, 20, 23, 26, 34, 38
Keystone Resistant Giant No. 3: 14, 36, 37, 38
King of the North: 10, 11, 12, 13, 18
Lady Bell: 14, 19
Liberty Bell: 30
Lincoln Bell: 30
Long Yellow Sweet: 12, 17, 38

Events Featuring Peppers

Hatch Valley Chile Festival
Labor Day weekend
Hatch Chamber of Commerce
Hatch, NM 87937

International Chile Conference
January
International Connoisseurs of Green and Red Chile
P.O. Box 3467
Las Cruces, NM 88003

Republic of Texas Chilympiad
Third weekend in September
Hays County Civic Center
San Marcos, TX 78666

The Whole Enchilada Fiesta
October
Las Cruces Chamber of Commerce
P.O. Box 519
Las Cruces, NM 88004

Wick Fowler Championship Chili Cookoff
First Saturday in November
Terlingua, TX 79852

World Championship Chili Cookoff
International Chili Society
P.O. Box 2966
Newport Beach, CA 92663

World Chile Faire
September
P.O. Box 879
Las Cruces, NM 88004

For listings of others, write:

Arizona Chili Society
221 S. Central–Lot #39
Avondale, AZ 85323

Calendar of Texas Events
Travel and Information Division
State Department of Highways and Transportation
Austin, TX 78701

Chile Appreciation Society International
c/o Caliente Chili, Inc.
P.O. Drawer 5340
Austin, TX 78763

International Connoisseurs of Green and Red Chile
P.O. Box 3467
Las Cruces, NM 88003

GLOSSARY

ACCRESCENT: continuing to grow after flowering.

ACHOCOLATADO: Spanish, meaning reddish-brown or chocolate colored.

ACHROMATIC: free from color.

ACUMINATE: long and pointed, tapering.

ADNATE: grown to, organically united with, another part, as stamens with the corolla tube or an anther in its whole length with the filament.

ANTHER: the pollen-bearing part of the stamen, borne at the top of the filament or sometimes sessile.

ANTHESIS: flowering; strictly, the time of expansion of a flower.

ARAWAKS: sometimes called Tainos; a spear- and dart-throwing group of American Indians who inhabited the Greater Antilles. They had come from the east bringing seed crops and agricultural practices originating in Meso-america. These had been obtained in a roundabout way after moving south through Central America, east across Tierra Firme, and then to the islands. Within twenty-eight years of the discovery, the Arawaks were virtually extinct (Sauer 1966).

ASYMMETRICAL: irregular arrangement of parts; inequality in number of whorls of a flower, as of sepals, petals, etc.

AUTOCHTHONOUS: sprung from the soil; native to a place; indigenous.

AXIL: upper angle that a petiole or peduncle makes with the stem that bears it.

BERRY: pulpy, indehiscent, few- or many-seeded fruit; the pulpy fruit resulting from a single pistil, containing one or more seeds but no true stone; e.g., tomato, grape.

CALYX: the outer circle of floral envelopes.

CAMPANULATE: bell shaped.

CAPSAICIN: the pungent principle in *Capsicum*; the vanillyl amide of Δ^6 8-methyl-nonenic acid,

$$\text{HO} \langle \rangle \begin{array}{c} \text{OCH}_3 \\ \end{array} \text{CH}_2\text{NHCO(CH}_2)\text{CH}=\text{CHCH(CH}_3)_2 \,,$$

(Nelson & Dawson 1923, 2179).

CARIBS: pre-Columbian American Indian bowmen, who came to inhabit the Lesser Antilles only a few generations before the discovery. They were more hostile than the Arawaks and, in the Spanish view, a Carib was one who practiced cannibalism, although this was not true in all of their domain.

CARMINATIVE: tending to relieve flatulence; warming.

CHALAZAL: the basal part of an ovule where it is attached to the funiculus.

COPROLITE: the petrified feces of extinct species.

CORDATE: heart shaped.

COROLLA: inner circle of floral envelopes; if the parts are separate, they are petals; if they are not separate, they are teeth, lobes, or divisions.

COTYLEDON: seed-leaf; the primary leaf or leaves in the embryo; in *Capsicum* it emerges on germination.

CROP: a broad term covering all that which is harvested regardless of its status as a domesticate. Both crop and weed are derived from the same progenitor.

CULTIVAR: a variety or race that has originated and persisted under cultivation; not necessarily referable to botanical species.

CULTIVATED: to cultivate means to conduct activities involving the care of a plant; it is concerned with human activities. Wild plants can be cultivated as well as domesticated ones; however, there is no genetic response.

CYATHIFORM: cup bearing; cup-shaped flowers; cup shaped, wider at the top than at the bottom.

DECIDUOUS: falling, as the leaves, at the end of one season of life; as leaves of nonevergreen trees.

DEHISCENCE: the method or process of the opening of a seed pod or anther.

DELTOID: triangular; deltalike.

DICHOTOMOUS: forked in one or more pairs.

DIFFUSIONIST: uses the deductive method to speculate beyond the available concrete evidence for transoceanic contact; uses similarities between the two areas as evidence of historical contact.

DIPLOID: having two sets of chromosomes in the somatic cells, as of all higher organisms; double the haploid number.

DISCOIDAL: a disk or disklike object; having only disk flowers or, in reference to stigmas, disk shaped.

DISSEPIMENT: a partition, as one of those that divide a compound pericarp into two or more cells.

DOMESTICATION: an evolutionary process operating under the influence of human activity. In plants there is genetic modification through selection. A domesticated type is entirely incapable of survival without the care of humans.

EMETIC: drugs or other means that produce vomiting.

ENDOSPERM: the albumen (starch-and-oil-containing tissue) of a seed; nutritive substance within the embryo sac of an ovule.

ENTIRE: margin is continuous, not in any way indented; whole.

FILAMENT: thread, particularly the stalk of the anther.

FLORILEGIUM (florilegia, pl.): collection of paintings of flowers.

FUNICULUS: the cord or stalk that connects the ovule or seed to the placenta of a plant.

GEOTROPICAL: a tendency for the roots of growing plants to turn toward the center of the earth.

GERMINATION: sprouting; beginning to grow.

GLABROUS: smooth, not hairy; glabrate, nearly glabrous.

HAPLOID: having the character of gametes with a reduced number of chromosomes; in contradistinction to the diploid with the doubled number found in somatic cells.

HOT CAP: individual plant covers to protect transplants.

IMBRICATE: overlapping, shingled.

INDEHISCENT: not regularly opening, as a seed pod or anther.

ISOLATIONIST: uses induction and admits documented evidence only while maintaining the position that the New World developed without any transoceanic contact with the Old World; a scientific approach.

LANCEOLATE: lance shaped; much longer than broad.

LEAF INDEX: width multiplied by one hundred, divided by length.

LITTORAL: of the seashore; *littoralis*.

LOBE: any part or segment of an organ; specifically, a part of a petal or calyx or leaf that represents a division to about the middle.

LOCULE: a small lobe; compartment or cell of an ovary; a descriptive term lacking morphological meaning.

LUX: the unit of illumination in the metric system.

MORPHOLOGY: that branch of biology which treats of the form and structure of plants and animals; the form of an organism considered apart from function.

MUCILAGINOUS: like musilage; gummy, soft, viscid.

NECTARY: the organ or gland of a plant that secretes nectar.

NUCELLUS: the body or essential part of a plant ovule, within which the embryo and its covering are developed.

NUCLEAR: pertaining to origins.

OBTUSE: blunt, rounded.

OVATE: with the outline like that of a hen's egg cut in two lengthwise.

OVULE: the body which after fertilization becomes the seed.

PATERIFORM: in the shape of a shallow, platelike vessel.

PEDICEL: stem of one flower in a cluster.

PEDUNCLE: stem of a flower cluster or of a solitary flower.

PERENNIAL: continuing through the year; lasting more than three seasons.

PERICARP: the wall of a ripened ovary; wall of a fruit, sometimes used to designate fruit.

PERIPHERIC: the outer wall or margin; the inner side or face of the ovary wall as opposed to the faces of its septa.

PERISTALSIS: a contractile muscular movement of any hollow organ of the body whereby the contents are gradually propelled toward the point of expulsion.

PETAL: one of the separate leaves of a corolla.

PETIOLE: leaf stalk.

pH: denoting the negative logarithm of the hydrogen-ion concentration, in grams per liter, of a solution; used in expressing relative acidity and alkalinity. The pH of pure water is 7 (neutral). To decrease acidity means decreasing the hydrogen-ion concentration, or a *rise* in the absolute value of pH.

PHYSIOLOGY: the branch of biology that treats of the vital phenomena manifested by animals or plants; the science of organic functions as distinguished from anatomy and morphology.

PISTIL: the ovule-bearing and seed-bearing organ, with style and stigma.

PLACENTA: the part or place in the ovary where the ovules are attached.

POLLINATION: the transfer of pollen from dehiscing anthers to the receptive stigma.

PROTOGYNOUS: a flower whose stigma is receptive to pollen before pollen is shed from anthers of the same flower.

PSYCHOTROPIC: acting on one's mind, e.g., a tranquilizer.

PUBESCENT: covered with short, soft hairs; downy.

RADICLE: the embryonic root below the cotyledon of a plant; the embyronic root of a germinating seed.

REPLICATION: that essential trait of repeating events.

REVOLUTE: rolled backward; margin rolled toward lower side.

ROTATE: wheel shaped.

RUBEFACIENT: causing redness of the skin.

SCABROUS: rough, not smooth.

SCARIFICATION: making slight incisions; to scratch.

SEPAL: one of the separate leaves of a calyx.

SEPTA: a partition; "septate" means divided by partitions.

SESSILE: not stalked; sitting.

SHAPE INDEX: length divided by width.

SIGMOID CURVE: curved like the letter *S*; Greek = sigma.

SOMATIC CELLS: pertaining to those elements or processes of an organism which are concerned with the maintenance of the individual as distinguished from the reproduction of the species.

STAMEN: the pollen-bearing male organ of the seed plant.

STIGMA: the part of the pistil that receives the pollen.

STYLE: the more-or-less elongated part of the pistil between the ovary and stigma.

SUCCULENT: juicy; fleshy; soft and thick in texture.

TOPONYM: a name derived from the name of a place.

TRUNCATE: appearing as if cut off at the end.

VAGAL: pertaining to the vagus, or pneumogastric nerve (10th cranial nerve), which controls throat, lungs, heart, stomach, and other abdominal motor secretory, sensory, and vasodilator fibers.

VALVATE: opening by valves or pertaining to valves; meeting of the edges without overlapping as leaves or petals in a bud.

WEED: a plant that grows in places disturbed by people, domesticated animals, or naturally.

WILD: has not been genetically manipulated by humans; however, it may be cultivated; may be spontaneous, not planted by humans.

ILLUSTRATED
GLOSSARY

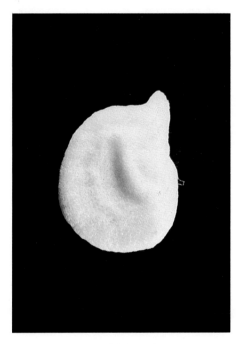 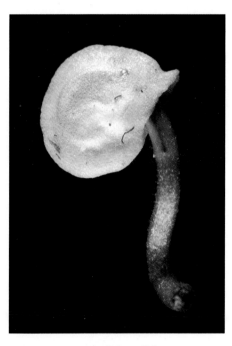

discoidal seed   seed with radicle

Capsicum Seed

A *Capsicum annuum* Group

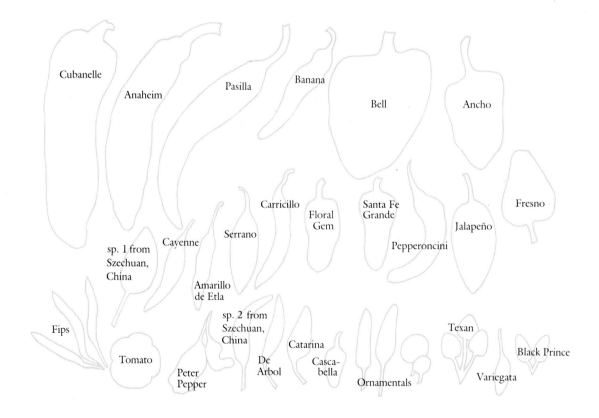

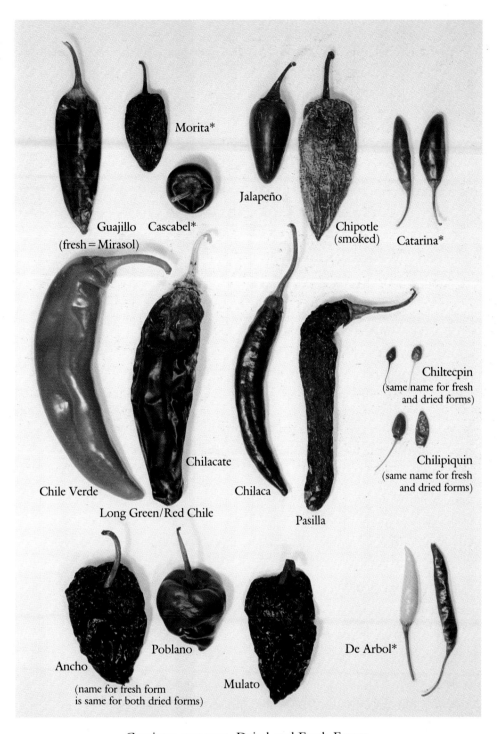

Morita*

Jalapeño

Guajillo   Cascabel*
(fresh = Mirasol)

Chipotle
(smoked)   Catarina*

Chiltecpin
(same name for fresh
and dried forms)

Chilacate

Chilipiquin
(same name for fresh
and dried forms)

Chile Verde

Long Green/Red Chile

Chilaca

Pasilla

Poblano

De Arbol*

Ancho
(name for fresh form
is same for both dried forms)

Mulato

Capsicum annuum, Dried and Fresh Forms

*Not used fresh.

C. annuum calyx   *C. annuum* corolla

C. frutescens calyx   *C. frutescens* corolla

Calyxes and Corollas of the Five Domesticated Species of *Capsicum*

C. baccatum calyx

C. baccatum corolla

C. chinense calyx

C. chinense corolla

C. pubescens calyx

C. pubescens corolla

exserted   same level   included

Stigma Position in Relation to Anthers at Full Anthesis

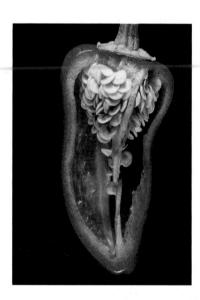

erect   pendent (declining)

Fruit Position   Cross Section of Fruit

one   two to three

Peduncle Number per Node

Position of Corolla at Anthesis

parallel to peduncle (pendent), *left*;
at right angles to peduncle (erect)

Shapes of Calyxes

cup shaped, *left*;
pateriform (saucer shaped)

BIBLIOGRAPHY

ACOSTA, J. DE
1590. *Historia natural y moral de las Indias en que se tratan las cosas notables del cielo, y elementos metales, plantas, y animales dellas: Y los ritos, y ceremonias, leyes, y gobierno, y guerras de los Indios.* Edited by Padre Ioseph de Acosta Religioso de la Compañía de Iesús. Seville.
1970. *The natural and moral history of the Indies.* Edited by C. R. Markham. New York: Lenox Hill Publishing Co. [Reprint of 1880 edition issued by Hakluyt Soc., London.]

ACTUARIUS, J.
1554. *Methodi mendeni de medicamentorum compositione Libri sex.* Cor. H. Mathisius. Venice.

ADAMS, C. F., AND M. RICHARDSON
1981. *The nutritive value of foods.* Home and Garden Bull. 72. Washington, D.C.: U.S. Dept. of Agriculture.

AGUIRRE BELTRÁN, G.
1973. *Medicina y mágica.* Mexico City: Inst. Nacional Indigenista.

AINSLIE, W.
1826. *Materia índica.* London: Longman, Rees, Orme, Brown, and Green.

ALVAREZ CHANCA, D. *See* Chanca, D. A.

AMERICAN PHARMACEUTICAL ASSOCIATION
1960. *Capsicum*: Cayenne pepper. In *National Formulary XI.* Washington, D.C.

AMERICAN SPICE TRADE ASSOCIATION
1966a. *A history of spices.* Englewood Cliffs, N.J.: American Spice Trade Assoc.
1966b. *What you should know about paprika.* Englewood Cliffs, N.J.: American Spice Trade Assoc.

ANDERSON, E.
1960. The evolution of domestication. In *Evolution after Darwin*, pp. 67–84. Chicago: Univ. Chicago Press.

ANGHIERA, P. M. D'
1493. *Decadas de nuevo mundo.* "Fifth Decade."
1904. *De orbo novo: The decades of the New World, or West India.* Vol. 5. Translated from Latin by Rycharde Eden. London: Hakluyt Soc.

AUCHTER, E. C., AND C. P. HARLEY
1924. Effect of various lengths of day on development and chemical composition of some horticultural plants. *Amer. Soc. Hort. Sci.* 21:199–214.

AVICENNA. *See* Husain, I. A. A.

BAILEY, L. H.
1923. *Capsicum. Gentes Herbarum* 1:128–129.
1933. *How plants get their names.* New York: Macmillan Co.

BAKER, H. G.
1971. Commentary: Section III. In *Man across the sea*, edited by C. L. Riley, J. C. Kelley, C. W. Pennington, and R. L. Rands, pp. 428–444. Austin: Univ. Texas Press.

BALBAA, S. I., M. S. KARAWYA, AND A. N. GIRGIS
1968. The capsaicin content of *Capsicum* fruits at different stages of maturity. *Lloydia* 31:272–274.

BALLARD, R. E., J. W. MCCLURE, W. H. ESHBAUGH, AND K. G. WILSON
1970. A chemosystematic study of selected taxa of *Capsicum. Amer. J. Bot.* 57:225–233.

BANCROFT, H. H.
1882. *Native races of the Pacific states of North America.* Vol. 2. San Francisco.

BARRACLOUGH, G. (ED.)
1982. *The Times concise atlas of world history.* Maplewood, N.J.: Hammond.

BATES, H., AND R. BUSENBARK
1970. *Finches and soft billed birds.* Neptune City, N.J.: T.F.H. Publishing Co.

BAUDIN, L.
1962. *Daily life in Peru.* New York: Macmillan Co.

BAUER, K. J.
1969. *Surfboats and horse marines: U.S. naval operations in the Mexican War, 1846–48.* Annapolis: U.S. Naval Inst.
1974. *The Mexican War, 1846–48.* New York: Macmillan Co.

BAUERNFEIND, J. C.
1975. Carotenoids as food colors. *Food Technol.* 29:48–49.

BENNETT, D. J., AND G. W. KIRBY
1968. Constitution and biosynthesis of capsaicin. *J. Chem. Soc.*, no. 442.

BESLER, B.
1613. *Celeberrimi eystettensis horti icones plantarum autumnalium.* Eichstätt: Norimb.

BESSER, W. S. J. G. VON
1811. *Catalogue des plantes du jardin botanique du Gymnase de Volhynie a Kryzemieniec.* Kremenets: Imprimerie de Gŷmnase.

BIRD, J. B.
1948. America's oldest farmers. *Natur. Hist.* 57:296–303, 334–335.
1967. Preceramic cultures in Chicma and Viru. In *Peruvian archaeology*, edited by J. H. Rowe and D. Menzel, pp. 54–61. Palo Alto, Calif.: Peek Publications.

BRAND, D. D.
1971. The sweet potato: An exercise in methodology. In *Man across the sea*, edited by C. L. Riley, J. C. Kelley, C. W. Pennington, and R. L. Rands, pp. 343–365. Austin: Univ. Texas Press.

BRAUER, O. H., AND R. W. RICHARDSON
1957. *El chile: Indicaciones generales para su cultivo.* Folleto de divulgación, no. 23. Mexico City: Sec. of Agr. and Livestock.

BRAVO, H.
1934. Estudio botánico acerca de las solanaceas mexicanas del género *Capsicum. Anales del Instituto de Biología* 5:303–321.

BRICKEL, E. D. (ED. CHM.)
1980. International code of nomenclature for cultivated plants, 1980. *Regnum vegtabile.* The Hague: Bohn, Sheltema, and Holkema.

BROWN, W. L.
1930. *Some effects of pimiento pepper on poultry.* Georgia Agr. Exp. Sta. Bull. 160.
1938. The influence of pimiento pigments on the color of the egg yolk of fowls. *J. Biol. Chem.* 122(3):655–659.

BRUMMETT, B.
1978. Processing outlook in Jalapeño and other pickling peppers. Paper presented at 2d Annual Texas Pepper Conf., McAllen, Tex.

BRYAN, H.
1982. Fluid drilling of pregerminated pepper seed. Paper presented at 6th National Pepper Conf., San Miguel de Allende, Mex.

BUBEL, N.
1978. *The seed-starter's handbook.* Emmaus, Penn.: Rodale Press.

BUKASOV, S. M.
1930. The cultivated plants of Mexico, Guatemala, and Colombia. *Bull. Appl. Bot., Gen., Plant Breed.* Suppl. 47:261–273. [In Russian, translated by N. P. Tarassuk.]

CAMP, W. H., V. R. BOSWELL, AND J. R. MAGNESS
1957. *The world in your garden.* Washington, D.C.: National Geographic Society.

CANDOLLE, A. P. DE
1852. *Prodromous.* 13:411–429. Paris: Masson.
1964. *The origin of cultivated plants.* London: Hafner Pub. Co. [Reprint of 1886 2d ed.]

CARTER, G. F.
1950. Plant evidence for early contacts with America. *Southwestern J. Anthropol.* 6:161–182.
1977. A hypothesis suggesting a single origin of agriculture. In *Origins of agriculture*, edited by C. A. Reed, pp. 89–133. The Hague: Mouton.

CASAS, B. DE LAS
1909. Apologética historia de las Indias. In *Historiadores de Indias*, by Marcelino Menéndez y Pelayo. Madrid.
1957–1961. *Historia de las Indias.* 2 vols. Biblioteca de Autores Españoles, vols. 95, 96. Madrid. [First published 1876, 5 vols., Madrid: Impr. de M. Ginesta.]

CHANCA, D. A.
1494. Letter to the municipal council of the city of Seville, Spain. In *The Letters of Christopher Columbus*, edited by R. H. Major, pp. 19–71. 2d ed. London: Hakluyt Society, 1870.

CHAPMAN, C. P.
1965. A new development in the agronomy of pimento. *Caribbean Quart.* 11(3–4):3–9.

CHILDRESS, M., AND C. CHILDRESS (EDS.)
1978. *Adventures in Mexican cookery.* San Francisco, Calif.: Ortho Books.

Chile Connoisseurs News
1974–1982. Vols. 4–22. La Mesilla, N.M.: International Connoisseurs of Green and Red Chile.

CIEZA DE LEÓN, P. DE
1864. Chronicle of Peru. In *The Travels of Pedro de Cieza de León, A.D. 1532–50 (Peru)*, edited by C. R. Markham, Part I (32). London: Hakluyt Soc. [First ed., Seville, 1553.]

CLUSIUS, C. *See* L'Éscluse, C.

COBO, B.
1653. Historia del Nuevo Mundo. In *Obras del P. Bernarbe Cobo de la compania de Jesús*, edited by F. Mateos, Part I of II. Madrid: Bibleoteca de Autores Españoles, 1964.

COCHRAN, H. L.
1932. Factors affecting flowering and fruit setting in the pepper. *Amer. Soc. Hort. Sci.* 29:434–437.
1935. Some factors which influence the germination of pepper seeds. *Amer. Soc. Hort. Sci.* 33:477–480.
1936. Some factors influencing growth and fruit setting in pepper (*Capsicum frutescens* L.). *Cornell Agr. Exp. Sta. Mem.* 190:1–39.
1938a. Flower and seed development in pepper. *Amer. Soc. Hort. Sci. Proc.* 77:449–451.
1938b. A morphological study of flower and seed development in pepper. *J. Agri. Res.* 56(6):395–419.
1940. Characters for the classification and identification of varieties of *Capsicum. Bull. Torrey Bot. Club* 67(8):710–717.

CODEX MENDOZA (MENDOCINO)
1938. *Codex Mendoza.* Edited and translated by James Cooper Clark. 3 vols. London: Waterlow.

COLUMBUS, C.
1493. The letter of Columbus to Luis de Sant Angel (Santangel) announcing his discovery (1493). *Harvard Classics* 43:22–28, 1910.

COOPER, J. E. (ED.)
1952. *With or without beans.* Dallas: W. S. Henson.

COPLEY, D. M.
1941. A new monograph for *Capsicum. Bul. Nat. Formulary Committee* 9(9):225–226, 9(10):300–301, 9(11):321–322.

CORLEY, W. L.
1970. *Evaluation of pepper plant introductions.* Southern Coop. Ser. Reg. Proj. S-9, Georgia Agr. Exp. Sta. Bull. 151.

CORLEY, W. L., AND A. H. DEMPSEY
1970. *Ornamental peppers for Georgia.* Univ. Georgia Coll. Agr. Exp. Sta. Res. Bull. 83.

COTNER, S.
1984. How to grow peppers like a pro. *Texas Gardener* 3(4):10–18.

CROSBY, A. W., JR.
1972. *The Columbian exchange: Biological and cultural consequences of 1492.* Westport, Conn.: Greenwood Press.

CURL, A L.
1962. The carotenoids of red bell peppers. *Agr. Food Chem.* 10:504–509.

D'ARCY, W. G.
1979. The classification of the Solanaceae. In *The biology and taxonomy of the Solanaceae*, edited by J. G. Hawkes, R. N. Lester, and A. D. Skelding, pp. 3–47. New York: Academic Press.

D'ARCY, W. G., AND W. H. ESHBAUGH
1973. The name for the common bird pepper. *Phytologia* 25(6):350.
1974. New World peppers (*Capsicum*-Solanaceae) north of Colombia: A résumé. *Baileya* 19(3):93–105.

DAVENPORT, W. A.
1970. A progress report on the domestication of *Capsicum* (chili peppers). *Proc. Assoc. Amer. Geogr.* 2:46–47.

DAVEY, B. L., M. L. DODDS, K. H. FISHER, C. SCHUCK, AND S. D. CHEN
1956. Utilization of ascorbic acid in fruits and vegetables. *J. Amer. Dietetic Assoc.* 32:1064–1068.

DEB, D. B.
1979. Solanacee in India. In *The biology and taxonomy of the Solanaceae*, edited by J. G. Hawkes, pp. 109–110. New York: Academic Press.

DECANDOLLE, A. *See* Candolle, A. P. de

DIEHL, A. K., AND R. L. BAUER
1978. Jaloproctitis. *N. Eng. J. Med.* 299(20):1137–1138.

DIERBACH, J. H.
1829. *Capsicum aviculare. Archiv des Apothekervereins* 30 (1):30.

DODOENS, R.
1583. *A new herball. Or history of the plants. Or cruydtboeck.* Translated and edited by H. Lyte. London.

DORAN, E., JR.
1971. The sailing raft as a great tradition. In *Man across the sea*, edited by C. L. Riley, J. C. Kelley, C. W. Pennington, and R. L. Rands, pp. 115–138. Austin: Univ. Texas Press.

DORLAND, R. E., AND F. W. WENT
1947. Plant growth under controlled conditions: VIII, Growth and fruiting of the chili pepper (*Capsicum annuum*). *Amer. J. Bot.* 34(8):393–401.

DUKE, J. A.
n.d. *Isthmian ethnobotanical dictionary.* Fulton, Md.: privately printed.

DUNAL, F. M.
1852. The Solanaceae. In *Prodromous*, by A. P. de Candolle, 13(1):411–429. Paris: Masson.

EKHOLM, G. F.
1964. Transpacific contacts. In *Prehistoric man in the New World*, edited by J. D. Jennings and E. Norbeck, pp. 489–510. Chicago: Univ. Chicago Press.

ELLIS, M.
1948. A study of peptic ulcer in Nigeria. *Brit. J. Surg.* 36:60–65.

EMBODEN, W. A., JR.
1960. A systematic study of the *Capsicum baccatum* complex. Master's thesis, Indiana Univ.
1961. A preliminary study of the crossing relationships of *Capsicum baccatum. Butler Univ. Bot. Study* 14:1–5.

ERWIN, A. T.
1929. A systematic study of the peppers *Capsicum frutescens* L. *Amer. Soc. Hort. Sci.* 26:128–131.
1932. The peppers. *Iowa Agr. Home Econ. Exp. Sta. Bull.* 293:120–152.
1937. Anthesis and pollination of *Capsicum. Proc. Amer. Soc. Hort. Sci.* 28:309.
1949. An interesting Guatemalan chili (*Capsicum guatemalense b. h.*). *Iowa Exp. Sta. Res. Bull.* 371:612–614.

ERWIN, A. T., AND C. C. LOUNSBERRY
1932. Nectaries of *Capsicum. Iowa State Col. J. Sci.* 6:227–285.

ESCH, T. A., AND D. E. MARSHALL
1983. Trash removal from mechanically harvested peppers. American Society of Agricultural Engineers. Paper no. 83-1072. June 26–29, 1983.

L'ÉSCLUSE, C. [CLUSIUS]
1601. *Rariorum plantarum historia.* Antwerp: C. Plantin.
1611. *Curae posteriores post mortem.* Antwerp.

ESHBAUGH, W. H., III
1964. A numerical taxonomic and cytogenetic study of certain species of the genus *Capsicum*. Ph.D. dissertation, Indiana Univ.
1968. A nomenclatural note on the genus *Capsicum. Taxon* 17:51–52.
1970. A biosystematic and evolutionary study of *Capsicum baccatum* (Solanaceae). *Brittonia* 22:31–43.
1971. A biosystematic and evolutionary study of *Capsicum pubescens* Ruiz & Pav. *Amer. Phil. Soc. Yearbook* (1971), pp. 315–316.
1975. Genetic and biochemical systematic studies of chili peppers (*Capsicum*-Solanaceae). *Bull. Torrey Bot. Club* 102(6):396–403.
1978. The taxonomy of the genus *Capsicum*-Solanaceae. *Acta Horticulturae* 15:13–26.
1979. Biosystematic and evolutionary study of *Capsicum pubescens* complex. *Nat. Geogr. Soc. Res. Rep.* 1970:143–162.
1980a. The taxonomy of the genus *Capsicum* (Solanaceae). *Phytologia* 47(3):153–166.
1980b. Chili peppers in Bolivia. *Plant Genet. Res. Newsletter* 43:17–19.

1980*c*. List of cultivars from Bolivian expedition. Typescript in files of the author.

In press. The genus *Capsicum* (Solanaceae) in Africa. *Bothalia*.

ESHBAUGH, W. H., AND P. G. SMITH
1971. A new variety of chili pepper: *Capsicum eximium* var. *tomentossum* (Solanaceae). *Baileya* 18(1):13–16.

ESHBAUGH, W. H., S. I. GUTTMAN, AND M. J. McLEOD
In press. The origin and evolution of domesticated *Capsicum* species. *Ethnobiology*.

ESHBAUGH, W. H., P. G. SMITH, AND D. L. NICKRENT
1983. *Capsicum tovarii* (Solanaceae), a new species of pepper from Peru. *Brittonia* 35(1):55–60.

F.A.O. *See* United Nations.

FERNÁNDEZ DE OVIEDO Y VALDÉS, G. *See* Oviedo y Valdés, G. F. de.

FINGERHUTH, K. A.
1832. *Monographia generis Capsici*. Dusseldorf: Arnz & Comp.

FISCHER, A.
1978. *Chili-lovers' cook book*. Phoenix, Ariz.: Golden West Publishers.

FISHBURN, M. T.
1981. *New Mexico chile peppers*. N.M. Crop and Livestock Reporting Service, N.M. Dept. Agri., Las Cruces, N.M.

FLANNERY, K. V.
1965. The ecology of early food production in Mesopotamia. *Science* 147(3663):1247–1256.

FLECKER, H.
1947. Injuries produced by plants in tropical Queensland. *Med. J. Australia* 1(25):636–637.

FLORES, I. M., AND B. P. CORTES
1966. *Taxonomía y distribución geográfica de los chiles cultivados en México*. Mexico City: Instituto Nacional de Investigaciones Agrícolas.

FLUCKIGER, F. A., AND D. HANBURY
1879. *Pharmocographia: A history of the principal drugs of vegetable origin, met with in Great Britain and British India*. 2d ed. London: Macmillan Co.

FRANCHET, A., AND L. SAVATIAT
1875. *Enumeratio plantarum*. 2 vols. Paris.

FREYRE, G.
1966. *The masters and the slaves: A study in the development of Brazilian civilization*. New York: Alfred A. Knopf.

FUCHS, L.
1543. *De historia stirpium commentarii insignes. Or new kreuterbuch*. Basel.

GAGE, T.
1928. *The English-American, his travail by sea and land; or, a new survey of the West India's*. Edited by A. P. Newton. London: Routledge. [Originally published in 1648.]

GARCIA, F.
1908. *Chile culture*. Coll. Agr. Mech. Bull. 67. Las Cruces, N.M.
1921. *Improved variety no. 9 of native chile*. Coll. Agr. Mech. Bull. 124. Las Cruces, N.M.

GARCILASO DE LA VEGA
1609. *Commentaries reales de los Incas*. Lisbon: P. Crasbeek.
1966. *Royal commentaries of the Incas*. Translated by H. V. Livermore. 2 vols. Austin: Univ. Texas Press.

GATHERCOAL, E. N., AND R. E. TERRY
1921. The *Capsicum* monograph in U.S. pharmocopoeia. *J. Amer. Pharm. Assoc.* 10:423–430.

GENTRY, J. L., AND P. C. STANDLEY
1974. Flora of Guatemala. *Fieldiana: Bot. (Capsicum)* 24 (10):12–18.

GEORGIA AGRICULTURAL EXPERIMENT STATION
1926. Utilization of fruit by-products. *Annu. Rep. Georgia Agr. Exp. Sta.* 39:149–151.
1927. Feeding pimientos to milk cows. *Annu. Rep. Georgia Agr. Exp. Sta.* 40:33.

GERARD[E], J.
1974. *The herball or general historie of plantes*. Reprint ed. Amsterdam and Norwood, N.J.: Theatrum Orbis Ltd. [Original edition published in 1597, London: John Norton.]

GERSON, R., AND S. HONMA
1977. Emergence response of the pepper at low soil temperature. *Enphytica* 27:151–156.

GHIGLIAZZA, M. M.
1948. *Invasión norteamericana en Tabasco (1846–1848): Documentos*. Mexico City: Imprenta Univ.

GILMOUR, J. S. L. (CHM.)
1969. *International code of nomenclature of cultivated plants*. Utrecht, Netherlands: Internat. Bur. for Plant Taxonomy and Nomenclature.

GIL Y SAENZ, M.
1892. *Historia de Tabasco*. Edited by J. M. Abalos. 2d ed. San Juan Bautista.

GOLDSCHMIDT, M.
1983. Interview. *On Campus*, Feb.–March issue. Austin: Univ. Texas.

GÓMARA, F. L. DE
1552. *La [h]istoria de las Indias y conquista de México*. Zaragoza.
1964. *Cortés: The life of the conqueror by his secretary, Francisco López de Gómara*. Translated and edited by L. B. Simpson. Berkeley: Univ. California Press.

GOMEZ, R. E., AND R. M. NAKAYAMA
1976. *Growing chile in home and market gardens*. N.M. State Univ. Coop. Ext. Ser. Guide 400H-206.

GORDE, R. B.
1967. Vitamin C content and capsaicin content of ten different chili varieties. *Nagpur. Agri. Col. Mag.* 42:53–54.

GRANT, V.
1981. *Plant speciation*. New York: Columbia Univ. Press.

GREENLEAF, W. H.
1975. The tabasco story. *Hortscience* 10(2):98.

GREENLEAF, W. H., M. H. HOLLINGSWORTH, H. HARRIS, AND K. S. RYMAL
1969. *Bighart: Improved variety of pimento pepper*. Agr. Exp. Sta. Leaflet 7B. Auburn, Ala.: Auburn Univ.

GREENLEAF, W. H., J. A. MARTIN, J. G. LEASE, E. T. SIMS, AND L. O. VAN BLARICOM
1970. *Greenleaf tabasco: A new tobacco etch virus resistant ta-*

basco pepper variety (C. frutescens L.). Agr. Exp. Sta. Leaflet 81. Auburn, Ala.: Auburn Univ.

GRIEDER, T.
1982. *Origins of pre-Columbian art.* Austin: Univ. Texas Press.

GRIFFEN, P. F.
1953. Geographical elements in the toponomy of Mexico. *Sci. Monthly* 76(1):20–23.

HALASZ, Z.
1963. *Hungarian paprika through the ages.* Translated by Lili Halapy. Budapest: Corvina Press.

HARLAN, J. R.
1971. Agricultural origins: Centers and non-centers. *Science* 174:468–474.
1975. *Crops and man.* Madison, Wis.: Amer. Soc. of Agronomy, Crop Soc. of Amer.

HAWKES, J. G., R. M. LESTER, AND A. D. SKELDING (EDS.)
1979. *The biology and taxonomy of the Solanaceae.* New York: Academic Press.

HAXTON, H. A.
1948. Gustatory sweating. *Brain* 71:16–25.

HEDRICK, U. P. (ED.)
1919. Sturtevant's notes on edible plants. *N.Y. Dept. Agr. Annu. Rep.* 2(2):134–140.

HEISER, C. B., JR.
1951. *Some like it hot.* New York: Amer. Mus. Natur. Hist.
1964. Los chiles y ajíes de Costa Rica y Ecuador. *Ciencia y Naturaleza* 7(2):50–57.
1965. Cultivated plants and cultural diffusion in nuclear America. *Amer. Anthropol.* 67:930–947.
1969a. *Nightshades: The paradoxical plants.* San Francisco: W. H. Freeman and Co.
1969b. Systematics and the origin of cultivated plants. *Taxon* 18:36–45.
1969c. Some considerations of early plant domestication. *Bioscience* 19:228–231.
1969d. Taxonomy. In *A short history of botany*, edited by J. Ewan, pp. 110–114. New York: Hafner Pub. Co.
1973. *Seed to civilization: The story of man's food.* San Francisco: W. H. Freeman and Co.
1976a. Peppers: *Capsicum* (Solanaceae). In *Evolution of crop plants*, edited by N. W. Simmonds, pp. 265–268. London: Longman.
1976b. Origins of agriculture. In *Encyclopedia of anthropology*, edited by D. E. Hunter and P. Whitten, pp. 8–10. New York: Harper and Row.
1976c. Domestication of plants and animals. In *Encyclopedia of anthropology*, edited by D. E. Hunter and P. Whitten, pp. 130–132. New York: Harper and Row.
1976d. Food and food crops. In *Encyclopedia of anthropology*, edited by D. E. Hunter and P. Whitten, pp. 174–175. New York: Harper and Row.
1979. *The gourd book.* Norman: Univ. Oklahoma Press.

HEISER, C. B., AND B. PICKERSGILL
1969. Names for the cultivated *Capsicum* species (Solanaceae). *Taxon* 18:277–283.
1975. Names for the bird peppers (*C. solanaceae*). *Baileya* 19:151–156.

HEISER, C. B., AND P. G. SMITH
1948. Observations on another species of cultivated pepper *C. pubescens* R. and P. *Proc. Amer. Soc. Hort. Sci.* 52:331–335.
1953. The cultivated *Capsicum* peppers. *Econ. Bot.* 7(3):214–227.
1958. New species of *Capsicum* from South America. *Brittonia* 10:194–201.

HEISER, C. B., W. H. ESHBAUGH, AND B. PICKERSGILL
1971. The domestication of *Capsicum*: A reply to Davenport. *Prof. Geogr.* 23(2):169–170.

HERNÁNDEZ, F.
1651. *Nova plantarum, animalium et mineralium Mexicanorum Historia, rerum medicarum novae.* Translated into Latin from 1628 edition by A. Reccho. Rome.
1943. *Historia de las plantas de Nueva España*, vol. 1. Mexico City: Inst. Biol. Univ. Autónomo.

HERNÁNDEZ ARMENTA, R.
1982. *Guía para cultivar chile áncho en el norte de Guanajuato.* Inst. Nac. de Inves. Agri. Fol. para Prod. Num. 1. San José Iturbide, Gto., Mexico.

HERRERA, A. (ED.)
1904. *Nueva farmacopea mexicana.* 4th ed. Mexico City: Sociedad Farmacéutica de México.

HEYERDAHL, T.
1963. Feasible ocean routes to and from the Americas in pre-Columbian times. *Amer. Antiquity* 28:482–488.
1964. Plant evidence for contracts with America before Columbus. *Antiquity* 38:120–133.

HOOVER, M. W.
1960. *Getting firmer peppers.* N.C. Agr. Exp. Sta. Res. Farming Progress Rep.

HOPPE, W. A., A. MEDINA, AND R. J. WEITLANER
1969. The Popoloca. In *Handbook of Middle American Indians*, edited by R. Wauchope, 7:489–498. Austin: Univ. Texas Press.

HORGAN, PAUL
1939. *The habit of empire.* Santa Fe, N.M.: Rydal Press.

HOWARD, F. D., J. H. MACGILLIVRAY, AND M. YAMAGUCHI
n.d. Nutrient composition of fresh California-grown vegetables. *Calif. Agr. Exp. Sta. Bull.* 788:6–17.

HUFFMAN, V. L.
1977. Volatile components and pungency in fresh and processed Jalapeño peppers. Ph.D. dissertation, Texas A&M Univ.

HUMBOLDT, F. H. A. VON
1811. *Essai politique sur le royaume de la Nouvelle-Espagne.* Paris.
1814. *Political essay on the Kingdom of New Spain.* Translated by J. Black. Vol. 1. London: Longman, Murat, Rees, Orms, and Brown.

HUNZIKER, A. T.
1950. Estudios sobre Solanaceae. I: Sinopsis de las especies silvestres de *Capsicum* de Argentina y Paraguay. *Darwiniana* 9:225–247.
1958. Synopsis of the genus *Capsicum*. VIII Congres Inter-

national de Botanique, Paris, 1954. *Proceedings* Sec. 4(2): 73–74.

1961*a*. Estudios sobre Solanaceae. III: Notas sobre los géneros *Physalis* L. y *Capsicum* L., con la descripción de las nuevas especies sudamericanas. *Kurtziana* 1:207–216.

1961*b*. Noticia sobre el cultivo de *Capsicum baccatum* (Solanaceae) en Argentina. *Kurtziana* 1:303.

1971. Estudios sobre Solanaceae. VII: Contribución al conocimiento de *Capsicum* y géneros afines (*Witheringia, Acnistus, Athenaea*, etc.), tercera parte. *Kurtziana* 6: 241–259.

1979. South American Solanaceae. In *The biology and taxonomy of the Solanaceae*, edited by J. G. Hawkes, pp. 54–55. New York: Academic Press.

HUSAIN, I. A. A.
1564. *Re medica omens*. Edited by J. P. Mongio and J. Costaeo. Venice.

HUTCHINSON, J.
1969. *Evolution and phylogeny of flowering plants*. New York: Academic Press.

IRISH, H. C.
1898. A revision of the genus *Capsicum* with especial reference to garden varieties. *Mo. Bot. Gard. Ninth Rep.* 9: 53–110.

IRISH, H. C., AND L. H. BAILEY
1927. *Capsicum*. In *The standard cyclopedia of horticulture*, vol. 1. New York: Macmillan Co.

JACKSON, B. D.
1895. *Index kewensis*. Vols. 1 and 2. Oxford: Clarendon Press.

JACKSON, B. J.
1964. *Guide to the literature to botany*. New York: Hafner Pub. Co.

JACOBS, M. B.
1944. *The chemistry and technology of food and food products*. Vol. 1, *Vitamins*; Vol. 2, *Herbs and spices*. New York: Interscience Pub.

JACQUIN, N. J.
1770–1776. *Hortus botanicus vindobonensis*. 3 vols. Vienna: C. F. Wappler.

JENSEN, W. A., AND F. B. SALISBURY
1972. *Botany: An ecological approach*. Belmont, Calif.: Wadsworth Pub. Co.

JENSON, R. J., M. J. McLEOD, W. H. ESHBAUGH, AND S. I. GUTTMAN
1979. Numerical taxonomic analysis of allozymic variation in *Capsicum* (Solanaceae). *Taxon* 28(4):315–327.

JETT, S. C.
1971. Diffusion versus independent development: The basis of controversy. In *Man across the sea*, edited by C. L. Riley, J. C. Kelley, C. W. Pennington, and R. L. Rands, pp. 5–53. Austin: Univ. Texas Press.

1973. Comment on Pickersgill's "Cultivated plants as evidence for cultural contacts." *Amer. Antiquity* 38:223–225.

JOHNSON, M. M.
1977*a*. *Freezing green chile*. N.M. State Univ. Coop. Ext. Ser. Guide 400E-311. Las Cruces: New Mexico State Univ.

1977*b*. *Canning green chile sauces*. N.M. State Univ. Coop.

Ext. Ser. Guide E-312. Las Cruces: New Mexico State Univ.

JONES, S. F.
1949. Spices: The essence of geography. *Nat. Geogr.* 95(3): 401–406.

JUSTICE, O. L., AND L. N. BASS
1978. *Principles and practices of seed storage*. U.S. Dept. Agr., Sci. Ed. Admin., Agr. Handbook no. 506. Washington, D.C.: U.S. Govt. Printing Ofc.

KAISER, S.
1935. Factors governing shape and size in *Capsicum* fruits: A genetic and developmental analysis. *Bull. Torrey Bot. Club* 62:433–454.

KALSEC, INC.
1982. Technical data sheets on Aquaresin *Capsicum*, domestic, and Oleoresin *Capsicum*, African. Kalamazoo, Mich.: KALSEC Inc.

KAPLAN, L., AND R. S. MacNEISH
1960. Prehistoric bean remains from caves in the Ocampo region of Tamaulipas, Mexico. *Bot. Mus. Leafl. Harvard Univ.* 19(2):33–56.

KARTTUNEN, F.
1983. *An analytical dictionary of Nahuatl*. Austin: Univ. Texas Press.

KENNEDY, D.
1972. *The cuisines of Mexico*. New York: Harper and Row.
1975. *The tortilla book*. New York: Harper and Row.
1978. *Recipes from the regional cooks of Mexico*. New York: Harper and Row.

KEW BOTANICAL GARDENS
1898. DCXIV.—Chillies. *Bul. Misc. Infor. Kew*, pp. 171–175.

KIRK, J.
1892. A report on the spice and other cultivation of Zanzibar and Pemba. F. Ol. Report, Misc. Series 226. *Kew Bull.* 1898.

KLOSS, J.
1971. *Back to Eden*. New York: Beneficial Books.

KRUKOFF, B. A., AND A. C. SMITH
1937. Notes on the botanical components of curare. *Bull. Torrey Bot. Club* 64:401–409.

KUBLER, G.
1962. *The shape of time: Remarks on the history of things*. New Haven: Yale Univ. Press.

KUNTZE, O.
1891. *Revisio generum plantarum* 2:449. Leipzig.

LABORDE CANCINO, J. A., AND P. POZO COMPODONICO
1982. *Presente y pasado del chile en México*. Pub. Especial Num. 85. Mexico City: Nac. de Invest. Agri.

LAFAVORE, M.
1983. A pepper talk. *Organic Gardening*. 31(1):34–38.

LAMARCK, J. B. P. A. DE M. DE
1804. [Fide Jussieu, *Annales du Musie d'Histoire Naturelle*], Paris. In *Tableau encyclopedique et methodique*. Part 22, *Botanique*, 3:58. Paris: Chez H. Agasse.

LANNING, E. P.
1967. A pre-agricultural occupation on the central coast of Peru. In *Peruvian archaeology*, edited by J. H. Rowe and

D. Menzel, pp. 42–53. Palo Alto, Calif.: Peek Publications.

LANTZ, E. M.

1946. *Effects of canning and drying on the carotene and ascorbic acid content of chilies.* Bull. N.M. Agr. Exp. Sta. 327.

LAS CASAS, B. DE. *See* Casas, B. de las.

LATHRAP, D. W.

1973. Gifts of the cayman: Some thoughts on the subsistence basis of Chavin. In *Variation in anthropology,* edited by D. W. Lathrap and J. Douglas, pp. 91–105. Urbana: Illinois Archaeological Survey.

1977. Our father the cayman, our mother the gourd: Spinden revisited, or a unitary model for the emergence of agriculture in the New World. In *Origins of agriculture,* edited by C. A. Reed, pp. 713–752. The Hague: Mouton.

LATORRE, D. L.

1977. *Cooking and curing with Mexican herbs.* Austin: Encino Press.

LAWRENCE, G. H. M.

1960. The cultivated species of solanum. *Baileya* 8 : 21–35.

1965. *Taxonomy of vascular plants.* New York: Macmillan Co.

LEASE, J. G., AND E. J. LEASE

1956. Factors affecting the retention of red color in peppers. *Food Technol.* 10 : 368–373.

1962. Effect of drying conditions in initial color, color retention, and pungency of red peppers. *Food Technol.* 16(11) : 104–106.

LEE, T. S.

1954. Physiological gustatory sweating in a warm climate. *J. Physiol.* 124 : 528–542.

LEWIN, S.

1976. *Vitamin C: Its molecular biology and medical potential.* New York: Academic Press.

LEWIS, O.

1960. *Tepoztlan.* New York: Henry Holt & Co.

LINNAEUS, C.

1737. *Hortus cliffortianus.* Amsterdam.

1753. *Species plantarum.* 1st ed. Stockholm.

1763. *Species plantarum.* 2d ed. Stockholm.

1767. *Mantissa plantarum.* Stockholm.

1783–1797. *Species plantarum.* Edited by C. L. Wildenow. 6 vols. Berlin: Impensis G. C. Nauk.

LIPPERT, L. F., AND R. S. SCHARFFENBERG

1964. Garden pepper (*Capsicum* sp.). In *Vegetable crops bibliographies: A comprehensive series.* Vol. 1. West Covina, Calif.: Bibliographic Assoc.

LIPPERT, L. F., P. G. SMITH, AND B. O. BERGH

1966. Cytogenetics of the vegetable crops. *Bot. Rev.* 32 : 24–55.

LLOYD, J. U.

1921. *Origin and history of all the pharmacopeial vegetable drugs, chemicals, and preparations with bibliography.* Vol. 1. Cincinnati: Caxton Press.

LONG, E.

1774. *A history of Jamaica. Or a general survey of the ancient and modern state of that island.* Vol. 3. London: Lowndes.

LONGBRAKE, T., S. COTNER, J. PARSONS, R. ROBERTS, AND W. PEAVY

1976. Keys to profitable pepper production. *Texas Agr. Ext. Ser. Fact Sheet* L-966. College Station: Texas A&M Univ.

LONG-SOLÍS, J.

1982. El *Capsicum* y su influencia cultura. Ph.D. dissertation, Univ. Ibero Americano, Mexico City.

LÓPEZ DE GÓMARA, F. *See* Gómara, F. L. de

MCBRYDE, F. W.

1971. *Cultural and historical geography of southwest Guatemala.* Westport, Conn.: Greenwood Press.

MCCLURE, S. A.

1982. Parallel usage of medicinal plants by Africans and their Caribbean descendants. *Economic Botany* 36(3) : 291–301.

MCGREGOR, R. A.

1982. *Calif. Vegetable Rev.* 3(2, 7) : 2.

MCGREGOR, S. E.

1976. *Insect pollination of cultivated crop plants.* U.S. Dept. Agr., Agr. Res. Ser., Agr. Handbook 496. Washington, D.C.: U.S. Govt. Printing Ofc.

MACKAY, E., G. J. MOUNTNEY, AND E. C. NABER

1963. Yolk color resulting from different levels of paprika extract in the ration. *Poultry Sci.* 42(1) : 32–37.

MCLEOD, M. J.

1977. A systematic and evolutionary study of the genus *Capsicum.* Ph.D. dissertation, Miami Univ.

MCLEOD, M. J., W. H. ESHBAUGH, AND S. I. GUTTMAN

1979a. A preliminary biochemical systematic study of the genus *Capsicum*-Solanaceae. In *The biology and taxonomy of the Solanaceae,* edited by J. G. Hawkes, R. N. Lester, and A. D. Skelding, pp. 701–713. New York: Academic Press.

1979b. An electrophoretic study of *Capsicum* (Solanaceae): The purple flowered taxa. *Bull. Torrey Bot. Club* 106(4) 326–333.

MCLEOD, M. J., S. I. GUTTMAN, AND W. H. ESHBAUGH

1981. LDH in *Capsicum* (Solanaceae) leaves. *Isozyme Bull.* 14 : 76.

1982. Early evolution of chili peppers (*Capsicum*). *Econ. Bot.* 36(4) : 361–368.

1983. Peppers (*Capsicum*). In *Elsevier plant isozyme monograph,* edited by S. D. Tanksley and T. S. Orton, pp. 361–368. Las Cruces, N.M.: New Mexico State Univ.

MCLEOD, M. J., S. I. GUTTMAN, W. H. ESHBAUGH, AND R. E. RAYLE

1983. An electrophoretic study of evolution in *Capsicum* (Solanaceae). *Evolution* 37(3) : 562–574.

MACMILLAN, H. G.

1962. *Tropical planting and gardening.* London: Macmillan and Co.

MACNEISH, R. S.

1964. Ancient Mesoamerican civilization. *Science* 143(3606) : 531–537.

1967. A summary of the subsistence. In *Environment and subsistence,* vol. 1 of *The prehistory of the Tehuacan valley,* edited by D. S. Byers, pp. 290–309. Austin: Univ. Texas Press.

1977. The beginning of agriculture in central Peru. In *The origins of agriculture,* edited by C. A. Reed, pp. 753–801. The Hague: Mouton.

MADSEN, W.
1960. *The virgin's children*. Austin: Univ. Texas Press.

MAGA, J. A.
1975. *Capsicum*. In *Critical reviews in food science and nutrition*, pp. 177–199. Cleveland: CRC Press.

MANGELSDORF, P. C.
1953. Review of *Agricultural origins and dispersals*, by Carl Sauer. *Amer. Antiquity* 19:87–90.

MANGELSDORF, P. C., AND D. L. OLIVER
1951. Whence came maize to Asia? *Bot. Mus. Leafl. Harvard Univ.* 14(10):263–291.

MANGELSDORF, P. C., R. S. MacNEISH, AND G. R. WILLEY
1964. Origins of agriculture in Middle America. In *Natural environment and early cultures*, vol. 1 of *Handbook of Middle American Indians*, edited by R. Wauchope, pp. 427–445. Austin: Univ. Texas Press.

MANNIX, D. P.
1978. Black cargoes: A history of the Atlantic slave trade, 1518–1865. New York: Penguin Books.

MARÍA, L.
1943. El chile: La planta de hortaliza más importante en la república mexicana. *Agr. y Ganado* 18(9):15, 17–26.

MARSHALL, D. E.
1977. *Estimates of harvested acreage, production, and grower value for peppers grown in the United States for 1976*. U.S. Dept. Agri., Agri. Res. Service, Mich. State Univ.
1981. Performance of an open-helix mechanical harvester in processing peppers. American Society of Agricultural Engineers. Paper no. 81-1069, June 21–24, 1981.

MARTIN, J. N., A. T. ERWIN, AND C. C. LOUNSBERRY
1932. Nectaries of *Capsicum*. *J. Res. Iowa State Coll.* 6(3):277–285.

MARTYR, P. *See* Anghiera, P. M. d'.

MASADA, Y., K. HASHIMOTO, T. IMOUE, AND M. SUZUI
1971. Analysis of the pungent principles of *Capcium annuum* by combined gas chromatography—mass spectrometry. *J. Food Sci.* 36:858.

MAYER, F.
1943. *The chemistry of natural coloring matters*. Translated by A. H. Cook. New York: Reinhold.

MAYR, E.
1970. *Populations, species, and evolution*. Cambridge, Mass.: Harvard Univ. Press, Belknap Press.

MEHRA, K. L.
1979. Ethnobotany of old world Solanaceae. In *The biology and taxonomy of the Solanaceae*, edited by J. C. Hawkes, pp. 161–170. London: Academic Press.

MERRILL, E. D.
1947. Pimenta dioica (Linné). *Contrib. Gray Herb.* 165:37.
1954. The botany of Cook's voyage. In *Chronica botanica*, edited by F. Verdoorn, 14(5–6):164–384. Waltham, Mass.: Chronica Botanica Co.

MICKO, L.
1898. Isolation of *Capsicum*. *Z. Unters. Nahr. Genussum Gebrauchsgegenstaende* 1:818.

MILLER, J. C., AND Z. M. FINEMAN
1937. A genetic study of some qualitative and quantitative characters of the genus *Capsicum. Proc. Amer. Soc. Hort. Sci.* 35:544–550.

MILLER, P.
1768. *The gardener's and botanist's dictionary*. 8th ed. London: Miller.

MIRACLE, M. A.
1967. *Agriculture in the Congo basin*. Milwaukee: Univ. Wisconsin Press.

MOLINA, A.
1970. *Dictionary of Nahuatl: Voca en lengua castillana y mexicana y mexicana y castillana*. 4th ed. Mexico City: Ed. Porrua.

MOLINA, J. I.
1782. *Compendio de la historia geográfica natural y civil reino de Chile*. Vol. 1. Bologna.
1973. *The geographical, natural, and civil history of Chile*. Translated from the original Italian by an American gentleman. New York: AMS Press. [Reprint of 1808 ed.]

MONTAGNE, P.
1968. *Larousse gastronomique*. New York: Crown Pub. Co.

MORGAN, W. A., AND J. G. WOODROOF
1927. Waste pimiento pepper for coloring egg yolks. *Georgia Agr. Exp. Sta. Bull.* 5(147):210–215.

MORISON, R.
1715. *Plantarum historiae universalis oxoniensis*. London: Paulum & Isaacum Vaillant.

MORISON, S. E.
1942. *Admiral of the ocean sea*. Boston: Little, Brown.

MORRIS, E. H.
1954. *Chile peppers: Fresh, frozen, canned, and dried*. Univ. Ariz. Agr. Ext. Ser. Circ. 221. Tucson: Univ. Arizona Press.

MORTON, C. V.
1938. *Capsicum*. In *Flora of Costa Rica*. Field Mus. Nat. Hist. Bot. Ser. Chicago.

MOSTER, J. B., AND A. N. PRATER
1952. Color of *Capsicum* spices. I: Measurement of extractable color. *Food Technol.* 6:459–463.

MOUNTAIN PASS CANNING CO.
1980. The old El Paso label. Paper presented at 5th National Pepper Conf., Las Cruces, N.M.

MUEHMER, J. K.
1982. Breeding peppers for Canada's special requirements. Paper presented at 6th National Pepper Conf., San Miguel de Allende, Mex.

MUEHMER, J. K., AND J. BRIMNER
1982. A simplified method of pregerminating pepper seeds in bulk. Paper presented at 6th National Pepper Conf., San Miguel de Allende, Mex.

MÚÑOZ FLORES, I., AND B. PINTO CORTÉS
1967. Taxonomía y distribución geográfica de los chiles cultivados en México. *Proc. Caribbean Region Amer. Soc. Hort. Sci.*, pp. 131–146.

NABHAN, G. P.
1978. Chiltepines! *El Palacio* (Museum of New Mexico) 84(2):30–34.

NAGLE, B. J.
1977. Color evaluation of selected *Capsicums*. Master's thesis, Texas A&M Univ.

NELSON, E. K.
1910. Capsaicin, the pungent principle of *Capsicum*, and the detection of *Capsicum. J. Ind. Eng. Chem.* 2:419–421.

1920. The constitution of capsaicin, the pungent principle of *Capsicum* III. *J. Amer. Chem. Soc.* 42:597–599.

NELSON, E. K., AND L. E. DAWSON
1923. The constitution of capsaicin, the pungent principle of *Capsicum. Amer. EHSM Soc. J.* 45:2179–2181.

NEW MEXICO AGRICULTURAL EXTENSION SERVICE
1958. Try these easy ways to peel chile. *N.M. Agr. Ext. News* 38:4–5.

ODLAND, M. L., AND A. M. PORTER
1941. A study of the natural crossing in peppers, *Capsicum frutescens. Proc. Amer. Soc. Hort. Sci.* 38:585–588.

O'NEAL, L. M., AND T. W. WHITAKER
1947. Embroideries of the early Nazca and the crop plants depicted on them. *Southwest J. Anthropol.* 3:294–321.

ORTIZ, E.
1979. *The book of Latin American cooking.* New York: Alfred A. Knopf.

OSOL, A., R. PRATT, AND M. D. ALTSCHULE
1973. *United States dispensatory.* 27th ed. Philadelphia: J. B. Lippincott.

OVIEDO Y VALDÉS, G. F. DE
1526. *Historia general y natural de las Indias.* Toledo.

1950. *Sumario de la natural historia de las Indias.* Edited, with introduction and notes by José Miranda. Mexico City: Fondo de Cultura Económica.

PARKINSON, J.
1640. *Theatrum botanicum.* London: T. Cotes.

PAUL, W. R. C.
1940. A study of the genus *Capsicum* with special reference to dry chili. *Tropic. Agr.* 94(1):10–18, 94(2):63–78, 94(3):131–145, 94(4):198–213, 94(5):271–281, 94(6):332–347.

PAULING, LINUS
1977. Albert Szent-Györgyi and Vitamin C. In *Search and discover: A tribute to Albert Szent-Györgyi*, edited by B. Karminer, pp. 43–53. New York: Academic Press.

PEAVY, W. S.
1983. Chili peppers: A hot addition to the home garden. *Texas Gardener* 2(4):50–53.

PETOSEED CO.
1978. *Seeds for the world.* Saticoy, Calif.: Petoseed Co.

PHILLIPS, P.
1966. The role of transpacific contacts in the development of New World pre-Columbian civilizations. In *Archaeological frontiers and external connections*, vol. 4 of *Handbook of Middle American Indians*, edited by R. Wauchope, pp. 296–315. Austin: Univ. Texas Press.

PICKERING, C.
1879. *Chronological history of plants.* Boston.

PICKERSGILL, B.
1966. The variability and relationships of *Capsicum chinense* Jacq. Ph.D. dissertation, Indiana Univ.

1969a. The archaeological record of chili peppers (*Capsicum* spp.) and the sequence of plant domestication in Peru. *Amer. Antiquity* 34(1):54–61.

1969b. The domestication of chili peppers. In *The domestication and exploitation of plants and animals*, edited by P. J. Ucko and G. W. Dimbleby, pp. 443–450. London: Gerald Duckworth.

1971. Relationships between weedy and cultivated forms in some species of chili peppers (genus *Capsicum*). *Int. J. Org. Evolut.* 25(4):683–691.

1972. Cultivated plants as evidence for cultural contacts. *Amer. Antiquity* 37:97–104.

1977a. Taxonomy and the origin and evolution of cultivated plants in the New World. *Nature* 268:591–595.

1977b. Chromosomes and evolution in *Capsicum*. In *Capsicum 77*, edited by E. Pochard, pp. 51–66. Compte rendus du 3ᵐᵉ Congrès EUCARPIA sur la génétique de la sélection du piment. Montfavet-Avignon, France: INRA.

1980. Some aspects of interspecific hybridization in *Capsicum*. Preliminary report presented at the Fourth EUCARPIA *Capsicum* working group meetings in Wageningen, The Netherlands.

PICKERSGILL, B., AND A. H. BUNTING
1969. Cultivated plants and the Kon Tiki theory. *Nature* 222:225–227.

PICKERSGILL, B., AND C. B. HEISER, JR.
1976. Cytogenetics and evolutionary change under domestication. *Phil. Trans. Royal Soc. London* 275:55–69.

1977. Origins and distribution of plants domesticated in the New World tropics. In *Origins of agriculture*, edited by C. A. Reed, pp. 803–835. The Hague: Mouton.

PICKERSGILL, B., C. B. HEISER, AND J. McNEILL
1978. Numerical taxonomic studies of variation and domestication in some species of *Capsicum*. In *The biology and taxonomy of the* Solanaceae, edited by J. G. Hawkes, pp. 679–699. New York: Academic Press.

PLINY, C. SEGUNDI
1945. *Natural history.* Book XI.24–XIV.27:19–23. Edited by T. E. Page, translated by H. Rackham. Cambridge, Mass.: Harvard Univ. Press.

POCHARD, E. (ED.)
1977. *Capsicum 77.* Comptes rendus du 3ᵐᵉ Congrès EUCARPIA sur la génétique de la sélection du piment. Montfavet-Avignon, France: INRA.

POCHARD, E., AND R. DUMAS DE VAULX
1979. Haploid parthenogenesis in *Capsicum annuum* L. In *The biology and taxonomy of the* Solanaceae, edited by J. G. Hawkes, pp. 455–472. New York: Academic Press.

POHLE, W. D., AND R. L. GREGORY
1960. Color of *Capsicum* spices. *Food Technol.* 14:245–247.

PORTER, C. L.
1967. *Taxonomy of flowering plants.* San Francisco: W. H. Freeman and Co.

POZO COMPODONICO, O.
1981. *Descripción de tipos y cultivares de chile (Capsicum spp.) en México.* Folleto Tec. 77. Mexico City: Inst. Nac. de Inves. Agri.

PRAIN, D.
1903. *Bengal plants*. Botanical Survey of India, vol. 2. Calcutta.

PURSEGLOVE, J. M.
1968. *Tropical crops*. New York: John Wiley and Sons.

QUAGLIOTTI, L.
1979. Floral biology of *Capsicum* and *Solanum melongena*. In *The biology and taxonomy of the Solanaceae*, edited by J. G. Hawkes, pp. 399–419. New York: Academic Press.

QUINBY, J. (ED.)
1958. *Catalogue of botanical books in the collection of Rachel McMasters Miller Hunt*. Vol. 1: *Printed Books 1477–1700*. Pittsburgh: Hunt Botanical Library.

QUINN, V.
1942. *Vegetables in the garden and their legends*. Philadelphia: J. P. Lippincott.

RANDS, R. L.
1969. Mayan ecology and trade: 1967–1968. In *Mesoamerican Studies*. Carbondale: Univ. S. Ill. Museum.

RAVINES, R.
1978. Agricultura y riego. *Technol. Andina*, pp. 102–105.

REDFIELD, R., AND A. VILLAS ROJAS
1962. *Chankom: A Maya village*. Chicago: Univ. Chicago Press.

REED, C. A. (ED.)
1977. *Origins of agriculture*. The Hague: Mouton.

REED, E. K.
1971. Commentary, Section I. In *Man across the sea*, edited by C. L. Riley, J. C. Kelley, C. W. Pennington, and R. L. Rands, pp. 106–111. Austin: Univ. Texas Press.

REHDER, A.
1927. The varietal categories in botanical nomenclature and their historical development. *J. Arnold Arboretum* 8: 56–68.

RICK, C. M.
1950. *Capsicum pubescens*: A little known pungent pepper from Latin America. *Mo. Bot. Gardens Bull.* 33:26–42.

RIES, M.
1968. *The hundred year history of Tabasco*. Avery Island, La.: McIlhenny Co.

RIKS, D.
1975. A tale of failure. *Bangkok Post Sunday Magazine*, Aug. 3, 1975.
1976. Some like it hot. *Off Duty—Pacific*, Feb. 1976.

RILEY, C. L., J. C. KELLEY, C. W. PENNINGTON, AND R. L. RANDS (EDS.)
1971. *Man across the sea*. Austin: Univ. Texas Press.

RIX, M.
1981. *The art of the plant world: The great botanical illustrators and their work*. Woodstock, N.Y.: Overlook Press.

ROSEGARTEN, F., JR.
1969. *The book of spices*. Wynnewood, Pa.: Livingston Pub. Co.

ROYS, R. L.
1931. *The ethno-botany of the Maya*. Middle American Research Series, no. 2. New Orleans: Tulane Univ.

ROZIN, P., AND P. SCHILLER
1980. The nature and acquisition of a preference for chile peppers by humans. *Motivation & Emotion* 4(1):77–101.

RUIZ, E.
1921. *Cultivo de chili*. Mexico City: Sec. of Agr. and Econ. Dev.

RUIZ, H., AND J. PAVON
1965. *Flora peruviana et chilensis*. 4 vols. Lehrey, N.Y.: F. A. Staflen and J. Cramen. [Reprint of 1797 ed. (Madrid).]

RUMPF, G. E. *See* Rumphius, G. E.

RUMPHIUS, G. E.
1741–1750. *Herbarium amboinense*. Edited by J. Burmann. Vol. 5. Amsterdam: F. Chansuion, J. Catuffe, and H. Vytwerf.

SAFFORD, W. E.
1917. Food plants and textiles of ancient America. In *Proceedings of 19th International Congress of Americanists*, pp. 12–30. Washington, D.C.
1927. Our heritage from the American Indians. *Smithsonian Inst. Ann. Rep. for 1926*, pp. 405–410.

SAHAGÚN, B. DE
1590. *Historia general de las cosas de la Nueva España* [Florentine Codex].
1963. *The general history of the things of New Spain; Florentine Codex*. Translated by A. J. O. Anderson and C. E. Dibble. School of Amer. Research (Santa Fe) Monogr., no. 14. Santa Fe, N.M.

SANCHEZ-PALOMERA, E.
1951. The action of spices on the acid gastric secretion, on the appetite, and on the caloric intake. *Gastroenterology* 18(2):254–268.

SANTAMARÍA, F. J.
1942. *Diccionario general de americanismos*. Mexico City: Editorial Pedro Roberdo.

SAUER, C. O.
1936. American agricultural origins: A consideration of nature and culture. In *Essays in anthropology presented to A. L. Kroeber*, pp. 279–297. Berkeley: Univ. California Press.
1950. Cultivated plants of South and Central America. In *Handbook of South American Indians*, edited by J. H. Steward, 5:487–543. Washington, D.C.: U.S. Govt. Printing Ofc.
1952. *Agricultural origins and dispersals*. New York: Amer. Geogr. Soc.
1966. *The early Spanish Main*. Berkeley: Univ. California Press.

SCHENDEL, G.
1968. *Medicine in Mexico: From Aztec herbs to betatrons*. Austin: Univ. Texas Press.

SCHERY, R. W.
1956. *Plants for man*. Englewood Cliffs, N.J.: Prentice-Hall.

SCHURZ, W. L.
1939. *The Manila galleon*. New York: E. P. Dutton & Co.

SCHWEID, R.
1980. *Hot peppers*. Seattle: Madrona Pub.

SENDTNER, O.
1846. Solanaceae et cestrineae. In *Flora brasiliensis*. 8 vols. Edited by Martius. Munich. [Reprint, 1967. New York: V. Von J. Cramer.]

SHANNON, E.
1977. *Chile disease control.* N.M. State Univ. Coop. Ext. Ser. Guide H-219. Las Cruces: New Mexico State Univ.

SHAW, F. J., AND S. A. KHAN
1928. Studies in Indian chiles: The types of *Capsicum. Mem. Dept. Agr. India Ser.* 16:59–82.

SHERRY, L.
1976. *Vitamin C: Its molecular biology and medical potential.* New York: Academic Press.

SHINNERS, L. H.
1956. Technical names for the cultivated *Capsicum* peppers. *Baileya* 4:81–83.

SIEVERS, A. F.
1948. Production of drug and condiment plants. *U.S. Dept. Agr. Farmers Bull.* 1999:73–75. Washington, D.C.: U.S. Dept. of Agriculture.

SIMPSON, L. B. (TRANS. & ED.)
1964. *Cortés: The life of the conqueror by his secretary, Francisco López de Gómara.* Berkeley: Univ. California Press.

SMITH, C. E., JR.
1967. Plant remains. In *Environment and subsistence*, vol. 1 of *The prehistory of the Tehuacan Valley*, edited by D. S. Byers, pp. 220–255. Austin: Univ. Texas Press.

SMITH, L., AND R. J. DOWNS
1966. *Solanaceas.* In *Flora illustrade catarinense*, edited by P. R. Reitz, pp. 12–24. Santa Catarina, Brazil.

SMITH, P. G.
1951. Deciduous ripe fruit character in peppers. *J. Amer. Soc. Hort. Sci.* 47:343–344.
1966. Peppers of Peru: A report to AID. *N. Carolina Bull.* 306 (Univ. North Carolina).
1978. Horticultural classification of peppers. Paper presented at 4th National Pepper Conf., Baton Rouge, La.

SMITH, P. G., AND C. B. HEISER
1951. Taxonomic and genetic studies on the cultivated peppers *C. annuum* L. and *C. frutescens. Amer. J. Bot.* 38:367–368.
1957a. Breeding behavior of cultivated peppers. *Amer. Soc. Hort. Sci.* 70:286–290.
1957b. Taxonomy of *Capsicum sinense* Jacq. and the geographic distribution of the cultivated *Capsicum* species. *Bull. Torrey Bot. Club* 84(6):413–420.

SMITH, P. G., C. M. RICK, AND C. B. HEISER
1951. *Capsicum pendulum* Will'd: Another cultivated pepper from South America. *Amer. Soc. Hort. Sci.* 57:339–342.

SORENSEN, K. A.
1977. *Pepper insects and their control.* N.C. State Univ., Agri. Ext. Ser., Insect Note, no. 30.

SPATH, E., AND S. F. DARLING
1930. Synthesis of capsaicin. *Ber. Chem. Ges.* 63B:737.

STADE, H.
1874. *The captivity of Hans State of Hesse in A.D. 1547–1555 among the wild tribes of eastern Brazil.* Translated by R. F. Burton. London: Hakluyt Soc.

STANDLEY, P. C.
1931. Flora of the Lancetilla valley, Honduras. *Field Mus. Nat. Hist. Bot. Ser.* 283(10):10–13, 341–343.
1938. Flora of Costa Rica. *Field Mus. Nat. Hist. Bot. Ser.* 18(Part 3):1038–1045.

STEVENEL, L.
1956. Red pepper, a too much forgotten therapeutic agent against anorexia, liver congestion, and vascular troubles (hemorrhoids, varices). *Bull. Soc. Pathol. Exot.* 49(5):841–843.

STONER, A. K., AND B. VILLALON
1977. The popular cultivated tomato and kinfolk peppers, eggplant. In *Gardening for food and fun*, pp. 139–146. Washington, D.C.: U.S. Dept. Agr.

STURTEVANT, E. L.
1885. Kitchen garden esculents of American origin: II, Peppers. *Amer. Nat.* 19:544–550.
1919. Notes on edible plants. *Rep. N.Y. Agr. Exp. Sta. 1919*, pp. 134–140. Albany, N.Y.: J. B. Lyon Co., State Printer.

SZENT-GYÖRGYI, A.
1939. *On oxidation, fermentation, vitamins, health, and disease.* Baltimore: Vanderbilt Univ.
1978. How new understandings about the biological function of ascorbic acid may profoundly affect our lives. *Executive Health* 14(8):n.p.

TELLO, J. C.
1960. *Chavin: Cultura matriz de la civilización andina* [part I, fig. 31]. Lima, Peru: Univ. San Marcos Press.

TERPO, A.
1966. Kritische revision der wildwachsenden arten und de kultivierten sorten der gattung *Capsicum* L. *Reportorium Specierum Novarum Regi Vegetabilis* 72:155–191.

THOMPSON, A. E. (ED.)
1971. ASTA-ASHS vegetable variety names. Amer. Seed Trade Assoc. and Amer. Soc. Hort. Sci.

THOMPSON, J. E. S. (TRANS.)
1969. *Travels in the New World.* Translation of Thomas Gage's *The English American.* Norman: Univ. Oklahoma Press.

THRESH, J. C.
1877. Note on capsaicin, the active principle of cayenne pepper. *Pharm. J.* 7(473):187–189.

TIMES-PICAYUNE
1947. *The original Picayune creole cook book.* New Orleans: Times-Picayune Pub. Co. [Reprint of 1901 ed.]

TOLBERT, F. X.
1972. *A bowl of red.* New York: Doubleday.

TOURNEFORT, J. P.
1700. *Institutiones rei herbariae.* 3 vols. Paris.

TOWLE, M. A.
1961. *The ethnobotany of pre-Columbian Peru.* Viking Fund Pub. in Anthropology, no. 30. Chicago: Aldine Pub. Co.

TRACY, W. W.
1902. A list of American varieties of peppers. *U.S. Dept. Agr. Bur. Plant Industry Bull.*, no. 6, pp. 5–19.

UNITED NATIONS, FOOD AND AGR. ORG.
1981. *F.A.O. Production Yearbook 1980.* Vol. 34. Rome: F.A.O.
In press. *Genetic resources of Capsicum: A global plan of action.* IBPGR Secretariat, Rome.

U.S. CIRCUIT COURT OF APPEALS
1922. B. F. Trappey et al. vs. McIlhenny Co. Fifth Circuit,

no. 3846, pp. 126–132, 160–162.

U.S. DEPARTMENT OF AGRICULTURE

1981a. *Agricultural statistics.* Washington, D.C.: U.S. Govt. Printing Ofc.

1981b. *Nutritive value of foods.* Sci. and Ed. Ad., Home and Garden Bull., no. 72. Washington, D.C.: U.S. Govt. Printing Ofc.

1982a. Spices. *Foreign Agri. Circ.* FTEA 1-82. U.S. Dept. Agr., Foreign Agr. Serv. Washington, D.C.

1982b. *National list of scientific plant names.* U.S. Dept. Agr., Soil Conserv. Serv. Washington, D.C.

U.S. DEPARTMENT OF COMMERCE

1978. *Census of agriculture.* Vol. 1: *Summary of state data.* U.S. Dept. Commerce, Bur. Census. Doc. no. 78-A-51. Washington, D.C.

U.S. DISTRICT COURT FOR THE EASTERN DISTRICT OF LOUISIANA

1917. Lowell R. Gaidry vs. McIlhenny Co., no. 15323.

VAN BLARICOM, L. O., AND J. A. MARTIN

1947. Permanent standards for chemical tests for pungency in peppers. *J. Amer. Soc. Hort. Sci.* 50:297.

VAVILOV, N. I.

1949–1950. The origin, variation, immunity, and breeding of cultivated plants. *Chron. Bot.* 13(1–6):1–168.

VERDOON, F.

1945. *Plants and plant science in Latin America.* Waltham, Mass.: Chronica Botanica Co.

VIEHOEVER, A., AND I. COHEN

1938. Mechanism of action of aphrodisiac and other irritant drugs. *Amer. J. Pharm.* 110:226–249.

VILLA, P.

1978. History and development of the green chile industry in California. Paper presented at 2d Annual Texas Pepper Conf., McAllen, Tex.

VILLALON, B.

1975. Virus disease of bell peppers in south Texas. *Plant Dis. Rep.* 59(10):859–862.

VIRANUVATTI, V., C. KALAYASIRI, O. CHEARANI, AND U. PLENGVANIT

1972. Effects of *Capsicum* solution on human gastric mucosa as observed gastroscopically. *Amer. J. Gastroenterology* 58(3):225–232.

VISUDHIPHAN, S., P. SITTITH, O. PIBOONNUKARINTR, AND S. TUMLIANG

1982. The relationship between high fibrinolytic activity and daily capsicum ingestion in Thais. *Amer. J. Clin. Nutr.,* pp. 1452–1458.

VÖLKER, O.

1955. The experimental red coloration of bird feathers with the rhodoxathin from the seed appendage of the yew tree (*taxus baccata*). *J. Ornithol.* 96:54–57.

WAFER, L.

1970. *A new voyage and description of the isthmus of America.* In *Wafer's Darien,* edited by G. P. Winship. New York: Burt Franklin. [First published in 1699, London: James Knapton.]

WATT, G.

1889–1896. *A dictionary of the economic products of India.* London: W. H. Allen & Co.

WAUCHOPE, R. (ED.)

1964–1976. *Handbook of Middle American Indians.* 16 vols. Austin: Univ. Texas Press.

WEIL, A.

1980. *The marriage of the sun and moon: A quest for the unity in consciousness.* Boston: Houghton Mifflin Co.

WHITAKER, T. W., AND G. F. CARTER

1954. Oceanic drift of gourds: Experimental observations. *Amer. J. Bot.* 41(9):697–700.

WHITE, B. H., AND V. R. GODDARD

1948. Green chili peppers as a source of ascorbic acid in the Mexican diet. *J. Amer. Diet. Assoc.* 24:666–669.

WILLDENOW, C. L.

1809. *Enumeratio plantarum horti regii botanici beroliensis.* 11 vols. Germany.

WILLEY, G. R., G. E. EKHOLM, AND R. F. MILLON

1964. The patterns of farming life and civilization. In *Natural environment and early cultures,* vol. 1 of *Handbook of Middle American Indians,* edited by R. Wauchope, pp. 446–498. Austin: Univ. Texas Press.

WILLIS, J. C.

1969. *A dictionary of the flowering plants and ferns.* 7th ed. London: Cambridge Univ. Press.

WILSON, C. M. (ED.)

1945. *New crops for the New World.* New York: Macmillan Co.

WINTER, E.

1968. *Mexico's ancient and native remedies: A handbook of testimonials and historic references for modern use.* Mexico City: Editorial Fournier S.A.

WYLDER, M. K.

1948. Botulism in New Mexico. *Amer. J. Dis. Child.* 75:203–205.

XIMÉNEZ, F.

1967. *Historia natural del reino de Guatemala compuesta por el reverendo padre Fray Francisco Ximénez.* Edited by J. de Pineda Ibarra. Guatemala City. [Reprint of 1722 ed.]

YACOVLEFF, E., AND F. L. HERRERA

1934. El mundo vegetal de los antiguos peruanos. *Revista del Museo Nacional* 3(3):241–323.

YOUNG, T. B., AND R. H. TRUE

1913. American-grown paprika pepper. *USDA Bull.* 43:26–50.

YULE, H., AND A. C. BURNELL

1903. *Hobson-Jobson: A glossary of colloquial Anglo-Indian words and phrases and of kindred terms, etymological, historical, geographical, and discursive.* Edited by W. Cooke. New Delhi: Munshiram Manoharlal Pub., 1979.

ZIMENT, IRWIN

n.d. Spicy foods and lung diseases. Paper in the files of the author, Olive View Medical Center, UCLA, Van Nuys, Calif.

ZUCKER, MARTIN

1981. The herbal prescription. *Cook's Magazine.* March–April, pp. 49–51.

INDEX